The Christian Experience

LIVING FAITH

MICHAEL KEENE

STANLEY THORNES (PUBLISHERS) LTD

LIVING FAITH:
The Christian Experience

Other books in the series:

The Catholic Experience
Christianity and Social Issues

Note: Throughout the series BCE (Before Common or Christian Era) and CE (Common or Christian Era) have been used in place of the traditional BC and AD.

Text © Michael Keene 1995

Original line illustrations © Stanley Thornes (Publishers) 1995

All rights reserved. No part of this publication may be reproduced or transmitted in any form or by any means, electronic or mechanical, including photocopy, recording, or any information storage and retrieval system, without permission in writing from the publisher or under licence from the Copyright Licensing Agency Ltd. Further details of such licences (for reprographic reproduction) may be obtained from the Copyright Licensing Agency Limited, of 90, Tottenham Court Road, London W1P 9HE.

First published in 1995 by:
Stanley Thornes (Publishers) Ltd
Ellenborough House
Wellington Street
CHELTENHAM GL50 1YW
England

98 99 00/10 9 8 7 6 5 4 3

A catalogue record for this book is available from the British Library

ISBN 0-7487-2188-6

Cover pictures used by permission of Colorbytes Inc. and Image Vault, © American Databankers Corp.

Typeset in 11/13 Galliard and Stone

Produced by AMR Ltd for Stanley Thornes (Publishers) Ltd

Printed and bound in China

Acknowledgements

The publishers are grateful for permission to use copyright material, as follows:

Quotations from the Revised English Bible ©, by permission of Oxford University and Cambridge University Press 1989.

Also the following for permission to reproduce copyright photographs: *Amnesty International:* pg 152, 153. *Andes Press Agency/Carlos Reyes:* pg 5, 9, 30, 31, 32, 35, 42, 43, 44, 78, 79, 82×2, 84, 87, 88, 92, 95, 104, 106, 111, 112, 117, 119, 132, 133, 134. *Cafod:* pg 148. Sally and Richard Greenhill: 147. *Hutchison Library:* pg 41, 52. *Jo MacLennan and Alex Keene:* pg 4, 6, 7, 8, 10, 11, 12, 13, 14, 18, 19, 22, 23, 24, 25, 26, 27, 28, 29, 33×2, 34, 36, 37, 38, 39, 40, 46, 47, 48, 49, 50, 51, 53, 54, 55, 56×2, 58×2, 59, 60, 61×2, 62, 63×2, 64, 65×2, 66, 67, 68, 69, 70, 71, 72, 73, 74, 75, 76, 77, 80, 81, 86, 89, 90, 91, 93, 94, 96, 97, 98, 101, 102, 103, 104, 107, 108, 109, 110×2, 113, 114, 115, 116, 118, 120, 121, 122, 124, 125, 126, 127, 128, 129, 130×2, 136, 137, 138, 139, 140, 141, 142, 143, 144, 145, 149, 150, 154, 155. *Mary Evans Picture Library:* pg 16, 17. *Murray White:* pg 85. *Popperfoto:* pg 20, 135. *Rex Features:* pg 45.

The publishers have made every effort to trace the copyright holders, but if they have inadvertently overlooked any, they will be pleased to make the necessary arrangements at the first opportunity.

Illustrations by Jane Jones

CONTENTS

UNIT ONE
JESUS OF NAZARETH
1.1 The identity of Jesus
1.2 The teaching of Jesus
1.3 The actions of Jesus
1.4 The crucifixion of Jesus
1.5 The resurrection of Jesus

UNIT TWO
THE CHRISTIAN CHURCH
2.1 The birth of the Christian Church
2.2 The different Christian Churches
2.3 The Roman Catholic Church
2.4 The Second Vatican Council
2.5 The Orthodox Church
2.6 The Church of England
2.7 The Nonconformists
2.8 The Evangelicals
2.9 The Charismatic Movement
2.10 The Ecumenical Movement

UNIT THREE
CHRISTIAN BELIEFS
3.1 The Creeds
3.2 The Trinity
3.3 The death of Jesus
3.4 The Holy Spirit
3.5 The Sacraments
3.6 The problem of suffering
3.7 Love
3.8 The Virgin Mary

UNIT FOUR
THE BIBLE
4.1 The Christian Bible
4.2 Putting the Bible together
4.3 Translating the Bible
4.4 Using the Bible

UNIT FIVE
INSIDE THE CHRISTIAN CHURCHES
5.1 Inside a Catholic church
5.2 Inside an Orthodox church
5.3 Inside an Anglican church
5.4 Inside a Nonconformist church

UNIT SIX
CHRISTIANS AND WORSHIP
6.1 Christians and worship
6.2 Christian leaders
6.3 Christian prayer
6.4 Holy Communion
6.5 The Eucharist
6.6 The Mass
6.7 The Divine Liturgy
6.8 The Lord's Supper
6.9 The monastic life
6.10 Taizé and Iona
6.11 Pilgrimages
6.12 Holy Places

UNIT SEVEN
BETWEEN BIRTH AND DEATH
7.1 Infant baptism
7.2 Confirmation
7.3 Adult baptism
7.4 A Wedding
7.5 A Funeral

UNIT EIGHT
CHRISTIAN CELEBRATIONS
8.1 The Christian year
8.2 Advent
8.3 Christmas and Epiphany
8.4 Lent
8.5 Palm Sunday and Maundy Thursday
8.6 Good Friday
8.7 Easter Sunday
8.8 Ascension Day and Pentecost
8.9 Harvest
8.10 Sunday

UNIT NINE
CHRISTIANITY IN TODAY'S WORLD
9.1 The Family
9.2 Marriage
9.3 Divorce
9.4 Sex
9.5 Contraception
9.6 Homosexuality
9.7 Abortion
9.8 AIDS
9.9 Drugs
9.10 Work
9.11 Leisure
9.12 The Elderly
9.13 Racial discrimination
9.14 World population
9.15 World hunger
9.16 War and Peace
9.17 Human Rights
9.18 The World in danger

1.1 THE IDENTITY OF JESUS

1 Jesus of Nazareth

In 163 BCE the Romans, under Pompey, conquered Palestine and occupied the country. This had happened to the Jews frequently throughout their long history, and they longed for God to send to them the much-awaited Messiah. Their Scriptures had been full of this mysterious figure who would deliver them from their enemies, so many Jews were expecting a military leader. Others, though, were looking for a prophet in the tradition of Moses, who had led their ancestors out of Egyptian slavery, or a king like the much-loved David.

When Jesus appeared many people were convinced that the Messiah had arrived. Jesus, however, was reluctant to apply the title to himself. He had no intention of leading a military uprising against the Romans nor was he a typical Jewish prophet or king. His 'kingdom' was spiritual and not political – the Kingdom of God which was to be set up in the hearts of the people.

After he left the earth his followers wasted no time in preaching that Jesus was the Messiah. It was this teaching which led to the final break between Judaism and Christianity. The Jews, as a whole, rejected the claim, but the Christians placed it at the centre of their preaching. They even took the Greek word for 'Messiah' (Christus – anointed by God) and turned it into a surname for Jesus.

Why were they so sure? The time they spent with Jesus had convinced them that he was the Messiah since he:
- fed large crowds miraculously;
- cast out demons;
- forgave sins;
- announced the coming of God's kingdom, just as their Scriptures had taught them the Messiah would do.

A *Jesus called himself the 'Light of the world'. What do you think he meant by this?*

Jesus – the Son of God and the Son of Man

The early Christians often called Jesus the 'Son of God', although the phrase only comes up occasionally in the Gospels. It highlighted the unique relationship that Jesus enjoyed with God – best expressed by the relationship between a father and a son (Mark 1.11; 9.7). Jesus shocked his disciples by even calling God 'Abba' (Daddy) – a term which spoke of the closest possible relationship.

For his part, however, Jesus preferred to call himself the 'Son of Man'. It was a phrase that was familiar to his listeners since it was used on several occasions in the Jewish Scriptures. More often than not it simply referred to 'humankind' but it also spoke of a figure of great spiritual authority who, at the end of time, would be given an everlasting kingdom to rule over by God.

Put these different terms together and we have some idea of how Jesus perceived himself and how others saw him. As the Messiah he had come to deliver the people from their sins. As God's Son he enjoyed a unique relationship with God and yet, as Son of Man, he identified himself totally with the human race. So Christians came to see in Jesus the unique person who was both fully God and fully human.

B *This kind of painting is called an icon and shows the 'Pantocrator' (Christ over all) and it is common in Greek Orthodox churches. Look at the photograph and carry out some research to discover just what the painting is intended to convey.*

ANSWER IN YOUR BOOKS ...

1. Why was Jesus reluctant to identify himself with the Messiah figure in the Jewish Scriptures for whom the people had long been waiting?
   What 'new meaning' did Jesus give to the idea of being the Messiah?
2. What claim was Jesus making above all others when he saw himself as God's Son?
3. What do we learn about the mission of Jesus from the titles of the Messiah, the Son of God and the Son of Man?

FIND OUT AND NOTE ...

Make a list of the different things that we can learn about Jesus from the following texts:

a) Mark 3.20-21
b) Mark 3.22-30
c) Mark 15.26
d) Mark 1.11; 9.27
e) Mark 9.7
f) Matthew 11.27

READ AND DECIDE ...

Read these two accounts from the New Testament:
- Jesus preaching in the synagogue. Luke 4.16-21.
- Jesus on trial before the High Priest. Mark 14.61-62.

From these two accounts we can discover both how Jesus saw himself and how others saw him. How was that?

IN THE GLOSSARY ...

Messiah; Prophet.

1.2 THE TEACHING OF JESUS

Jesus was recognised as an outstanding teacher by his own disciples and also by the people who referred to him as 'rabbi' (teacher). Technically, though, he was not a rabbi. Jewish men who wanted to enter that honourable profession went through an extended period of training. In Jesus, the people recognised a considerable gift for teaching as well as a distinctive emphasis which marked his teaching out from that of others. At the beginning of his ministry he taught in the Jewish places of worship (synagogues) but when that was no longer possible he began to preach in the open-air. The people brought their questions about the Jewish Law (the Torah) to him and in reply he taught them about such issues as paying taxes to the Romans (Mark 12.13-17); adultery (John 7.53-8.11); marriage and divorce (Mark 10.1-12). By bringing their questions about the Torah to Jesus the people were, in effect, treating him like a rabbi. This was probably one of the ways in which he most annoyed the Jewish authorities.

Our only information about this teaching comes from the four Gospels. For a long time the information in the Gospels was kept alive by word of mouth in the Christian community before it was written down. Jews were familiar with the 'oral tradition', as this process was called, and this had a very distinguished history in Judaism. The teachings of all their great prophets and leaders had been kept alive in this way for centuries. Now they formed the backbone of the Jewish Scriptures.

Parables – and other ways of teaching

Along with other spiritual teachers of the day Jesus mainly taught in parables – human stories that were intended to have a spiritual meaning. The Jewish holy books were full of such stories – called 'mishnah'. With one exception (Mark 4.1-20), Jesus left his stories open for his listeners to draw their own conclusions.

Jesus also used other devices in his teaching:

a) *Short, memorable sayings:* see, for example, Luke 4.23 and 6.39.
b) *Vivid and familiar images:* in the so-called 'Sermon on the Mount', for instance, Jesus spoke of light, salt, birds, flowers and a city set on a hill among other familiar images. You can locate these for yourself in Matthew chapters 5 to 7. Jesus used different but equally familiar images in John's Gospel, describing himself as 'the true vine'; the 'good shepherd'; 'bread' and 'life-giving water'.
c) *Exaggeration:* Jesus often exaggerated deliberately to emphasise the point he was making, as you can see from Matthew 5.29; 5.30 and 19.24.

A *What do you think are the qualities of a good and effective teacher?*

The message

So what was Jesus trying to say through his parables, sayings, images and exaggerations? His whole teaching was concerned with one message – that God's kingdom had come. Jesus himself had ushered in that kingdom and he was now concerned to tell the people how they could belong to it. Mark summed this up beautifully:

> 'The time has arrived; the kingdom of God is upon you. Repent, and believe the Gospel.' (1.15)

His Jewish listeners would have understood the message. For centuries their ancestors had been waiting for the coming of God's Messiah and Jesus was announcing that their wait was over. Yet Jesus had not only come to call the religious and self-righteous into the kingdom – he had also come for those on the edge of society. No wonder that his message was welcomed by the prostitutes, the tax-collectors and the demon-possessed. It was for them that God's time had come.

IN YOUR OWN WORDS …

This stained-glass window illustrates one of the most well-known and important parables of Jesus – the Good Samaritan.

a) Read, and carefully consider, each of the following parables:

- The parable of the Good Samaritan. Luke 10.25-37.
- The parable of the lost son. Luke 15.11-32.
- The parable of the mustard seed. Mark 4.3-34.
- The parable of the sower. Mark 4.1-20.
- The parable of the two sons. Matthew 21.28-32.

Describe, in your own words, three of these parables and explain what you think Jesus was trying to say in each case.

b) On occasions Jesus suggested that he spoke in parables to 'obscure' the truth, not to make it clearer. Why do you think that Jesus chose to deliver most of his teaching in the form of parables? Could there be some truth in the idea that they made the truth more difficult to understand?

ANSWER IN YOUR BOOK …

1. How did Jesus teach the people?
2. What message lay at the heart of the teaching of Jesus?
3. Three Jewish terms are mentioned here – a rabbi, a synagogue and the Torah. Explain each of them in a sentence.

IN THE GLOSSARY …

Synagogue; Torah; Gospel; Parable.

1.3 THE ACTIONS OF JESUS

In his sermon in the synagogue in Nazareth, at the outset of his ministry, Jesus read a passage from the prophet Isaiah which said that the Messiah would bring:

> '...good news to the poor...release for the prisoners...recovery of sight for the blind...' (Luke 4.18)

The miracles that Jesus performed were an important ingredient in this message. They were also one of the main causes of the opposition that he encountered.

Whose power?

Whilst people seem to have accepted that Jesus performed miracles, there was considerable debate about the source of his power and authority. The Jews believed that there were 'good' and 'false' prophets, and they felt that Jesus firmly belonged in the latter category. That is why we find the scribes insisting, in Mark 3.22-26, that Jesus was performing miracles by the power of Satan, not God. At the end of the 1st century the Jewish writer, Josephus ('The Antiquities of the Jews'), confirmed that Jesus had extraordinary powers as:

> '...a doer of wonderful deeds and a teacher of those who receive the truth gladly...'

However, Josephus himself did not come to any conclusion about the origin of his power.

Miracles?

The most striking feature about the life of Jesus presented in the four Gospel accounts is the emphasis which each of them places upon the miracles. We frequently meet a Jesus who uses his power to cure illness, cast out evil spirits and control the unruly elements of nature with a single word of command. In the biblical sense, a 'miracle' is any 'event' which appears to defy the laws of nature. Why, then, did miracles figure so prominently in the ministry of Jesus? Here are four reasons:

A *This stained-glass window portrays a well-known miracle performed by Jesus. Decide which one it is and then find out where it is recorded in the New Testament. Write up your own description of it.*

a) He was deeply moved by the needs of the people. He:
- fed 5,000 men, women and children miraculously from loaves and fish because '...his heart went out to them, because they were like sheep without a shepherd' (Mark 6.30-44);
- healed two blind men who cried out to him (Matthew 9.27-31);
- brought Lazarus back to life after being '...moved with indignation and deeply distressed' (John 11.17-44).

b) He responded to the faith of people. For example:
- A Roman Army centurion expressed his belief that Jesus did not need to come to his house to cure his servant – "You need only to say the word and my servant will be cured." (Matthew 8.5-13)
- A woman, who had been haemorrhaging for twelve years, tried to touch his cloak saying "If I just touch his cloak I will be healed." (Luke 8.43-48)

c) He performed miracles to instil faith in people. He saved his disciples from a storm for this very reason – Mark 4.35-41.

d) He performed miracles to tell the people that the Kingdom of God had come. When John the Baptist was in prison he sent messengers to Jesus to find out whether he really was the Messiah. Jesus replied by telling the messengers to remind John the Baptist of the miracles that Jesus was performing. They were the final proof that God's rule on earth had begun.

1 · JESUS OF NAZARETH

B What do you think people might call a 'miracle' today? Do you think that 'miracles' still happen? Give some reasons for your answer.

ANSWER IN YOUR BOOK ...

1. Why did Jesus perform miracles?
2. Why do you think that people associated miracles with the coming of God's kingdom?
3. How did Jesus show his authority in the Gospels over illness, evil spirits, the forces of nature and death?

FIND OUT AND NOTE ...

Study each of these miracles carefully:
- Healing miracles
  Mark 2.3-12.
  Luke 18.35-43.   Matthew 8.5-13.
- Miracles over nature
  Mark 6.35-44.
  Luke 18. 48-51.   Matthew 8.23-27.
- Bringing the dead to life
  Luke 7.11-15.
  John 11.1-44.   Mark 5.22-24.

In the case of each miracle:
a) describe any unusual features;
b) discover whether faith was required from the person healed – or from someone else;
c) see whether any important statements by Jesus were attached to the miracle.

DISCUSS AMONG YOURSELVES ...

Jesus performed several miracles because of the needs of the people concerned. Here are three examples:

a) '...his heart went out to them, because they were like sheep without a shepherd...' (Mark 6.30-44)

b) 'As he went on from there Jesus was followed by two blind men, shouting, 'Have pity on us, Son of David.' (Matthew 9.27-31)

c) '...he was moved with indignation and deeply distressed...' (John 11.17-44)

Look up each of these miracles. What do you think really 'moved' Jesus in each case? Discuss among yourselves situations in our world today that might move Jesus in a similar way.

IN THE GLOSSARY ...

Synagogue; Satan; Messiah; Gospel; Prophet.

1.4 THE CRUCIFIXION OF JESUS

Jesus knew that he had aroused bitter opposition during his ministry – most of it coming from the religious leaders. He also knew that matters would come to a head if he visited Jerusalem, the city which stood at the heart of the Jewish faith. To go there during the great Jewish festival of Passover was added provocation. Jerusalem, though, was a city about which Jesus cared deeply:

> "O Jerusalem, Jerusalem, city that murders the prophets and stones the messengers sent to her! How often I have longed to gather your children, as a hen gathers her brood under her wings; but you would not let me." (Luke 13.34)

What happened in the city, during the last few days of his life, is crucial to understanding the whole ministry of Jesus.

Towards death

In one of his parables (Mark 12.1-12) Jesus compared the nation of Israel with a vineyard which was carefully looked after by its owner before being let out to tenants. When the owner sent his servants to collect his share of the harvest they were beaten up. Eventually, the owner sent his own son but the tenants killed him. The parable is teaching that Jesus, as God's Son, was aware that he would also share this fate.

When Jesus tried to tell his own disciples what lay ahead they could not understand it. Even those disciples closest to him, Peter, James and John, could not come to terms with the idea of a suffering and dying Messiah. This was not surprising. They still had so much to learn about Jesus, for after he left the earth, his undeserved suffering and death were to become the very heart of the early Church's message.

Who was responsible for the death of Jesus? Should the blame be laid at the feet of the Jewish leaders, the Jewish people or the Roman leaders? The question is far from being simply academic. For centuries the Jews, as a nation, were blamed for the death and the most barbaric persecution was directed against them. The Holocaust, in the Second World War, in which 6,000,000 Jewish men, women and children died, was the culmination of a long process of anti-semitism. The truth is that the New Testament presents the death of Jesus as God's plan – and largely leaves it at that.

A Why do you think that many people looking at the death of Jesus on a cross might conclude that his whole life had been a failure?

Death

The Gospels record two 'trials' of Jesus:

a) *The appearance before the High Priest, Caiaphas, and members of the Sanhedrin.* As the Jews had no power to put anyone to death this was hardly a real trial. It was simply an attempt to put some evidence together to set before Pontius Pilate, the Roman Emperor's representative in Jerusalem.

b) *The appearance before the Roman procurator, Pilate.* Three charges were laid against Jesus:
- that Jesus had misled the people;
- that Jesus had encouraged the people not to pay their taxes to Rome;
- that Jesus had claimed to be a king.

Pilate was not concerned with whether Jesus was guilty or not. His only concern was a political one. Would the Jews riot if he released Jesus and so destroy his own position as the 'upholder of peace'? Rather than take that risk he sentenced Jesus to death. Jesus was duly executed along with two other criminals. The only surprising thing was that he died so quickly – within six hours of being nailed to the cross. Criminals often lingered there for twenty-four hours or more.

B *This sculpture is illustrating an event in the sequence which led to the death of Jesus. Can you work out what is happening?*

ANSWER IN YOUR BOOK ...

1. Look up the parable of the vineyard in Mark 12.1-12. Retell it in your own words and explain why you think that Jesus told this parable so close to the end of his ministry.
2. Explain why Jesus appeared before both a Jewish and a Roman court.
3. Why do you think that the disciples and others found it very difficult to come to terms with the idea of God's son, the Messiah, suffering and dying?

READ AND DECIDE ...

Read each of these accounts of the death of Jesus carefully:
- Matthew 27.11-56.
- Mark 14.53-15.39.
- Luke 22.66-23.49.
- John 18.12-19.42.

a) List the details about the death of Jesus which occur in more than one Gospel.
b) Write an essay of about 500 words entitled 'The Death of Jesus of Nazareth' from the notes that you make.

FIND OUT AND NOTE ...

Find out what anti-semitism is. What link does it have with the death of Jesus?

IN THE GLOSSARY ...

Jerusalem; Passover; Messiah; High Priest; Pontius Pilate.

1.5 THE RESURRECTION OF JESUS

Did the crucifixion of Jesus make his life and ministry meaningless? According to the New Testament, his disciples were given the answer to this question through various resurrection 'appearances'. This is why the belief that Jesus returned from the dead, three days after he was crucified, stands at the very heart of the Christian faith. The early Church believed that Jesus was living through the Holy Spirit in the Christian community which began after the Day of Pentecost.

A *What do you think the early Christians understood by the resurrection of Jesus?*

The Gospels and the resurrection

Each of the four Gospels reports the fact that, three days after Jesus was put to death and buried, the tomb was empty. They do not all, however, tell quite the same story. Perhaps this is not surprising since the resurrection of Jesus seems to have taken his followers completely by surprise. The Jews did not hold any clear belief about life after death. As with all of the material in the Gospels, each of the evangelists (Gospel-writers) selected and shaped their accounts to emphasise their own particular view about Jesus.

The Gospels do not explain what happened to the body of Jesus. All we have is an empty tomb and we are left to make of that what we will. The Gospels are much more interested in the 'appearances' of Jesus after his resurrection to various individuals and groups of people. Quite in what form Jesus 'appeared' to them is also an open question. There was certainly a very real change in Jesus after his resurrection: it took people longer to recognise him (compare John 20.14 and Luke 24.13-35); he walked through locked doors (John 20.19-23) and he appeared and disappeared at will (Luke 24.36).

According to the New Testament Jesus appeared to:

1 Mary Magdalene and the 'other Mary' (Matthew 28.1-10).
2 Mary Magdalene, Salome and Mary, the mother of James (Mark 16.1-8).
3 Two disciples walking from Jerusalem to Emmaus (Luke 24.13-35).
4 The eleven disciples (Mark 16.14; Luke 24.36-49).
5 Five hundred of his followers (1.Corinthians 15.6).
6 James (1.Corinthians 15.7).
7 All of the apostles (1.Corinthians 15.7).

The meaning of the resurrection

The importance of the resurrection of Jesus lies in its meaning. According to the New Testament it is important in three clear ways:

a) It provides the proof that Jesus was who he claimed to be – God's Messiah. Preaching to a Jewish audience on the Day of Pentecost Peter declared:

> 'Let all Israel then accept as certain that God has made this same Jesus, whom you crucified, both Lord and Messiah.' (Acts 2.36)

b) It is the event that releases upon humankind a new kind of power – the power of God's Holy Spirit. Only after Jesus returned from the dead could this power be experienced.

c) It guarantees that at the end of time all of Jesus' followers will also return to life. This is why Paul calls the resurrection of Jesus:

> '…the first fruits of the harvest of the dead…' (1.Corinthians 15.20)

B *Making an Easter garden is an old tradition. What do you think Christians today understand by the resurrection of Jesus?*

ANSWER IN YOUR BOOK …

1. What do you think are the main problems which Christians have to face when they claim that Jesus rose from the dead?
2. Look up the various references in the New Testament to the 'appearances' of Jesus after he rose from the dead. Can you draw any conclusions from these appearances?
3. What effect do you think the resurrection of Jesus might have on Christian believers today?

READ AND DECIDE …

Paul refers to the resurrection of Jesus in 1.Corinthians 15.3-7 and adds a personal note at the end:

'…what I received I passed on to you as of first importance; that Christ died for our sins according to the Scriptures; that he was buried, that he was raised on the third day according to the Scriptures, and that he appeared to Peter, and then to the Twelve. After that, he appeared to more than five hundred of the brothers at the same time, most of whom are still living, though some have fallen asleep. Then he appeared to James, then to all the apostles, and last of all he appeared to me also, as to one abnormally born.'

a) Twice here Paul uses the phrase 'according to the Scriptures' although none of the New Testament was written at the time. To what do you think he was referring?
b) It is not possible to match up the appearances recorded here with those found in the Gospels. Two of the 'appearances' here do not appear in the Gospels. Which are they? Does it matter?
c) What did Paul mean when he spoke of himself as being '…one abnormally born'? Read Luke's account of Paul's encounter with the risen Christ in Acts 9.1-9. Does this count as 'evidence' for the resurrection of Christ?
d) Return to 1.Corinthians 15. This time read 15.12-34. What does Paul insist are the consequences of the resurrection of Christ?

IN THE GLOSSARY …

Pentecost; Holy Spirit.

2.1 THE BIRTH OF THE CHRISTIAN CHURCH

The Jewish festival of Passover (Pesach), during which Jesus died, was followed fifty days later by the annual festival of Pentecost (the Feast of Weeks). Luke described what happened at this particular Pentecost in the Acts of the Apostles. We have no other record of this momentous event in the history of the Christian Church.

The Day of Pentecost

For several weeks after the death of Jesus his followers huddled together in Jerusalem waiting for the spiritual power that he had promised them:

> 'You will receive power when the Holy Spirit comes upon you.' (Acts 1.8)

In the supernatural experience that followed two 'pictures' are used to describe the event:

> 'Suddenly there came from the sky what sounded like a strong, driving **wind**, a noise which filled the whole house where they were sitting.' (Acts 2.2)

> 'And there appeared to them **flames** like tongues of fire distributed among them and coming to rest on each of them.' (Acts 2.3)

In a sermon later that day Peter, the leader of the first Christians, made four points about Jesus:

a) He was the Messiah. (Acts 2.36)
b) The Messiah had been crucified and brought back to life by God. (Acts 2.24)
c) Jesus had now been given the highest place in heaven. (Acts 2.32-33)
d) All those who repent of their sins and believe the Gospel are forgiven by God. (Acts 2.38)

These four beliefs became the corner stone of the Church's preaching. On the first day alone 3000 people were converted. Later, when Paul succeeded Peter as the Church's leader, he founded Christian communities all around the Mediterranean Sea. The Gospel also spread into Europe.

A *This banner suggests the Holy Spirit as a wind. By looking at Acts 2.1-3, explain what characteristics you think this symbol is intended to portray.*

B *Within a few decades of the death of Jesus there were Christian communities spread all around the Mediterranean Sea. Which event led to such a rapid growth of the Christian Church?*

Some tough times

The spread of Christianity was certainly not trouble free. The new Church faced problems from the beginning. Amongst the most pressing was the relationship between the new faith of Christianity and the old faith of Judaism. For some years after the death of Jesus his disciples remained firmly within the Jewish faith. They took part in the regular worship of the Temple; they observed the Jewish festivals; they worshipped regularly in the synagogue on the Sabbath and they lived by the law of Moses. At the same time they proclaimed that the Messiah had come, had been crucified and brought back to life.

Although nearly all the first Christians were Jews, an increasing number of non-Jews (Gentiles) were being converted to the faith. Questions began to be asked about how they should be treated. Should they, for instance, be asked to accept certain Jewish practices, such as circumcision? Church leaders travelled to Jerusalem in 49 CE to investigate the problem.

In 64 CE Nero, the Roman Emperor, began the first real persecution of the Church and both Peter and Paul died before it ended. For many Christians the persecution was an indication that Jesus was about to return to the earth, but when this did not happen they began to develop a Church organisation for the first time. Then, in 325 CE, the Emperor Constantine was converted to Christianity and things were never the same again.

ANSWER IN YOUR BOOK ...

1 How does Luke explain what happened to the followers of Jesus on the Day of Pentecost?
2 What were the key elements in the message preached by the early Christians?
3 Why do you think that the Christians linked their first experience of persecution with the return of Christ to the earth?

FIND OUT AND NOTE ...

Read Acts 2.1–42.

a) What did the 'last days' refer to and what had God promised to do in them and where?
b) How did the early Christians know that Jesus was God's Messiah?
c) Why was Jesus put to death and who, according to the writer of the Acts of the Apostles, was responsible?
d) Why was Jesus raised from the dead?
e) What did Peter tell the crowd to do?

READ AND DECIDE ...

Read Acts 15.1–35.

a) Why was a Council called in Jerusalem?
b) What did Paul and Barnabas tell the believers in Phoenicia and Samaria – and what was their response?
c) What did those opposed to Paul and Barnabas maintain at the Council?
d) What did Peter tell the Council?
e) What advice did James give to the Council?
f) What was in the letter sent out to all non-Jewish believers from the Council? Why do you think this directive has been called 'an uneasy compromise'?

IN THE GLOSSARY ...

Passover; Pentecost; Jerusalem; Messiah; Gospel; Gentile.

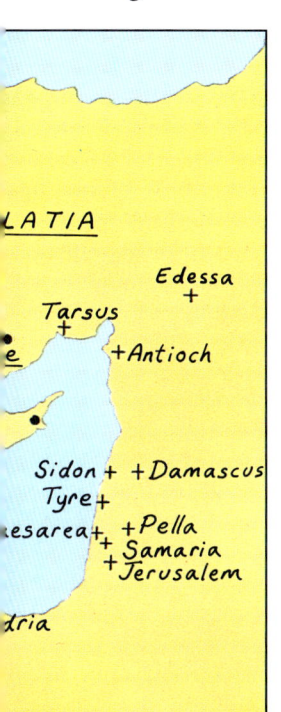

2.2 THE DIFFERENT CHRISTIAN CHURCHES

After the downfall of the Roman Empire in 410, power in the Church shifted from the West to the East. However, a Council of Bishops, meeting at Chalcedon in 451, adopted a resolution that many Eastern bishops could not accept. As a result, the Church began to show its first real signs of disintegration with the formation of the Eastern Oriental Church. It was not until 1054, though, that the split between East and West became final when the 'Great Schism' took place. The Orthodox Church broke away from the Roman Catholic Church over three main areas of disagreement:

a) The claim of the Pope in Rome to have supreme authority over the whole Church.
b) The desire of Rome to become the leading centre of Christianity.
c) A change by Rome in the wording of the Creed which Eastern Christians considered to be untouchable.

So Christendom broke into two parts. The Orthodox Church was formed and the breach between it and the Catholic Church has never been healed.

The Reformation

In the centuries that followed the Great Schism dissatisfaction began to build up in the Catholic Church. Matters came to a head in 1517 when Martin Luther, a German monk, nailed a list of 95 theses (grievances) to the door of his church in Wittenburg. In these 'theses' Luther argued that:

1. A Christian is a person who has faith in God without needing to buy salvation through purchasing indulgences. This belief is called 'Justification by Faith'.
2. Christians can pray directly to God for forgiveness without needing to go through a priest.
3. The Bible, and not the Church, is the supreme authority for all Christians.

This protest against the power of the Catholic Church led to the birth of the Protestant movement and a further splintering of the Church worldwide. As a result of the Reformation Luther was excommunicated from the Catholic Church. However, churches were soon formed in Germany based on his teaching. In this country Henry VIII rejected the authority of the Pope although the disagreement was over a personal and not a spiritual matter – the Pope refused to grant Henry a divorce. He declared himself to be Head and Protector of the Church and the Church of England (or Anglican Church) was later formed under Elizabeth I.

The Nonconformists

Before long the Church of England was to splinter and break up. The new Churches were called Nonconformist because they did not 'conform' to the teaching of the Church of England. Amongst these Churches were:

a) The Baptist Church, which was largely based on the belief that only adults, and not children, should be baptised.
b) The Quakers, formed by George Fox in the middle of the 17th century, with a simple and largely silent form of worship.
c) The Methodist Church, which was born in the 18th century after the death of John Wesley, a Church of England minister.
d) The Salvation Army, which sprang out of Methodism in 1865.

All of these Nonconformist Churches remain a part of the Christian scene today. Others, however, are still coming into existence. In the 1970s the House Church Movement was formed and it now has over 20,000 members in this country alone. Today, in fact, there are more than 20,000 different Churches worldwide – a far cry from the vision of their founder who prayed that all his followers might be one (John 17.11).

A What was Luther particularly protesting about when he nailed his 95 theses to the door of his church in Wittenburg?

2 · THE CHRISTIAN CHURCH

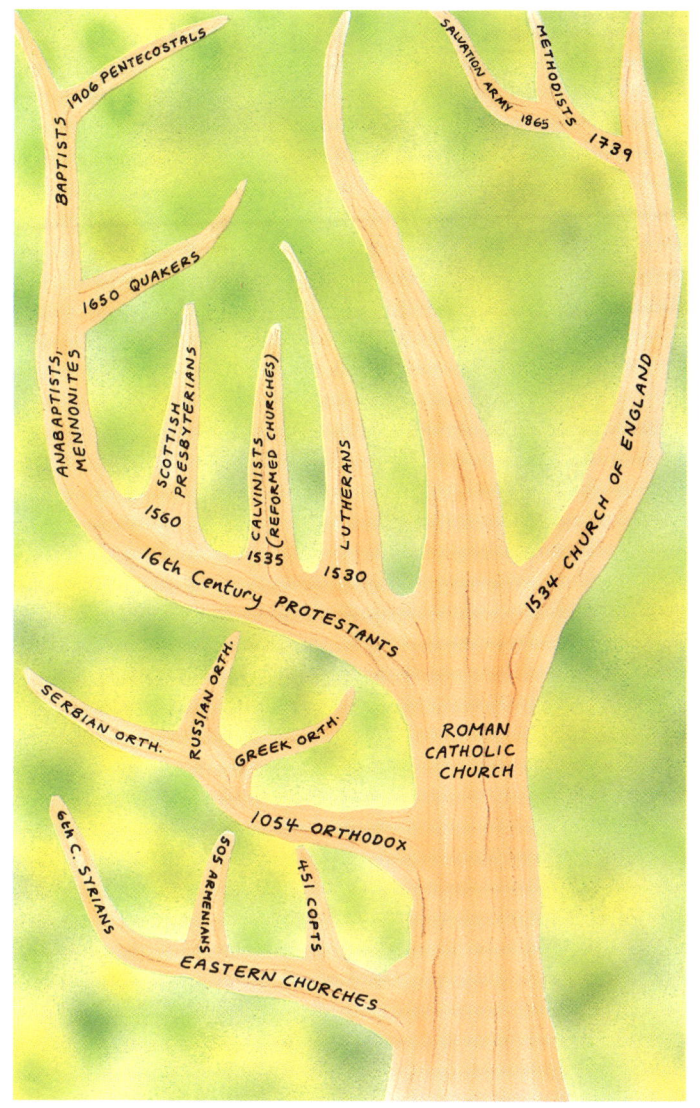

B The Methodist Church is based on the teachings of John Wesley. Find out as much as you can about this important 18th century religious leader.

COMPLETE A CHART ...

The chart above shows just how the main Christian Churches have grown. Copy it into your book and then answer these questions:

a) Why do you think an analogy is drawn here between the breaking-up of the Christian Church and a tree with its branches?

b) What is the foundation on which the Christian Church is based?

c) What happened as a result of the Great Schism in 1054?

d) What did the Protestants protest about?

e) What was the break between the Roman Catholic and the Protestant Church called?

ANSWER IN YOUR BOOK ...

1 What is meant by the Great Schism and why did it come about?

2 What was the Reformation?

3 Who are the Nonconformists and where did their name come from?

IN THE GLOSSARY ...

Eastern Orthodox Church; Roman Catholic Church; Great Schism; Pope; Creed; Indulgence; Priest; Protestant; Excommunication; Church of England; Anglican Church; Nonconformist; Methodist Church; Salvation Army; House Church Movement.

2.3 THE ROMAN CATHOLIC CHURCH

There are some 900 million Roman Catholics in the modern world and they make up more than 50% of the Christian Church. Although this Church is worldwide, it is strongest in North America, South America and Europe.

Why 'Roman Catholic'?

The name of this Church is significant in two ways:

1. It is 'Roman' because it recognises the Pope, the Bishop of Rome, as its leader. The pope governs the Church worldwide with his advisers, the cardinals, bishops and committees in their individual dioceses. Catholics believe that the Papacy and its authority comes directly from Jesus Christ himself who appointed Peter to be the first head of the Church. This same Peter became the first Bishop of Rome. By reading Matthew 16.18-20 you can see why this direct line of succession from Peter to the present Pope is thought to be so important by Catholics. The powers given originally by Jesus to Peter are believed to be transferred directly to his successors in the Papal Office (Papal Succession) by the 'Laying on of Hands'. This allows the Pope to speak 'infallibly' (by divine authority without error) on occasions. This only happens when he is speaking about matters of belief and delivers his statement 'ex cathedra' (from the throne). When he does so the new belief becomes binding on all Roman Catholics and becomes part of the official teaching of the Church.

A The altar in a Roman Catholic church is the focal-point of the building. Can you find out why it occupies the central place?

2. It is 'Catholic' because the word means 'universal' and Catholics see themselves as being the one true Church – Christians in other Churches are 'separated brethren'.

A little history

By the 5th century the Bishop of Rome was claiming to have authority over the whole Christian Church – a claim that was disputed by other bishops. It was this claim which led to the Great Schism and the Pope's authority being confined to churches in the western part of Christendom. In the centuries that followed there was increasing corruption in the western Church and this was a major factor in the breakaway of the Protestants during the Reformation.

The Protestant Reformation was followed by a Catholic Counter-Reformation in which the Church tried to win back the hearts and minds of the people. The Roman Catholic Church prided itself on being the 'repository of truth' – a body which did not change. This was strongly maintained until 1958 when an aged and little-known Italian was surprisingly elected Pope. He became Pope John XXIII and set up the Second Vatican Council (see Unit 2.4).

Catholic beliefs

Roman Catholics believe that all of their beliefs are rooted in the teaching of Jesus Christ and his Apostles. A few of these beliefs, however, have only been 'officially' accepted comparatively recently – such as the Immaculate Conception (1854) and the Assumption of the Blessed Virgin Mary (1950). Roman Catholics would maintain, however, that the Church had actually believed these doctrines since the time of the Apostles. In addition, the Church also places a considerable emphasis on the following:

a) The Mass as the central act of church worship and the occasion when the sacrifice of Christ on the cross is re-enacted – a belief which is called 'transubstantiation';
b) The importance of the saints and the Virgin Mary;
c) The belief in heaven and purgatory;
d) The use of the rosary as an aid to prayer.

B You will find a statue of the Virgin Mary in every Catholic church. Find out as much as you can about her and the place she occupies in Roman Catholic devotion and worship.

ANSWER IN YOUR BOOK ...

1. Why are Roman Catholics so called?
2. Why does the Pope occupy an important place in the Roman Catholic Church?
3. What beliefs are particularly important to Roman Catholics?

READ AND DECIDE ...

Read Matthew 16.13-20 carefully.

a) What declaration did Simon Peter make about Jesus?
b) How did Jesus respond to that declaration?
c) What does Jesus declare that he will build his Church on?
d) What did Jesus promise to give to Peter? What do you think he meant by this promise?
e) Why do you think that this promise to Peter is particularly important to the Roman Catholic Church?

FIND OUT AND NOTE ...

Two events are mentioned in this unit which have had enormous repercussions for the life of the Christian Church. They are the following:

a) The Great Schism.
b) The Protestant Reformation.

Find out more about these and write an account on each of them.

IN THE GLOSSARY ...

Bishop; Cardinal; Laying on of hands; Altar; Protestant; Roman Catholic Church; Transubstantiation; Mass; Purgatory; Rosary; Virgin Mary.

2.4 THE SECOND VATICAN COUNCIL

In 1958 a 76 year old Italian cardinal, Angelo Roncalli, took the title Pope John XXIII when he was elected to the Papal office. The other cardinals who supported him thought that they had elected a 'caretaker' Pope who would look after the Church for a year or two. Instead, he set up a special Council of the Roman Catholic Church to look at its worship and witness its entry into the second half of the 20th century.

Pope John XXIII thought that the Council could 'open the windows of the Church and let in some fresh air'. The word 'aggiornamento' began to emerge as the keynote of the Council. It simply meant 'bringing the Church up-to-date'. In terms of the Catholic Church it meant a call for it to return to its sources; to rediscover its faith and traditions and to work out what they meant in relation to the modern world.

Between 1962 and 1965 over 2500 bishops, abbots and cardinals met together in St Peter's Basilica in the Vatican City. These sessions are known as the Second Vatican Council since the first such Council of the Church had been held between 1869 and 1870. Although Pope John XXIII died in 1963, his successor, Pope Paul VI, continued with the Council until its discussions were completed in 1965.

The Second Vatican Council

At the end of the Council there were no less than sixteen major statements. These statements changed so much in the Roman Catholic Church that the Council

A What do you think Pope John XXIII might have had in mind when he called the Second Vatican Council?

has been described as a 'watershed' (turning-point) in the Church's history. The Roman Catholic Church could never be quite the same again. In particular:

a) The way in which the Church understood itself was changed. Through baptism all people, clergy and laity (ordinary people in the congregation), shared the same faith and responsibility to share that faith with others. The laity were encouraged to play a full part in the Church's life for the first time by forming a partnership with the clergy. The whole Catholic community, clergy and laity, was described as the 'pilgrim people of God'.

b) Changes were made in the worship life of the Church. For centuries, every act of worship had been conducted in Latin but now this was dropped. Worship was to take place in the usual language of the people in the congregation. This was especially important for Catholics in Asia and Africa. Catholics were encouraged to spend more time studying the Bible and to place it at the centre of their worship. This was very important in improving relations between the Catholic Church and the Protestant Churches. The censorship of reading matter for Catholics by the Church largely became a thing of the past.

c) Roman Catholics were encouraged to think differently about other branches of the Christian Church and other religions. Christians from different Churches should treat each other with tolerance and trust – and the same should be true of all contacts between Catholics and followers of other religions.

d) The Church pledged itself to be fully involved in the problems of society. The Council called for:
- nuclear weapons to be abolished;
- the Arms Trade to be halted;
- a fairer distribution of the world's resources;
- racism, in any form, to be opposed;
- a bridge to be built between Communism and the Church.

At the same time the important beliefs of the Church were left untouched – among them the infallibility of the Pope, the Virgin Birth, the importance of the Virgin Mary and the rejection of all that 'devalues human life', including artificial means of birth-control, abortion and euthanasia.

ANSWER IN YOUR BOOK ...

1. What was the Second Vatican Council?
2. How did the Second Vatican Council seek to change the relationship between the clergy and the laity?
3. What recommendations did the Council make about the relationships between the different Christian Churches and the relationship of the Roman Catholic Church to other Faiths?

DISCUSS AMONG YOURSELVES ...

Here are three quotations from the Council for you to discuss:

a) 'Virginity must be regarded as a gift from God.'
b) 'From the moment of conception life must be guarded with the greatest possible care.'
c) 'All who are baptised have the right to be honoured as Christians.'

FIND OUT AND NOTE ...

a) Take one of the doctrines which was left untouched by the Second Vatican Council and find out just what Catholics believe about it.
b) Invite a Roman Catholic priest and/or a Catholic layman or laywoman to tell you just how the recommendations of The Second Vatican Council have been put into practice.

WHAT DO YOU THINK?

When Pope John XXIII called the Second Vatican Council he declared that he wanted it to:

'...open the windows and let a breath of fresh air blow through the Church.'

How did the Second Vatican Council carry out the wishes of Pope John XXIII?

IN THE GLOSSARY ...

Cardinal; Pope; Laity; Virgin Birth; Virgin Mary; Abortion.

2.5 THE ORTHODOX CHURCH

Within a few centuries of the death of Christ cities like Rome, Antioch, Alexandria and Constantinople had become great Christian centres. As this happened differences in outlook were becoming apparent between the western church, under the authority of the Bishop of Rome, and the Eastern Orthodox (right-thinking) Churches which valued their independence. A split first appeared in the 7th century and this was completed by the Great Schism in 1054. The Church was now irreparably divided into two bodies. Today the Orthodox Church, a family of self-governing Churches, has 150,000,000 believers who are mainly found in eastern Europe, Russia and around the eastern Mediterranean. Each Orthodox Church – such as the Russian, Serbian, Armenian and Greek Churches – is led by a senior bishop who is usually known as a 'patriarch'. Among the patriarchs special honour is given to the Patriarch of Constantinople, based in Instanbul, who is the spiritual leader of the whole family. As a result, he is known as the 'Ecumenical Patriarch'. The two broad families into which the Orthodox Church is divided are:

1. The Oriental Orthodox Church with some 30,000,000 believers.
2. The Eastern Orthodox Church with 120,000,000 members.

The intention is that the two 'families' should merge in 1995 and become one Orthodox Church.

Orthodox beliefs

The basic belief of Orthodoxy is implied in its name – 'orthos' meaning 'rightly' and 'doxadzein' meaning 'glorify'. Orthodox believers see themselves as those who 'rightly glorify' God. They draw their beliefs from two main sources:

❖ The Holy Scriptures.
❖ The Traditions of the Church.

Along with the Roman Catholic Church, the Greek Orthodox Church places a very high premium on the value and importance of tradition. The faith, expressed in the teachings and worship of the Church, is that which was once 'delivered to the Apostles'. Although there are minor disagreements over belief between the different Orthodox Churches, there is total agreement over what really matters. All Orthodox Christians believe that:

a) God is a Trinity – three persons in the single Godhead. Orthodox believers share this conviction with almost every other Christian denomination (see Unit 8.2).

A *The two families of the Orthodox Church are due to unite. Why do you think it has taken them so long to reach this decision?*

b) Jesus Christ, the second person in the Trinity, was both fully God and fully man.
c) The Church is holy and spans both heaven and earth. Jesus Christ, the Apostles, martyrs and other holy ones form the foundation of the Church. All believers, living and dead, are part of the one Church.
d) All worship must centre around the Sacraments. There are seven such sacraments or, as the Orthodox Church prefers to call them, 'mysteries'. The Divine Liturgy, the most important Orthodox service, is celebrated every Sunday and on all feast days. It is seen as the re-enactment of the birth, life, death and resurrection of Jesus.
e) Men and women must worship God with all their senses. The Divine Liturgy makes full use of drama with incense, the voice of the priest chanting the words and the songs of the choir and congregation in reply. All singing, incidentally, is unaccompanied. Icons (religious pictures) also play a very important role in Orthodox worship. During the service worshippers move around to pray in front of them, bow, and kiss them as a mark of respect and honour.

B *How does the meaning of the word 'Orthodox' help us to understand the distinctive approach of Orthodox believers to Christianity?*

ANSWER IN YOUR BOOK ...

1. When did the Orthodox Church split away from the Roman Catholic Church?
2. Into which two 'families' is the Orthodox Church divided and what is due to happen to them?
3. Which beliefs do Orthodox believers have in common?

WHAT DO YOU THINK?

a) Why do you think that it is important for the Orthodox Church to be able to trace its beliefs and traditions back to the earliest days of Christianity?
b) Why do you think that it has been important for each Orthodox Church to be independent, taking its name from the country in which it has been situated?

FIND OUT AND NOTE ...

a) Which two sources does the Orthodox Church recognise for its authority? Which other Church also derives its teachings from the same two authorities?
b) Can you discover two beliefs or practices in the Orthodox Church which are derived from tradition alone?
c) Why do you think that the Orthodox Church prefers to call the sacraments 'mysteries'?
d) Orthodox believers hold a distinctive view of the Church. What is it?

IN THE GLOSSARY ...

Bishop; Eastern Orthodox Church; Great Schism; Trinity; Apostles; Sacraments.

2.6 THE CHURCH OF ENGLAND

In 597 Pope Leo I sent Augustine from Rome to bring the Christian Gospel to England. When he landed he was astonished to find the Christian faith well established, although in a very different form from the one that he had brought with him. He discovered a Celtic form of Christianity which kept very close to nature, the seasons and the earth. Augustine had brought a highly disciplined and controlled form of Christianity under the authority of the Pope. Inevitably, there was considerable suspicion and mistrust between the two very different approaches to Christianity. Eventually, though, the Roman form prevailed and Christians in this country reluctantly accepted the authority of the Pope at the Synod of Whitby, held in 664.

The Church of England

While the German Catholic monk, Martin Luther, was protesting on the Continent against the power and corruption of the Catholic Church, King Henry VIII was having his own battle with the Pope. The issue was whether the King could divorce his wife, Catherine of Aragon, and when the Pope refused to grant the request the King declared himself to be:

> 'Especial Protector, only and supreme lord, and, as far as the law of Christ allows, even supreme head of the Church.'

In the years that followed steps were taken to break Rome's power over the Church in England:

1. Two Acts of Parliament, in 1536 and 1539, authorised the dissolution of the monasteries, the real seats of Catholic power in Great Britain. It was claimed that they were corrupt, but the real reason for their dissolution was that their wealth was needed to ease Henry's financial problems.

2. Although many traditional Catholic practices remained, Protestant ideas began to gain ground. Publications filtered through from Protestant Europe and this influenced the decision to place a Bible in every parish church in the country. The official translation used was that of Miles Coverdale in 1539.

3. The Book of Common Prayer, largely the work of Thomas Cranmer, had gone through three revisions by 1662. These changes gradually removed most of the Catholic teaching in the book. The Book of Common Prayer was to provide the basic services for the Church of England until the publication of the Alternative Service Book in the early 1980s.

4. Under Elizabeth I the Church of England became the Established (Official) Church in England. It retains this position today, although there have been increasing calls, both from within and outside the Church of England, for it to be disestablished. Its leaders are appointed by the Prime Minister, with the Archbishop of Canterbury officiating on State occasions and its bishops sitting in the House of Lords. Serious changes to the Church, such as the recent legislation to ordain women, have to be debated and passed by Parliament, and this makes change in the Church a slow and cumbersome process.

A *This is a traditional parish church. When this church is described as being part of the 'Established Church' what does that mean?*

Beliefs

A statement drawn up in the 16th century, called The Thirty-Nine Articles, still forms the basis for the belief of the Church of England. The Lambeth Conference (a meeting of Anglican leaders which assembles every ten years), reduced these beliefs in 1888 to just four:

a) That the Scriptures contain all 'things necessary to salvation'. This was the distinguishing mark of the Reformation. The Church of England is a 'reformed' Church.

b) That the Creeds (statements of belief) contain all that an Anglican needs to believe.

c) That just two sacraments, Holy Communion and baptism, should be celebrated.

d) That bishops are appointed by God to have special authority within the Church. This means that the Church of England is an 'episcopal' Church.

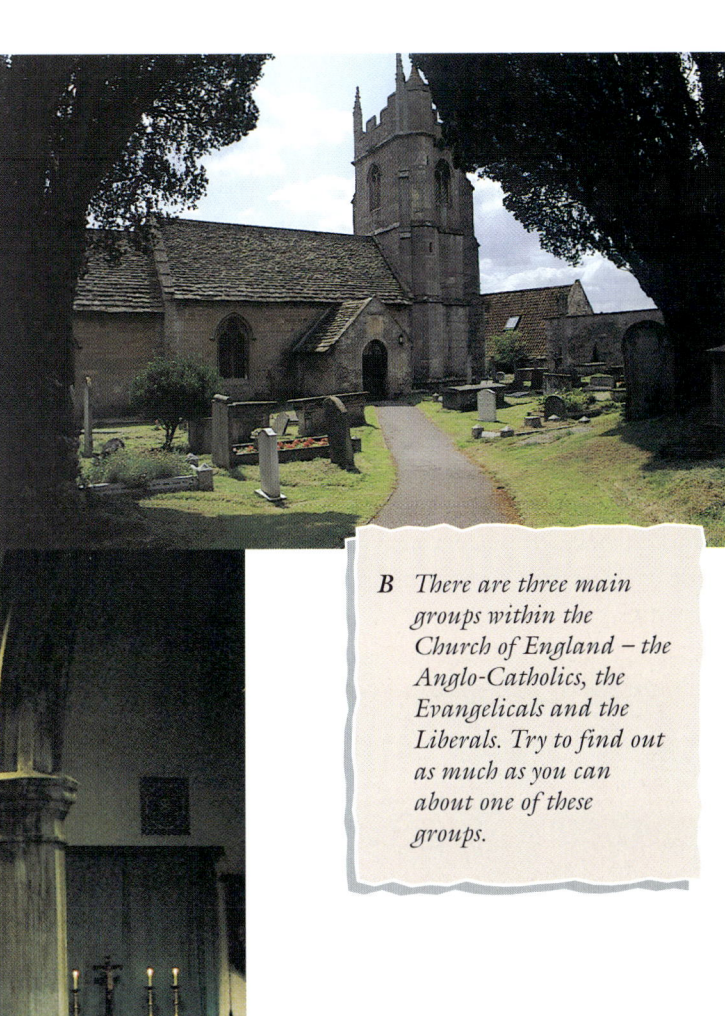

B There are three main groups within the Church of England – the Anglo-Catholics, the Evangelicals and the Liberals. Try to find out as much as you can about one of these groups.

ANSWER IN YOUR BOOK ...

1. How did the Church of England come into existence?
2. What steps were taken to destroy the power of the Catholic Church after the Church of England broke its ties with Rome?
3. List two ways in which the Church of England is treated differently from other Churches in this country.

FIND OUT AND NOTE ...

a) Can you find out more about each of the following:
  - The arrival of Christianity in England.
  - The Establishment of the Church of England.
  - The Book of Common Prayer.
  - The part played by the Archbishop of Canterbury in the Church of England.

b) Is there a priest or a lay person in your area who has left the Church of England as a result of the decision to ordain women to the priesthood? If so, invite him/her in to answer some of your questions. For instance:
  - Which branch of the Church of England do they come from?
  - Why could they not accept the Church's decision to ordain women?
  - What do they intend to do in the future?

To balance things out, if possible, also invite a newly ordained female priest in to explain why she thinks the Church of England made the right decision on the issue.

IN THE GLOSSARY ...

Pope; Church of England; Monastery; Book of Common Prayer; Established Church; Bishop; Thirty-Nine Articles; Creed; Sacrament; Holy Communion; Anglo-Catholics; Evangelicals.

2.7 THE NONCONFORMISTS

A number of Protestant Churches, known as Nonconformist or Free Churches, grew out of the Church of England and other Churches from the 17th century onwards. Among them were the Quakers, the Methodist Church and the Salvation Army.

The Quakers

The Quakers were a Protestant denomination founded in the middle of the 17th century by George Fox. He wanted his followers to return to the simple lifestyle and faith of the early Christians. He initially called his movement 'The Society of Friends' because he wanted its members to be friends of God and of each other. They were dubbed 'Quakers' by a judge who, at Fox's trial in 1650, was told to 'tremble at the voice of the Lord.' The title, intended as an insult, was taken to symbolise the devotion and submission of the 'Friends' to God and so was widely adopted.

The Quakers soon developed a simple way of worshipping. They saw no need for priests since each man and woman can follow their 'inner light' by which God guides all people into truth. This 'inner light' is really the voice of God's Holy Spirit. Sunday worship is mainly made up of silence which is only broken by the voices of those who believe that God's Spirit has prompted them to speak.

The Methodist Church

Methodism is the Protestant denomination which came into existence through the preaching and teaching of the Anglican clergyman John Wesley (1703-1791). Wesley first received the nickname 'Methodist' when he was studying at Oxford because of the methodical way in which he read and studied the Bible. After becoming a priest, Wesley had his own 'heart-warming' experience of God which convinced him that his sins had been forgiven. This inspired him to ride the length and breadth of the country on horseback preaching to large crowds in the open-air. Thousands of people were converted, but, after Wesley's death, these people were not made welcome into the Church of England. Instead they formed their own Methodist Church, installed their own ministers and found that they had ready-made congregations.

In 1969 there was an attempt to re-unite the Methodist Church with the Church of England. Clergy of the Church of England voted against it but exploratory talks are planned to take place again in 1995. The Methodist Church continues, in its worship and witness, to place a heavy emphasis on the necessity for each person to respond personally to the Christian Gospel.

A What is distinctive about the Quaker style of worship?

The Salvation Army

The Salvation Army was founded by William Booth, a Methodist minister, as the 'Christian Mission' in London's East End in 1865. It was given the name 'Salvation Army' in 1878 and was organised along military lines with a general (initially William Booth himself), colonels, adjutants and corporals. Two years later it adopted its distinctive uniform and brass bands. Within a short time the Salvation Army had spread to other towns and cities as well as establishing its work overseas. Today it has workers in 74 different countries.

In many ways the Salvation Army has been a pioneer amongst Christian Churches. It concentrated its efforts on the neediest areas and conducted open-air meetings, accompanied by brass bands, an effective way of contacting the masses. At the same time it found work for prisoners released from prison, needy women and children, and teenagers who had left home with nowhere to go. It also set itself up as a campaigner against the evils of alcohol, gambling and smoking. Many of these activities have been financed through selling the Salvation Army's newspaper 'War Cry' on the streets and in public houses.

ANSWER IN YOUR BOOK ...

1. Why do you think that Nonconformist Churches are also called 'Free Churches'?
2. Why do you think that, throughout his lifetime, John Wesley was very reluctant to leave the Church of England and start another new Church?
3. What do you think William Booth saw as the advantages of organising his movement along military lines? What does this say about the work that he was trying to do?

FIND OUT AND NOTE ...

Invite a Salvation Army officer in to speak to your class. Try to find out the following:

a) Why the Salvation Army was founded in the first place and what social problems it was trying to tackle in 19th century Britain.
b) How the work of the Salvation Army has changed over the years and which problems it is most deeply involved with today.
c) What the main beliefs of the Salvation Army are.
d) What the Salvation Army is doing locally in your area.

COMPLETE A CHART ...

In this unit you have been introduced to three Nonconformist Churches. Draw up a chart like the one below to tabulate the information you have discovered.

CHURCH	FOUNDER	WHEN FORMED	BELIEFS
METHODIST			
QUAKERS			
SALVATION ARMY			

IN THE GLOSSARY ...

Free Church; Salvation Army; Methodist Church.

2.8 THE EVANGELICALS

Evangelicals are Christians of any denomination who believe that a person becomes a Christian by committing themselves to Jesus Christ after they have undergone a 'conversion experience'. This group of Christians is now the fastest-growing in the Christian Church with one in four believers now claiming to be Evangelical. The group has only really become established within the Church during the second half of the 20th Century.

Evangelical beliefs

The beliefs held by Evangelicals are more clearly defined than those of any other Christian group. Below are some which are considered to be the most important:

a) A belief in the Bible as the inspired and faultless Word of God. When the books of the Bible were first being written each writer was inspired by the Holy Spirit and so could only write the truth. It was the 'truth' then and remains the 'truth' today. The Bible is without error and carries the full authority of God. When people read the Bible openly God speaks to them, hence the favourite Evangelical description of the Bible as the 'Word of God'. Great emphasis is also placed on the preaching of the Bible in the sermon and this is the central element in any Evangelical service. Evangelicals believe that the Bible itself, when presented in the power of God's Spirit, is able to challenge and convince those listening of their own sinfulness and of God's power to forgive.

b) A belief that the Bible is at the centre of their own devotional life. Evangelicals often talk of having a 'Quiet Time' every day when they read a passage from the Bible, reflect upon it and pray. Because God speaks to them mainly through the Bible, Evangelicals believe that it is very important to know it thoroughly. Bible-studies are a prominent feature of Evangelical church-life.

c) A belief that the Bible tells us all that we need to know about God and ourselves. Humankind was created by God: we were created and we did not evolve from lower forms of life. Every human being is born with a sinful nature (Original Sin) which he/she has inherited from the first man and woman who disobeyed God in the Garden of Eden. Because of that act of disobedience, everyone stands under the condemnation of God. But God, in his mercy, sent Jesus Christ to be the Saviour of the world. Christ died 'in our place' and so took the punishment of God for our sins. This doctrine is called 'justification by faith' and was first emphasised by the Apostle Paul and Martin Luther. The same Jesus, who died to save those who believe, will return to the earth at some future time to be its judge. This is called the 'Second Coming'.

A These Evangelical beliefs are displayed outside a church. Why do you think that this particular church feels that it is necessary to do this?

WHAT WE BELIEVE

About God:
God is the Creator of all things. He is powerful, loving and pure, and He is one God in three Persons– Father, Son and Holy Spirit.

About Jesus Christ:
He is Gods Son, and is both fully human and fully divine. He died on the cross in the place of sinners, He rose again from the dead, He is alive today, and He will one day personally return to earth as the Judge of every person.

About the Holy Spirit:
He is fully divine and makes the work of Jesus Christ real in the lives of believers.

About Ourselves:
Every person is a sinner by nature and therefore separated from God and under his judgment, God invites every person to turn from their sin and trust in Jesus Christ as Saviour. All who believe in Him are saved, but those who do not turn to Him in repentance and faith remain under Gods judgement.

About the Bible:
The Bible is Gods living Word and is therefore totally true. Through it He speaks to the world today, It contains all that we need to know about God, and about how we can be made right with Him and live to please Him.

d) Everyone must respond to this 'Good News' (Gospel) for themselves. Evangelicals believe that being 'converted' is the start of a new life. Those converted are also expected to share their faith with others and this is called 'evangelism'. Evangelism can take place through large rallies or meetings; in church services; on the streets; in the work-place or in the home. Whatever the chosen method, Evangelicals are constantly seeking to introduce other people to Jesus Christ.

B *It is Easter Sunday and this group of Evangelicals are setting out to share their faith with others in their area. What is the 'faith' that they are sharing?*

READ AND DECIDE ...

Evangelicals place a great emphasis upon a personal experience of God. Here are two Evangelicals talking about particular aspects of their own experience. Read what they have to say carefully:

a) Anne, 21. 'I was converted to Christ at a meeting three years ago. Since then I have grown as a Christian by setting aside regular times for prayer, reading my Bible and meeting other like-minded Christians. Next year I hope to go to college to study to be a missionary. That is what I believe God is calling me to do.'

* What do you think Anne means when she speaks of being 'converted to Christ'?
* Why do you think that praying, reading the Bible and meeting with other Christians are important means of spiritual growth?
* What do you understand by the term 'missionary'?

b) Don, 24. 'I became a Christian when I was just eight years old. Since then I have become a great believer in prayer. Time and time again I have discovered that God answers my prayers – whether it is to do with my family, my work or my love-life. God always seems to be intervening in my life.'

There are several phrases in these two quotes which other Christians might feel uncomfortable using. Can you work out what they are and say why you think they might make some people feel this way?

ANSWER IN YOUR BOOK ...

1. What are the distinctive beliefs which Christians who are Evangelicals hold?
2. Why do Evangelicals often refer to the Bible as the 'Word of God'?
3. What is 'evangelism' and what forms might it take in the Evangelical community?

IN THE GLOSSARY ...

Evangelical; Bible; Holy Spirit; Original Sin; Gospel; Evangelism; Missionary.

2.9 THE CHARISMATIC MOVEMENT

Since the late 1960s many Protestant and Roman Catholic churches have been affected by the Charismatic Movement. This movement emphasises the role of the Holy Spirit in giving Christians an intense experience of God. Charismatics are people who feel and want to express an uninhibited joy in their Christian faith. They do this in public worship as they dance, sing, clap their hands, look in anguish heavenwards and shout out during the service. The real keynote of every charismatic service is that of active participation – by everyone present!

A Why do you think that some Christians feel the need to participate in services like this, whilst others do not?

The Gifts of the Spirit

The Pentecostal Movement is thought to have begun in a small Methodist church in Los Angeles in 1906. Christians there experienced what came to be known as the 'baptism of the Holy Spirit' and were speaking in tongues and prophesying. When the movement spread to Great Britain it started in the Anglican Church but soon spread beyond this. The following two Churches were formed:

1. The Assemblies of God were formed in 1924 with an emphasis on self-government within each church.
2. The Elim Church, formed in 1926, emphasised a central form of government.

For a long time these intense religious experiences largely stayed within the Pentecostal Movement but, in the early 1960s, Christians in other denominations also started to claim that they had received the gifts of the spirit. As a result, the Charismatic Movement was born.

What 'gifts' are we speaking about? When the Christian Church was born on the Day of Pentecost, the first disciples felt the power of God come on to them, giving them the courage to go out and give witness to Jesus. On that day they also spoke in the different languages of the people gathered to listen to them in Jerusalem. This was the first recorded example of 'speaking in tongues'.

From 1.Corinthians 12.1-11 we learn about the different gifts which Paul believed God had given to the Church. Among them were the following:

a) *Healing* – there are people who pray for those who are ill and people who 'lay hands on them' so that their health can be restored. Healing meetings are common in Charismatic churches.
b) *Prophecy* – people in Charismatic churches pass on God's message to other members of the congregation. This message may concern the present or the future.
c) *Speaking in tongues* – this is used in public and private prayer, where a person suddenly finds themselves speaking in an unknown language.
d) *Interpretation* – in every congregation where someone speaks in tongues, there should be someone with the gift of interpretation so that they can tell the people God's message.

B In this church the priest is praying for sick people. What do you think he might be asking God on their behalf?

There are also other gifts which are mentioned in the New Testament. These include the gifts of faith, wisdom, teaching and discernment. Whatever gift a person is given by God, they have it for just one reason – to be used for the benefit of the church to which they belong.

Satanic powers

Charismatic Christians believe not only in the almighty power of God but also in the more limited power of Satan, the Devil. They are convinced that people can be controlled by demons today, just as Jesus believed. Demon-possession can make people violent but God, in his mercy, has given some people the power to cast them out (exorcism). In Charismatic teaching there is a close link between sickness and the activity of evil spirits. There are some people with the gift of healing, as Paul promised, and healing services are common in charismatic circles. Those people who have this particular gift often find themselves fighting against the powers of darkness before they bring wholeness to a person.

READ AND DECIDE ...

Read 1.Corinthians 12.1-11 before answering these questions:

a) What is meant by 'gifts of the Holy Spirit'?
b) Where do all the 'gifts of the Spirit' come from?
c) Why is each manifestation (gift) of the Holy Spirit given by God?
d) Ten 'gifts of the Spirit' are mentioned here altogether. What are they?
e) Take any three of the 'gifts of the Holy Spirit' and try to explain what you think their value might be in a Christian community today.
f) Can you offer any explanation for the resurgence of interest in the 'gifts of the Holy Spirit' in the last two or three decades?

ANSWER IN YOUR BOOK ...

1. What is the Charismatic Movement and where did it come from?
2. What do Charismatics believe about sickness and suffering?
3. Explain what is meant by: baptism in the Holy Spirit; speaking in tongues; exorcism and prophecy.

IN THE GLOSSARY ...

Charismatic Movement; Protestant; Holy Spirit; Pentecostal Movement; Satan; Exorcism.

2.10 THE ECUMENICAL MOVEMENT

The world's Christians are divided into three main groups – the Orthodox Church, the Roman Catholic Church and the Protestants. For centuries the relationship between them has been characterised by persecution and bloodshed. During the 20th century, though, strenuous efforts have been made to bring them closer together. These efforts have been made along two parallel lines:

1. The Ecumenical Movement has sought to heal the serious breaches and differences of opinion between the various Churches.
2. On a local level, different churches have worked together on various projects to make their witness in the community more effective.

> **A** Can you explain what the word 'ecumenical' means? Why do you think that the symbol of the World Council of Churches shows a cross in a boat?

The Ecumenical Movement

The Ecumenical Movement has been a serious attempt to heal the breaches between the different Churches. Its name comes from the Greek word 'oikumene' which means 'whole world' and expresses the hope that Christians worldwide can find some basis for genuinely understanding each other and even uniting.

This movement towards greater unity began very optimistically in Edinburgh in 1910 when the different Churches met to decide how they could work together more effectively on the mission-field. It was agreed that they should stop competing against one another for converts, as they had been doing for a long time. A later conference, at Lausanne in Switzerland in 1927, began to explore ways in which the Churches could move closer together. A considerable step towards this goal was taken in 1948 when the World Council of Churches was formed.

To begin with, 148 Churches joined the World Council, united in a common belief of Jesus Christ as God and Saviour. Today over 300 Churches belong to the organisation, the Orthodox Church having joined in 1961. The Roman Catholic Church has sent observers to WCC meetings since 1968 but has never formally joined. The organisation, therefore, represents less than 50% of Christendom and this has always been a major drawback. The World Council of Churches has always been a controversial movement. Over the years it has tackled many important issues at its meetings and attracted criticism from other Churches for doing so. Among these issues have been:

❖ financial support for those fighting racism;
❖ the need to send help to those countries torn apart by war or poverty;
❖ measures to tackle the worldwide problem of refugees;
❖ the moral and spiritual problems raised by advances in science and technology.

Successes

The larger Churches are still very wary of each other and are far from uniting. However, there have been some successes among the smaller Churches:

a) In 1947, Anglicans, Methodists and some Baptists and Lutherans united to form the Church of South India.
b) In 1972, Congregationalists and Presbyterians united to form the United Reformed Church.
c) In 1990, the Orthodox and Oriental Orthodox Churches announced that they would unite, having been separated since the 5th century.

Yet two attempts to unite the Methodist and Anglican Churches, in 1969 and 1972, failed dismally when Anglicans rejected the plans. Talks between the Anglican and Roman Catholic Churches have made little progress, and relationships between the Catholic and Orthodox Churches remain frosty. Although Christians of different denominations do work together at local level on many projects, the Ecumenical Movement, as such, is making little progress.

B *This photograph shows a United Reformed Church. Which two Churches combined to form this Church? When did this happen?*

ANSWER IN YOUR BOOK ...

1. How did the movement towards a closer bond between the Churches, and possible unity, get under way?
2. What ecumenical successes have there been along the way?
3. Why do you think that Christians from different denominations often find it easier to work together than to unite with each other?

FIND OUT AND NOTE ...

a) Make a list of the advantages/disadvantages that there might be in having so many Churches. Do you think that the Church would have a greater impact if it was united?
b) Find out about any activities in your area which involve Christians working together across Church and denominational barriers. In recent years there has been a movement called 'Churches Together'. Is this movement involved in any inter-Church activities in your area?
c) Write a report of any activities that you can find under the title 'Christians work and worship together'.

C *This is a sheltered housing project for the elderly, supported by churches of all denominations What other social needs might churches work on together?*

IN THE GLOSSARY ...

Ecumenical Movement; Orthodox Church; Roman Catholic Church; Baptists.

3.1 THE CREEDS

Asked to describe what a Christian is, most of us would state the main beliefs of the religion: 'To be a Christian you must believe…'. Others would point out that, while such beliefs are important, they are not the essence of Christianity. This, they maintain, is to be found in how people live, how they treat others and how committed they are to the Christian community, the Church.

Whatever answer is given to the question, there can be no doubting the importance of religious belief. It is the means by which the Church has always distinguished between those who are 'orthodox believers' and those who hold unorthodox views, many of whom would still call themselves Christian. In the past, people who have held unorthodox views (heretics), have often been excommunicated by the Church. The Church has only been able to do this because it has had a clear statement of its own belief – the Creeds.

The Creeds

There was another reason why such statements of belief became an important feature of the Church in the first few centuries of its history. When people came forward to be baptised they were expected to declare their Christian belief. To help them, certain 'formulae' were developed and the Creeds grew out of these. Two Creeds in particular were incorporated into the Church's worship:

1. *The Nicene Creed* – this was produced by a Church council which Constantine summoned at Nicea in 325 CE. It is still often used in Anglican and Catholic worship and also at Orthodox baptisms.
2. *The Apostles Creed* – this Creed had nothing to do with the Apostles, although its roots are probably found in the first two centuries of the Church's existence. It is still used in Roman Catholic and Anglican churches.

Using the Creeds

Whilst the Creeds are of little importance to Nonconformists, they continue to play an important role in other Churches. During most Anglican and Catholic services the people turn towards the altar and recite one of the Creeds together. They declare that what unites them as Christians is far more important than any differences they may have. It is strange, though, that there has been little attempt to revise the Creeds, even though the way that people feel and think about their Christian faith has altered a great deal over the centuries.

Both of the Creeds are concerned with those doctrines, or beliefs, which stand at the heart of the Christian Faith:

a) The oneness of God.
b) The Incarnation of Jesus – the birth of God.
c) The life, suffering and death of Jesus.
d) The resurrection of Jesus.
e) The return of Jesus Christ to the earth to be its judge.
f) The Holy Spirit.
g) The 'Holy, Catholic and Apostolic' Church.

A The Apostles Creed speaks of '…the Father Almighty, creator of heaven and earth.' What is meant by this statement?

3 · CHRISTIAN BELIEFS

ANSWER IN YOUR BOOK...

1. Why was it felt necessary for the Church to have a clear statement of its beliefs in the Creeds?
2. What do we know about the Apostles and Nicene Creeds?
3. Why do you think many churches still make use of the Creeds when you consider that its worshippers may not believe everything that they are saying?

READ AND DECIDE...

The earliest indications we have of the beliefs of the early Christians come from the speeches recorded in the Acts of the Apostles and from the writings of Paul. Read each of the following carefully:

- Acts 3.12-16
- Acts 10.34-43
- Acts 17.16-34
- Philippians 2.6-11

a) Make a list of all the beliefs about God, Jesus Christ and the Holy Spirit that you can find in these passages.
b) In just two paragraphs sum up the beliefs that seem to have been held by the early Christians.
c) How do these statements seem to compare with statements in the Apostles and Nicene Creeds?

WHAT DO YOU THINK?

Here is an extract from the Nicene Creed:
'We believe in one God...We believe in one Lord, Jesus Christ...God from God, Light from Light, true God from true God...of one being with the Father...For us men and our salvation he came down from heaven; by the power of the Holy Spirit he became incarnate of the Virgin Mary and was made man. For our sake he was crucified under Pontius Pilate; he suffered death and was buried. On the third day he rose again...He will come again in glory...we believe in the Holy Spirit ...we believe in one holy, catholic and apostolic church...'

a) Whereas the Apostles Creed speaks throughout of 'I believe' the Nicene Creed has 'We believe'. Do you think there is any significance in this difference?
b) Draw up your own list of statements in the Nicene Creed about:
   - God
   - Jesus Christ

Then write an essay with the title 'The beliefs of the early Christians.'

B *The Nicene Creed speaks of Jesus as becoming 'incarnate of the Virgin Mary and was made man'. Why do you think that this 'mystery' is at the very centre of Christianity?*

IN THE GLOSSARY...

Heretic; Excommunication; Creed; Nicene Creed; Apostles Creed; Apostle; Roman Catholic Church; Anglican Church; Nonconformist; Incarnation; Holy Spirit; Virgin Mary; Pontius Pilate.

3.2 THE TRINITY

Christianity is built upon the foundational belief that there is just one God. This belief, which Christians share with both Jews and Muslims, is called 'monotheistic'. Christians believe that this one God has been revealed throughout history in three different 'persons' – as God the Father, God the Son and God the Holy Spirit. The relationship which binds together these three distinct, and yet perfectly united, members of the Godhead is known as the 'Trinity': a belief unique to Christianity.

Christians have laboured over the centuries to give a precise statement of their belief in the Trinity. Their one concern has always been to clearly state that the Trinity is made up of one God who appears in three different forms.

God the Father

The Bible opens with the words:

> 'In the beginning God created the heaven and the earth…'

From these words in Genesis, through to the closing words of Revelation, and taking in all the teaching of Jesus along the way, certain 'truths' about God are emphasised:

1 That God is the 'giver' of all life. Without God, life would not exist. Whether we are talking about the universe, the world, nature or humanity, they all owe their initial, and continual, existence to God.
2 That God is the Father of everything. This was the word that Jesus used more than any other to refer to God – his Father. Just as a human father cares for his children so God, the divine Father, cares for and loves the whole of creation.
3 That God is a person who takes a personal interest in all that he has made.

A *How might the familiar scene in this photograph help Christians to understand the love which God has for creation?*

God the Son

All men and women are sons and daughters of God since, as Genesis tells us, we are all made in the image of God. Jesus, however, is uniquely the Son of God. The Incarnation, God taking on human flesh, is the mystery that stands at the very centre of the Christian Faith. As God, Jesus was born into a Jewish family in Palestine, put to death by Pontius Pilate and brought back to life by God three days later. At some future time the same Jesus will return to the earth again, this time as its king and judge (an event known to Christians as 'The Second Coming'). History, and the whole of life as we know it, will end when Jesus returns.

God the Holy Spirit

According to John's Gospel, Jesus promised his followers a 'Comforter' when he left the earth. Christians believe that this promise was honoured on the Day of Pentecost when the Holy Spirit became God's power on earth. He also told them that he would send an 'Advocate' who would tell his followers what to say when they were brought before emperors, tribunals and other courts of law. This, again, was to be the work given to the Holy Spirit.

To sum up, then, Christians believe that:

a) God the Father created the world and sent his Son, Jesus Christ, to save it.
b) God revealed himself to the world through Jesus Christ, his Son.
c) God gives life and achieves his purposes in the world through the Holy Spirit.

3 · CHRISTIAN BELIEFS

B *You can hardly be in any doubt that these people come from the same family. The family 'likeness' is undeniable. The Bible says that we are made in the 'image of God'. What do you think this means?*

READ AND DECIDE ...

At the very heart of the Christian faith stands an inconceivable mystery – that God was born as a human being. This is how Paul describes it:

> 'He was in the form of God;
> yet he laid no claim to equality with God,
> but made himself nothing, assuming the form of a man.
> Bearing the human likeness,
> sharing the human lot,
> he humbled himself
> and was obedient,
> even to the point of death,
> death on a cross!'
> (Philippians 2.5-8)

a) How do you understand these words?
   'He was in the form of God;
   yet he laid no claim to equality with God...'
b) How do you think that Jesus humbled himself and took on the form of a servant?
c) What was the ultimate act of humility by Jesus?
d) Consult Philippians 2.9-11 and then describe what happened to Jesus after his death.
e) Why do you think that the doctrine of the Incarnation stands at the very centre of the Christian Faith?

ANSWER IN YOUR BOOK ...

1 What do Christians mean when they speak of the Trinity?
2 What do Christians believe about God the Father?
3 What do Christians mean when they speak of the 'incarnation' of God?

IN THE GLOSSARY ...

Trinity; Bible; Incarnation; Holy Spirit; Pentecost.

3.3 THE DEATH OF JESUS

The Creeds, which have played a crucial role in the Christian Church for centuries, contain much more than historical information. Above all, they express the commitment of Christian believers to a God who has acted in the world – both to create it and to save it. This is why the Creeds are particularly taken up with Jesus Christ, and, in particular, his death.

Jesus – his death

The crucifixion is central to any understanding of Jesus and his mission. In our Western form of Christianity the sufferings of Jesus on the cross have emphasised the way in which God and human beings have been brought together (reconciled). Other pictures taken from the New Testament show us how this salvation works:

a) Jesus died as an innocent man – he did not deserve to die. He did not commit any sin but is pictured in the Gospels as a dumb and helpless lamb who is put to death. Jewish people would have been familiar with this image from the Old Testament, where the perfect lamb was slaughtered on the altar so that its blood could be used as a sacrifice to offer to God for the sins of the people. This happened every year but Jesus, as the perfect Lamb of God, died just once to secure an eternal sacrifice.

b) The death of Jesus was a victory over all the powers of evil. Through it, people can be set free from the power of sin.

c) By his death Jesus was able to pay the penalty that God had placed on humankind for its sinfulness.

d) The death of Jesus was a means of 'buying back' (redeeming) the sinful past of humankind.

All of these pictures came from the religious faith which formed Christianity – Judaism. In the New Testament the death of Christ was spoken of as an 'Atonement', a making at-one-ment, or a 'bringing together in harmony'.

We are, of course, only speaking in pictures. The most effective pictures of the death of Jesus are those which come out of Christian worship, especially through Holy Communion. In the 'Mass', for instance, the death of Christ is seen as an 'eternal' act in which Christians share as they worship together.

A These Christians are witnessing to their faith by carrying a cross on Good Friday. What do you think they are trying to tell others about Jesus Christ?

3 · CHRISTIAN BELIEFS

The Mass itself is a sacrifice in which the death of Jesus is re-enacted. The emphasis is different, however, in the Protestant service of Holy Communion since the stress is upon the once-and-for-all death of Jesus. This death provides God's free forgiveness for all who believe. Holy Communion then becomes an occasion for thanksgiving to God.

B *This photograph shows a crucifix from a Roman Catholic church. It shows Jesus on a cross. Why do you think that crucifixes are found in many churches, and how might Christians use them in their own devotional lives?*

ANSWER IN YOUR BOOK ...

1. What different 'pictures' are used in the New Testament to explain the significance of the death of Jesus?
2. What is the basic difference in the understanding of the death of Jesus between the Catholic Mass and the Protestant Holy Communion?
3. What does the word 'atonement' mean, and what is its connection with the death of Jesus?

WHAT DO YOU THINK?

Take another look at the different images that are portrayed in the New Testament to explain aspects of the death of Jesus. Which of them do you think are particularly useful – and why?

READ AND DECIDE ...

As you might expect, the writings of Peter and Paul in the New Testament are full of references to the death of Jesus. Here are just four examples:

a) 'There (on the cross) he disarmed the cosmic powers and authorities and made a public spectacle of them, leading them captives in his triumphal procession.' (Colossians 2.15)

b) 'Christ died for us while we were yet sinners and that is God's proof of his love for us.' (Romans 5.8)

c) 'For if, when we were God's enemies, we were reconciled to him through the death of his Son, how much more, now that we have been reconciled, shall we be saved by his life.' (Romans 5.10)

d) 'You were set free by Christ's precious blood, blood like that of a lamb without mark or blemish.' (1.Peter 1.18)

Using the material in the text to help you, as well as the quotations above, write about 500 words on the meaning of the death of Christ and its importance to Christian believers.

IN THE GLOSSARY ...

Creed; New Testament; Holy Communion; Mass; Protestant.

3.4 THE HOLY SPIRIT

Whilst Christians generally agree that God exists as a Trinity, different groups and denominations place a particular emphasis on one member of the Godhead or another. As we have seen, Pentecostalists and those belonging to the Charismatic Movement stress the work and gifts of the Holy Spirit such as speaking in tongues, healing and prophecy. For most Christians, however, the simple truth is that each member of the Godhead is equal but is revealed to the world at different times and in different ways.

The Holy Spirit

What do Christians believe about the Holy Spirit?

They believe the word 'spirit' means 'power' and that the Holy Spirit is the living and visible embodiment of God's power in the world today. When Luke described how the Holy Spirit was given to the first disciples in Jerusalem, he used several telling phrases:

> '...a sound like the blowing of a violent wind...a crowd came together in bewilderment...utterly amazed... amazed and perplexed.' (Acts 2.2-5)

Luke is desperately trying to find words to convey the 'power' of the event. All who were there were amazed at the power of God's descent. Yet it was not power in the normal sense of the word. To speak of the Holy Spirit as 'God's power' is to refer to the power of God's unconditional love. Christians in the New Testament were people 'filled with God's Spirit' and the love of God.

To begin with, being filled with God's Spirit led to some rather unusual behaviour. It was thought by many, for example, that the Christians on the Day of Pentecost were drunk (Acts 2.13). Peter countered this accusation by pointing out that it was still early in the morning before the same Christians went on to show what it really meant by the way that they lived, preached and died.

From the beginning of its life the Christian Church was called 'the body of Christ' – a figure of speech often used by Paul. Believers were baptised into that body by the Holy Spirit using the traditional baptismal formula:

> 'I baptise you in the name of the Father, of the Son and of the Holy Spirit.' (Matthew 28.19)

Whilst individual believers are given some of the 'gifts of the Holy Spirit', these are intended to be used for the benefit of the 'Body of Christ' – the Church. You can discover this for yourself by reading 1.Corinthians 12.27-30. The Church is the body into which all believers have been baptised by God's Spirit and in which there is no difference between Jews and Greeks, between slaves and free people. In God's sight, and in God's Church, all men and women are equal.

The Holy Spirit then, is with us as the one who makes the power of God known to the world. He is steadily building up the Kingdom of God which Jesus himself started. Then, at the end of time, as Jesus returns, the work of the Holy Spirit will be over.

A *What does this banner from Uganda suggest about the activity of God's Spirit in today's world?*

3 · CHRISTIAN BELIEFS

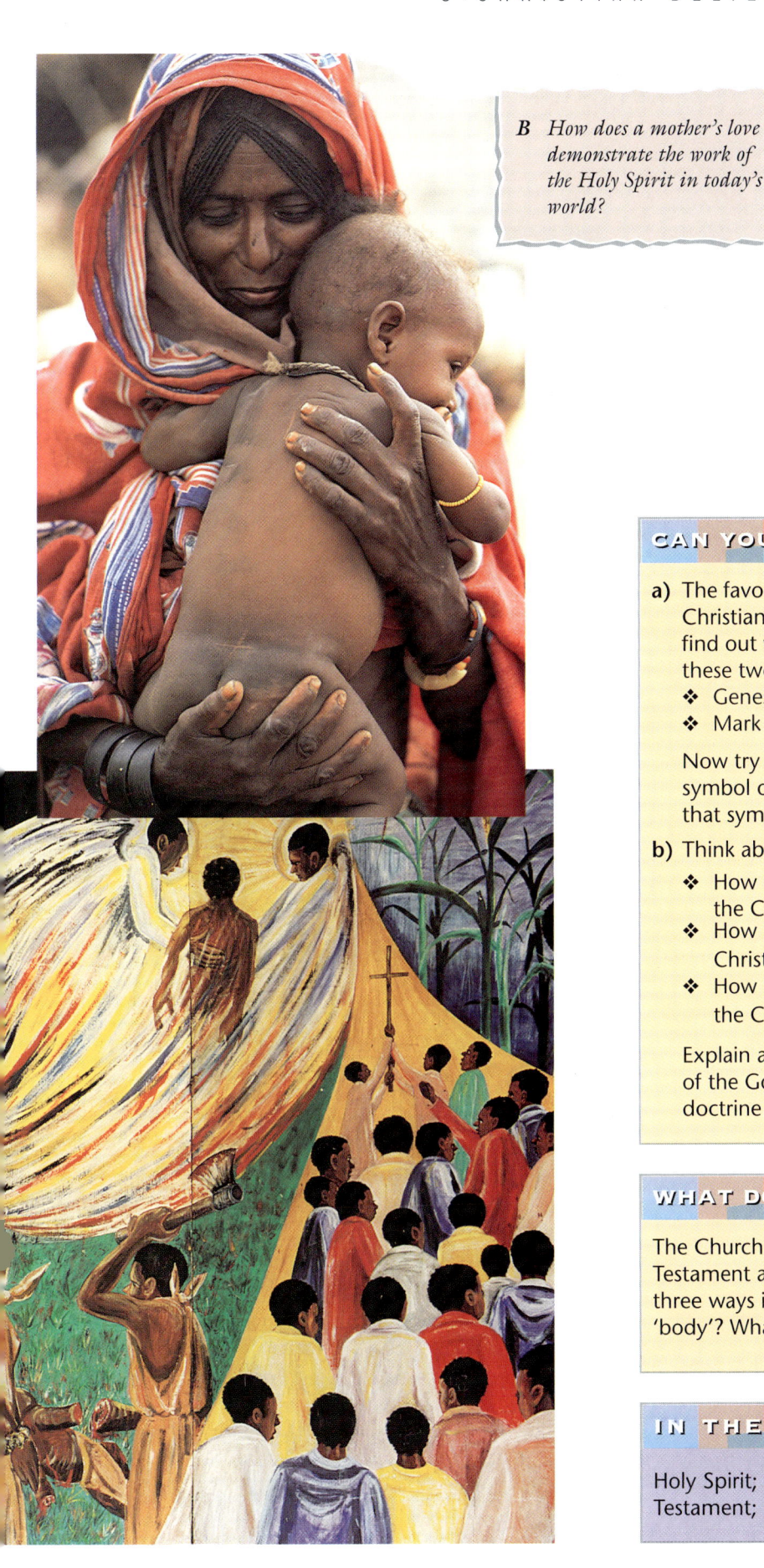

B How does a mother's love demonstrate the work of the Holy Spirit in today's world?

ANSWER IN YOUR BOOK ...

1. How did the first Christians receive the Holy Spirit and how was this misinterpreted by others?
2. What was Paul referring to when he wrote about the 'Body of Christ'? How is this linked with the Holy Spirit?
3. How does the work carried out by the Holy Spirit link up with that of the two other members of the Trinity – God the Father and God the Son?

CAN YOU EXPLAIN?

a) The favourite 'picture' of the Holy Spirit in the Christian tradition has been that of a dove. You can find out why the dove was chosen by looking up these two Biblical references:
- ❖ Genesis 8.8-12
- ❖ Mark 1.10

Now try to explain why the dove was chosen as a symbol of the Holy Spirit and what the meaning of that symbol is.

b) Think about and try to explain the following:
- ❖ How has God the Father been revealed through the Christian tradition?
- ❖ How has God the Son been revealed through the Christian tradition?
- ❖ How has the Holy Spirit been revealed through the Christian tradition?

Explain also how the activities of the three members of the Godhead have been brought together in the doctrine of the Trinity?

WHAT DO YOU THINK?

The Church community is often described in the New Testament as the 'Body of Christ'. Can you think of three ways in which the community resembles a 'body'? What does the Holy Spirit have to do with this?

IN THE GLOSSARY ...

Holy Spirit; Charismatic Movement; Jerusalem; New Testament; Pentecost; Trinity.

3.5 THE SACRAMENTS

The Sacraments stand at the very heart of worship for most Christians. These are ceremonies, or rituals, which can be traced back to the ministry of Jesus or the worship of the early Christian Church. Since then they have been used by the Church as the main means of channelling God's grace directly to countless worshippers – usually through actions involving a material element like oil, water or bread.

The most well-known definition of a sacrament came from St Augustine (354-430):

> 'A sacrament is the visible form of an invisible grace…'

The definition is important because it introduces us to the two most important ingredients of every sacrament:

a) *The physical or material element* – this is the part of the sacrament that you can feel, see, taste and smell. Here are two examples:
   - During the service of Holy Communion a worshipper drinks a small quantity of wine and eats a piece of bread. By using these elements a believer can share in the death of Jesus.
   - When babies are baptised (infant baptism), water is poured over them to symbolise their cleansing from sin.
b) *The spiritual or invisible element* – the physical elements used in a sacrament are only important as they bring spiritual realities within the reach of each worshipper. The ceremonies have little value in themselves.

The Sacraments

Christians disagree over just how many sacraments (channels of divine grace) there are. The seven sacraments which the Roman Catholic and Orthodox Churches recognise are:

1. Holy Communion – also called the Eucharist, the Divine Liturgy or the Mass;
2. Infant baptism;
3. Confirmation;
4. Penance;
5. Marriage;
6. Ordination to the priesthood;
7. Holy Unction.

A *Which sacrament is being celebrated here and which physical elements are being used in the service?*

Most Protestant Churches recognise just two of these, Holy Communion and baptism, as sacraments. These are the only two, they maintain, which can be traced back to Jesus himself. Most of the Free Churches celebrate Holy Communion (called the Breaking of Bread or the Lord's Supper) and baptism. The Salvation Army and the Quakers, alone among the Free Churches, do not celebrate any of the sacraments.

The Sacraments – one by one

Four of the sacraments – Holy Communion (Units 6.5-6.8); Baptism (Units 7.1 and 7.3); Confirmation (Unit 7.2) and Marriage (Unit 7.4) are covered later in the book. The other three are:

a) *Penance* – in Roman Catholic and some Anglican churches, people regularly confess their sins to a priest to find forgiveness with God. Roman Catholics do this at least once a year although many go to 'Confession' far more frequently. As part of the path to forgiveness the priest often gives them a penance (penalty) to perform.
b) *Ordination* – this is the sacrament by which people become priests. The service is always conducted by a bishop as it involves 'the laying on of hands', which only a bishop can do.
c) *Anointing the sick (Holy Unction)* – this sacrament is given to those people who are either sick or dying. The priest anoints the person with oil and prays over them.

3 · CHRISTIAN BELIEFS

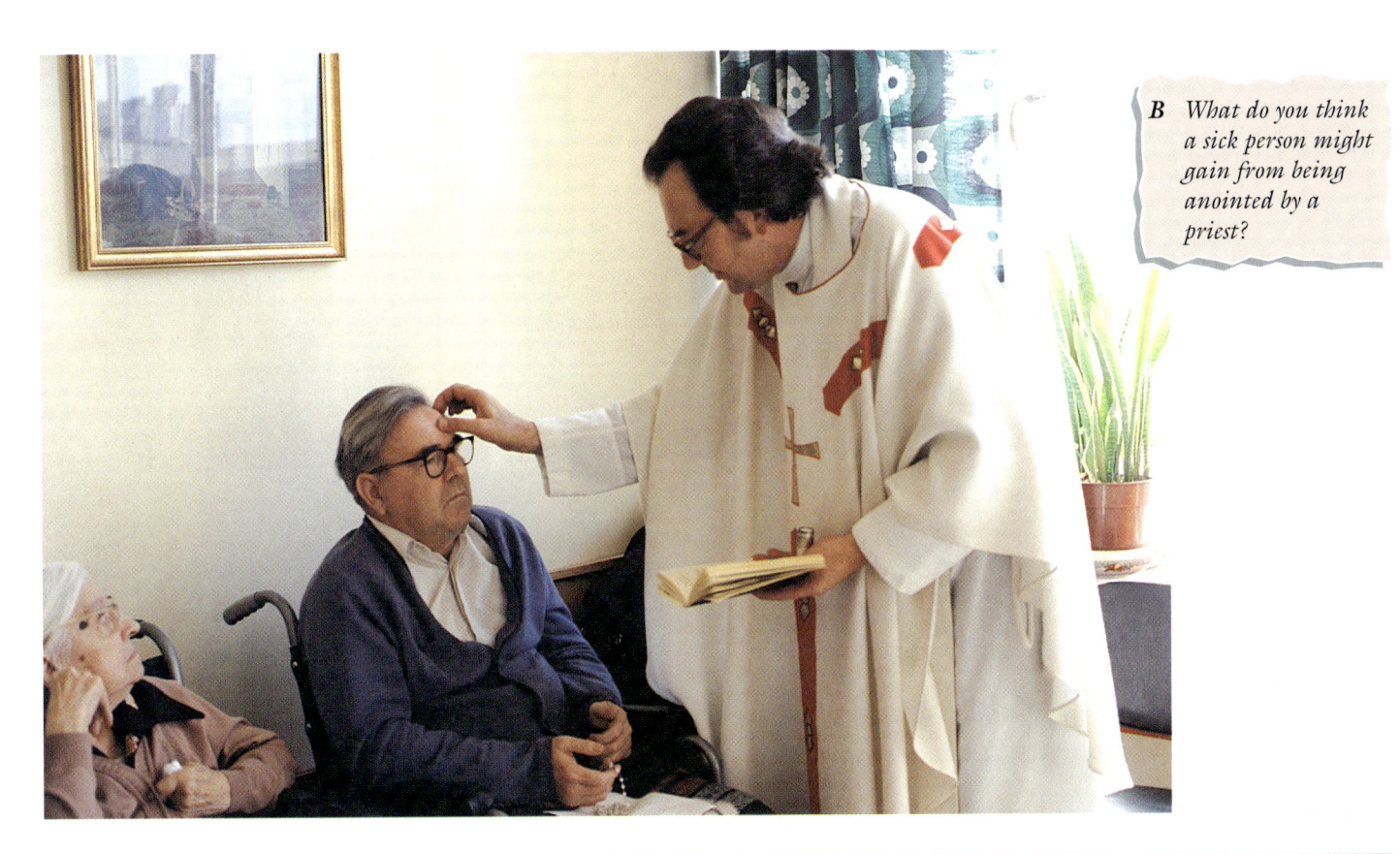

B What do you think a sick person might gain from being anointed by a priest?

ANSWER IN YOUR BOOK ...

1. How would you define a sacrament?
2. Why do you think that the Church has always maintained that God's blessing comes through a bringing together of the material and the spiritual? What does this tell you about the importance of both?
3. Write one sentence for each of the following: Holy Communion; Infant Baptism; Confirmation; Penance; Holy Unction.

DISCUSS AMONG YOURSELVES ...

Many Christians would say that administering the sacraments is the most important task of a minister or priest. Can you understand why the sacraments should still play a central part in the worship life of the Church?

You may want to invite two or three ministers from different denominations in to help you to answer these questions. It might also be interesting to hear from a member of the Salvation Army or the Quakers, explaining why their Church does not use any sacraments.

COMPLETE A CHART ...

As we have seen, a sacrament combines both physical and spiritual elements. Draw up a table like the one below and fill in the relevant information for each of the sacraments.

SACRAMENT	PHYSICAL ELEMENTS	SPIRITUAL GRACE
1		
2		
3		
4		
5		
6		
7		

IN THE GLOSSARY ...

Sacrament; Infant Baptism; Eucharist; Divine Liturgy; Mass; Confirmation; Penance; Ordination; Holy Unction; Protestant; Breaking of Bread; Lord's Supper; Salvation Army; Priest; Bishop; Laying on of hands.

3.6 THE PROBLEM OF SUFFERING

Christians believe that God made and sustains all forms of life. Why then is there suffering? Look at any moment in history and you will find an immense amount of suffering – most of it undeserved and without purpose! Take four examples:

1. Natural disasters (volcanoes, earthquakes, floods etc.) which kill millions of people and over which the human race has no control.
2. Babies and adults dying from hunger and malnutrition who have had the misfortune of being born in the wrong place at the wrong time. Hunger is directly responsible for 20 million deaths each year.
3. Children born with incurable diseases or massive handicaps through no fault of their own or their parents.
4. Parents snatched away from their families prematurely through illness or accident.

There are innumerable examples. It is not just the 'fact' of suffering that causes such anguish to the Christian believer. It is also the 'unfairness' of it all. Some people suffer much more than others. There are many who have never known a minute free from pain or suffering. Why does it happen? Is there some purpose to it all or is there no reason behind it? These are problems that believers in the Christian God cannot evade. An explanation could be:

> **Either** God does want to remove suffering but cannot – in which case he is not all-powerful.
> **Or** God can remove all suffering but does not want to – in which case he cannot be all-loving.

Christianity and suffering

Suffering is a universal problem and a constant source of anxiety to anyone who believes in God – whatever faith they belong to. Every religion puts forward its own answers to the problem of suffering. Christianity is no exception although many of its answers have been inherited from the much older faith of Judaism. Here are some of the answers found in the Bible:

a) *God alone knows the reason for suffering*. At the end of the Book of Job the author reaches his conclusion: suffering is a mystery and to ask

A *When you see a young person confined to bed or to a wheel-chair, what questions does that raise in your mind? Why do most people find the suffering of children and young people particularly distressing?*

questions about it shows a lack of faith in God. Yet, how can anyone witness suffering on any scale and fail to ask searching questions?

b) *Suffering is a direct consequence of sin*. This can hardly explain why some children die before reaching their first birthday or why others are born with a lifetime of suffering ahead of them.

c) *Suffering comes from the activity of Satan*. Who, though, created Satan? If it was God, why did he do it knowing the havoc that Satan would cause?

d) *Sin and suffering come from human free-will*. People must be free to choose wrong as well as right. In so doing they may bring much suffering on themselves. This does not explain natural disasters or illness which suddenly strikes.

No single answer appears to cover the full extent of suffering. Those who continue to believe in God, despite the suffering that they find and often experience, must have compelling reasons for doing so. The traditional Christian answer is to fall back on their faith at this point.

3 · CHRISTIAN BELIEFS

B Can there ever be any answer to suffering on this scale?

DISCUSS AMONG YOURSELVES …

There is no conclusive answer to the problem of suffering. You may decide, however, that one or two of the suggested answers do provide some insight into the problem. Read the text through again before breaking up into small groups. Look again at each of the answers which Christians have put forward to the problem of suffering.

a) What are the arguments in favour of each suggested answer?

b) What are the arguments against each answer?

c) Do you find any of these answers more persuasive than the others? If so, why?

READ AND DECIDE …

Here are two perspectives on suffering for you to think about:

a) There is an old story about a man going to Joseph the carpenter, father of Jesus, in a dream and complaining about the cross (burden) that he was carrying through life. 'It is much too heavy for me to carry,' he said. Joseph took the cross from him and asked him to choose another. The man looked through all the other crosses in Joseph's workshop and, after a long time, finally picked another up. 'This one is just right for me,' he said. 'That's funny,' Joseph said with a smile, 'It's the one you brought in.'

❖ Sum up what this story is saying about suffering. Do you agree with it?

b) Contrary to popular belief, Job was not a very patient man. He did, however, face his suffering with considerable courage. This is what he said about it:
 'Naked I came from the womb,
 naked I shall return whence I came.
 The Lord giveth and the Lord taketh away;
 blessed be the name of the Lord.'
 (Job 1.21)

❖ What point is this quotation making about suffering? Do you agree with it?

ANSWER IN YOUR BOOK …

1 How would you describe the dilemma that suffering causes to those who believe in a loving and powerful God?

2 Which forms of suffering cause you most concern? Why?

3 Perhaps the most well-known 'answer' to suffering is that found in the Book of Job. What did he say?

IN THE GLOSSARY …

Bible; Satan.

3.7 LOVE

'Love' is probably the most over-used and abused word in the English language. In everyday usage it covers everything from tender devotion to selfish lust. Used properly, however, the word conveys many feelings which show that human beings have a spiritual as well as a physical dimension. Christians believe that, at one end of the scale, we may be related to animals but, at the other, we are able to enjoy communion with God. That makes human beings unique. It follows that when we treat the whole of creation, including our fellow human beings, lovingly we are behaving as God intended. Conversely, we are being inhuman if we act without any real measure of care and love.

As Christians know only too well, love can be destroyed like all good and perfect things. The love between parents and children can be beautiful – but it can so easily become destructive and possessive. Friendships can enhance the lives of the people concerned – or they can degenerate rapidly as one person in a relationship uses the other. Sexual love can be amongst the most exquisite experiences given to the human race – or it can simply be a way of obtaining personal pleasure and satisfaction. Even the claim that people 'love God' has often been used to cloak some appalling and inhuman behaviour.

For genuine Christians, though, life is a journey in which two changes gradually take place:

a) Human love expressed towards the whole of creation is purified.
b) Human love is brought closer and closer to that love which God has for us.

Real love

Christian teaching is very clear. Love is the greatest and most important of all the virtues. As Paul wrote when discussing the three great Christian virtues – faith, hope and love:

> 'The greatest of them all is love.'
> (1.Corinthians 13.13)

Paul also said that even if a person has all the other virtues, including faith and hope, yet does not have love, he or she is nothing. He or she has no value in the sight of God:

> 'I may have faith enough to move mountains; but if I have no love, I am nothing.'
> (1.Corinthians 13.2)

There is no limit to love. Jesus summed up the demand that God makes in the simplest terms:

> 'Love the Lord your God with all your heart, and with all your soul, and with all your strength, and with all your mind; and your neighbour as yourself.'
> (Luke 10.27)

This saying of Jesus introduces us to another theme in his teaching about love. We should love God, we should love our neighbour and we should love ourselves. In Christian terms this means loving ourselves as Christ loved us, seeing ourselves as Christ saw us and giving ourselves to others

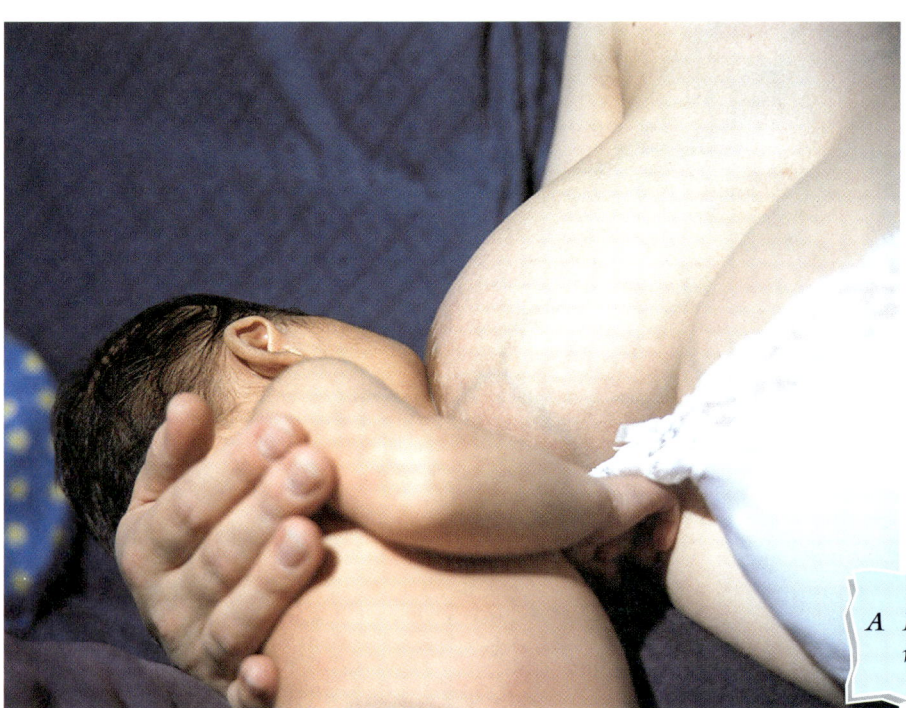

A How would you describe the very special love which exists between a mother and her baby?

as Christ gave himself for us. As John wrote:

> 'This is what love really is: not that we have loved God, but that he loved us and sent his Son as a sacrifice to atone for our sins. If God thus loved us, my dear friends, we also must love one another.'
> (1.John 4.10, 11)

Indeed, if you look up 1.John 4.20, you will discover that it is quite impossible for someone to love God unless they love their neighbour first.

B Do you think there is any real difference between the ways in which a mother and a father come to love their own children?

ANSWER IN YOUR BOOK ...

1. What do you think Augustine meant when he said: 'Love God and do what you will.'
2. Do you agree with the idea that love is the greatest and most important of all the virtues?
3. How many different 'kinds' of love can you think of? Can you illustrate each of them with an example? Do they have anything else in common apart from using the same word to describe them?

IN YOUR OWN WORDS ...

Using l. John 4.20 as the basis for your answer, can you explain, in your own words, the link in Christian behaviour between:

a) loving God?
b) loving one's neighbour?
c) loving oneself?

DISCUSS AMONG YOURSELVES ...

C.S.Lewis, a well-known Christian author of the 20th century, believed that there were four distinct kinds of love:

- *Affection* – the tender love between a parent and child; the feeling between an old person and a pet.
- *Friendship* – a close companionship between two people.
- *Erotic love* – a passionate, sensual love.
- *Charity* – the love which is God himself and is poured into our hearts by the Holy Spirit.

Think about each of these kinds of love for a moment.

a) Is 'affection' a suitable term to describe the feelings of a father or a mother towards their new-born child?
b) Would you put the love between a parent and child on the same level as that between someone and their pet?
c) What do you think is the difference in love between parents and children and:
   - the feeling of deep friendship between two people;
   - the intensity of feeling between two lovers.
d) How would you explain the link between the love of God and the other 'loves' that we have mentioned?

IN THE GLOSSARY ...

Holy Spirit.

3.8 THE VIRGIN MARY

It seems likely that Mary was little more than a teenager when she was betrothed (engaged) to Joseph, a carpenter. According to the Gospels, the Angel Gabriel appeared to tell her that she was soon to become the mother of the Messiah by a process which we call 'the Virgin Birth'. Following the announcement Mary travelled to Bethlehem, a small village, and gave birth to Jesus in a stable.

Years later, when Jesus became a public figure, Mary went with him to Cana and Capernaum and witnessed some of the miracles he performed. On another occasion she appeared with the rest of her family to try to persuade Jesus not to preach and heal in public. She failed in her mission. She then disappeared from the Gospel story until the last hours of the life of Jesus, when she watched from a distance as he was crucified.

The Virgin Birth

There was a very strong tradition, reflected in Matthew and Luke's Gospels, that Jesus was not conceived through normal sexual intercourse between Joseph and Mary. Instead they refer to the Holy Spirit impregnating Mary – see Matthew 1.20 and Luke 1.35. This is why the Apostles Creed can speak of Jesus being:

> '…born of the Virgin Mary.'

There are two opinions in the modern Christian Church about the Virgin Birth:

a) There are those who accept the idea without question. They accept that it would make the birth of Jesus almost, if not totally, unique. They argue that one would expect something very special and miraculous for the birth of Jesus. After all, as God's Son, he was a totally unique person.

b) There are those who believe that Jesus was conceived and born in the normal way. Otherwise, how could Christians claim that Jesus was totally human. They believe that the story of the Virgin Birth grew out of the mistaken idea among many early Christians that sexual intercourse was basically sinful, and that this sinful nature was passed on from parent to child.

Beliefs about Mary

Apart from believing in the 'perpetual virginity' (that Mary remained a virgin for the whole of her life) Roman Catholics have added two further beliefs about Mary in recent years:

1. That Mary was born without original sin so that she might be the perfect recipient for the infant Jesus. This belief, known as the 'Immaculate Conception', sets Mary apart from the rest of the human race since everyone else is born with natural sinful tendencies.
2. At the end of her life, because of her perfect holiness, Mary was taken up into heaven, body and soul, by the power of God. This belief, which Catholics share with Orthodox believers, is called the 'Bodily Assumption' of Mary. Both Churches celebrate the Assumption of Mary into heaven on August 15th.

Because of the great respect which Catholics and Orthodox Christians have for the Virgin Mary she plays a very important role in their religious devotions and worship:

A Take a close look at this statue and describe the virtues of the Virgin Mary that it tries to show.

3 · CHRISTIAN BELIEFS

a) They pray to her so that she can represent them before God.
b) They call her the 'Mother of God' (Theotokos) because she was the bearer of God's Son.
c) They have statues and icons of her in church and often carry them in festival processions.
d) They dedicate altars and shrines in her honour and often have side-chapels set aside to house them.

B *How do Catholic and Orthodox believers express their reverence for the Virgin Mary?*

READ AND DECIDE ...

You can now compare what you see in the photograph of the Virgin Mary with this prayer which is often used in Catholic churches:

> 'Alone of all women, Mother and Virgin, Mother most happy, Virgin most pure, now we sinful as we are, come to see thee who are all pure, we salute thee, we honour thee as how we may with our humble offerings; may the Son grant us that by imitating thy most holy manners, we also, by the grace of the Holy Ghost, may deserve spiritually to conceive the Lord Jesus Christ in our inmost soul, and once conceived never to lose him. Amen.'

a) What do many Christians mean when they speak of the 'Virgin' Mary?
b) How do many Christians solve the problem of Mary being both 'Virgin' and 'Mother'?
c) What is the main difference between the Virgin Mary and those who are now honouring her?
d) What is the believer trying to imitate when he or she follows the example of the Virgin Mary?

ANSWER IN YOUR BOOK ...

1. What part did Mary play in the life of Jesus?
2. What is meant by the doctrine of the Virgin Birth and why does this belief separate Christian from Christian?
3. What is meant by the 'Immaculate Conception' and the 'Bodily Assumption' of the Virgin Mary?

IN THE GLOSSARY ...

Virgin Mary; Virgin Birth; Holy Spirit; Apostles Creed; Immaculate Conception; Bodily Assumption of Mary; Icon.

4.1 THE CHRISTIAN BIBLE

The Bible is a collection of books made up of two parts – the Old Testament with 39 books and the New Testament with 27. There was a gap of at least 200 years between the writing of the last book in the Old Testament and the first book in the New Testament. In addition to the 66 books of the Bible, the Jerusalem Bible, used by Roman Catholics, includes seven books from the Apocrypha including Tobit, Judith, and I and II Maccabees. Protestants do not believe that these books carry the authority of Scripture.

The Old Testament

The early Christians were Jews and so were very familiar with the Jewish Scriptures. The same Scriptures are included in the Christian Bible, although the books are in a different order. Christians refer to this part of their Bible as 'The Old Testament' (Agreement) although Jews find this title offensive. It suggests that the message of the Old Testament has been superseded by that of the New Testament – a belief which Jews repudiate. Christianity, it must be pointed out, is the only religious faith which includes holy books from another faith in its own Scriptures. The books of the Old Testament are divided into three groups:

1 *The books of the Law (the Torah)* – the first five books of the Jewish Scriptures – Genesis, Exodus, Leviticus, Deuteronomy and Numbers – contain the most important elements of the Jewish faith. They begin with the story of the creation of the world and the formation of the Jewish nation under Abraham. Then follows the account of the delivery of the Israelites from Egyptian slavery by Moses. The hurried exit from Egypt and the journey to the Promised Land (the Exodus) is celebrated each year during the festival of Pesach (Passover). This is followed by the giving of the Law to Moses on Mount Sinai and the Jewish conquest of the Promised Land (Canaan).

2 *The Prophets* – a 'prophet' was a man or woman who declared the word and message of God to the people, whether they wanted to hear it or not! There are many books based on the lives of prophets in the Old Testament, although none of them, as far as we know, were written by the prophets themselves. These books are usually divided into two groups:

> **A** *Why do you think that the early Christians incorporated the Jewish Scriptures into their own Bible?*

- ❖ The major prophets – three of the prophets, Isaiah, Jeremiah and Ezekiel, have substantial books in the Old Testament named after them.
- ❖ The minor prophets – there are 12 books at the end of the Old Testament which convey the words of the so called 'minor prophets', including Amos, Joel and Habakkuk.

3 *The Writings* – including Psalms, Proverbs and wise sayings such as the Book of Ecclesiastes.

The New Testament

The New Testament contains 27 documents in all – four Gospels, the Acts of the Apostles, 21 letters or epistles (including 13 which carry the name of Paul) and the Book of Revelation. Most of these books were written within a generation or two of the death of Jesus.

a) Of the four Gospels, three present a similar picture of Jesus and they are called Synoptic Gospels (Matthew, Mark and Luke). We gain a very different picture of Jesus from the 4th Gospel – John's.

b) The Acts of the Apostles, written by Luke, is a record of the early Church from the ascension of Jesus into heaven through to the death of Paul.

c) We do not know how many of the Epistles in the New Testament were written by Paul since several which bear his name were certainly not written by him. There are also letters by Peter and John, among others.

d) The Book of Revelation claims to be a record of a vision given by God to John on the island of Patmos. It is quite unlike any other book in the New Testament.

B Why do you think that most Christians believe that the Bible is unique?

ANSWER IN YOUR BOOK ...

1 What is the most important part of the Jewish Scriptures and what does it contain?

2 Several books in the New Testament were not accepted as authoritative for over 300 years. What do you think the early Christians were looking for in those books which were going to carry the authority of 'Scripture'?

3 Write short notes on each of the following: The Old Testament; The New Testament; The Torah; The Synoptic Gospels and the Epistles.

DISCUSS AMONG YOURSELVES ...

Christians and Jews have long disagreed over the description of the first part of the Bible as 'The Old Testament'. Why do you think that Jews strongly object to this title?

READ AND DECIDE ...

This quotation is from the Bible about the Bible:
'But for your part, stand by the truths that you have learned and are assured of. Remember from whom you learned them; remember that from early childhood you have been familiar with the sacred writings which have power to make you wise and lead you to salvation through faith in Christ Jesus. All inspired Scripture has its use for teaching the truth and refuting error, or for reformation of manners and discipline in right living...' (2.Timothy 3.14-16)

a) Make a list of the different claims that are made for the 'Holy Scriptures' in this verse.

b) Put this important verse into your own words:
'...remember that from early childhood you have been familiar with the sacred writings which have power to make you wise and lead you to salvation through faith in Christ Jesus.' (v.15)

c) What do you understand by the following statement?
'All inspired Scripture has its use for teaching the truth and refuting error, and for reformation of manners and discipline in right living...' (v.16)

IN THE GLOSSARY ...

Old Testament; New Testament; Apocrypha; Torah; Exodus; Passover; Synoptic Gospels; Epistle.

4.2 PUTTING THE BIBLE TOGETHER

A The scribe has always been an important member of the Jewish community since he copies the scrolls of Scripture which are placed in the Ark in the synagogue. Can you find out how these scrolls are treated?

Every religion has its collection of writings which it considers to be authoritative and inspired. The collection itself is called the 'Canon' (from the Greek word meaning 'a measuring rod'). 'The Canon of Scripture' is that standard against which all Christian belief and behaviour can be tested. That is why the Christian Church needed to establish those holy books whose authority it was going to accept.

To begin with the Church adopted the Jewish Scriptures because it believed that they all pointed to the coming of the Messiah – Jesus. Most of the early Christians had, in any case, been taught as Jews to treat them as authoritative. Although the Jewish Canon was not finally fixed until the Synod of Jamnia, held in 90 CE, there was general agreement about the content of the Jewish Scriptures by the time of Jesus.

The New Testament Canon

The early Christian writers scoured the pages of the Old Testament for evidence which pointed towards Jesus as God's Messiah. The most prolific of these writers was Paul, who sent letters to churches and individuals that he had helped towards faith in God. His letters were taken up with teaching and combatting errors which, even at this early stage in the Church's history, were beginning to occur. The first of his letters preserved in the New Testament, 1.Thessalonians, was probably written about 49 CE – some 16-17 years after Jesus had been put to death. Paul was a tireless missionary preacher before he was executed in the Neronian persecution of 64 CE.

The Gospels were written after the Epistles. The first written account of the life and teaching of Jesus,

Mark's Gospel, was written between 65 and 70 CE, around 40 years after Jesus died. In the meantime, the information had been kept alive in the memories, conversations and preaching of those who believed. Scholars call this the oral tradition. Mark's Gospel was soon followed by Matthew's and Luke's between 70 and 80 CE. Luke also wrote an account of the life and witness of the Early Church (the Acts of the Apostles) which follows the four Gospels in the New Testament.

Then, towards the end of the 1st century, John put together his own highly individual account of the ministry of Jesus, John's Gospel. The same John also wrote three letters which were preserved by the early Christians. At the end of his life this same author found himself on the island of Patmos where he had a bizarre vision of heaven (the Book of Revelation or the Apocalypse). By the end of the 1st century most, if not all, of the books of the New Testament were written.

The Canon of the New Testament

For a long time, books written by the apostles and early followers of Jesus were highly valued and used widely by the Church in its worship, although no attempt was made to bring them together into one authoritative book. By the end of the 2nd century most of the books were accepted as special, with some disagreement over a few of them. In 367 Athanasius, an influential Eastern Church leader, set out the Canon and it contained 27 books. This was confirmed at the Synod of Carthage in 397. All together there were 66 books in the Christian Bible, and that is the way it has remained. The Roman Catholic Church accepted this decision although it did not formally accept the Canon of Scripture until the Council of Trent in the 16th century.

ANSWER IN YOUR BOOK ...

1 What was the attitude of the early Christians towards the Jewish Scriptures and what use did they make of them?
2 What is meant by the word 'Canon'?
3 How did the New Testament come to be written?

IN YOUR OWN WORDS ...

Answer each of these questions in your own words:

a) What did the 'Canon of Scripture' give to the Christian Church?
b) What happened at the Synod of Jamnia and why was it important for the Christian Church?
c) What was finally settled at the Synod of Carthage?
d) What is unusual about the dating of the Gospels? How was the information about Jesus kept alive before the Gospels were written?
e) How did the Church progress towards defining a Canon of its own Scriptures?

WHAT DO YOU THINK?

Why do you think that the Christian Church felt the need to have an accepted Canon of Scripture, having done without one for three hundred years?

IN THE GLOSSARY ...

Messiah; New Testament; Old Testament.

B How did the Church finally decide which books to include in the Bible?

4.3 TRANSLATING THE BIBLE

Most of the Old Testament was originally written in Hebrew while the New Testament was in Greek. Around the 3rd century BCE the first translation of the Jewish Scriptures into Greek was made and this was called the Septuagint. According to tradition, Ptolemy Philadelphus (285-246 BCE) commissioned seventy-two Jewish scholars in Alexandria to make the translation and they completed it in seventy-two days. The translations were identical although the scholars worked independently of each other! The Septuagint was for those Jews who had been 'dispersed' across the ancient world and so did not know Hebrew.

Into Latin

While the documents in the New Testament were written in Greek, Jesus taught in Aramaic. There are a few traces of this language left in the New Testament. Soon, however, Latin became the language of the Western Church and a Latin version of the Bible, the Vulgate, became the only version people were allowed to use. This was made by St Jerome at the request of Pope Damascus. The Gospels were translated in 384 CE and the whole Bible was completed by 404 CE. The Council of Trent declared it to be the undisputed Word of God, containing the authoritative text of the Scriptures. Most of the people, however, could neither speak nor understand Latin.

Translating the Bible into English

There were two important events in the 15th and 16th centuries which greatly affected the subsequent history of the Bible:

a) The invention of printing around 1450. Instead of being copied out by hand, the Bible could now be printed.

b) The beginning of the Protestant Reformation from 1517 onwards. This upheaval was inspired by the Bible and it left the Reformers with an overwhelming desire to place the Bible in the hands of as many people as possible.

The translation and printing of the Bible in English became imperative. William Tyndale (1494-1536) saw the ignorance of the clergy and laity alike and declared:

> "... it is impossible to establish the lay people in any truth, except the Scripture is plainly laid before their eyes in their mother tongue".

He moved to Antwerp, in Belgium, and began to print the New Testament in English from 1525 onwards. Under incredibly difficult conditions he published a translation that was both clear and in the language of the people.

Just before Tyndale died in prison, a translation of the whole Bible in English, the Miles Coverdale version, was circulating. In 1539 the Great Bible was placed, by royal decree, in every parish church in England. The Geneva Bible, published in 1560 by a

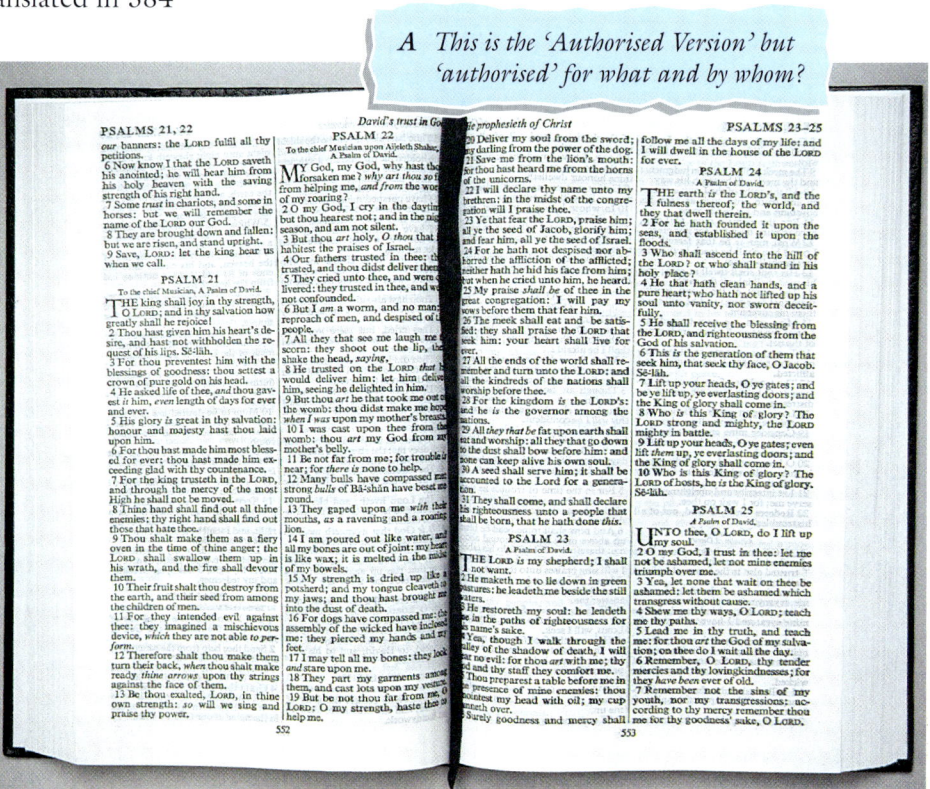

A *This is the 'Authorised Version' but 'authorised' for what and by whom?*

group of Protestant exiles in Geneva, was the first to translate the Bible directly from the original languages.

In 1611 all existing translations were superseded by the Authorised Version of the Bible. It proved to be so good that it was unchallenged for three centuries. Forty-seven scholars, under the inspiration of King James 1, used all the existing versions in many languages and made constant reference to the original texts. The feel of the translators for poetry and prose rhythm meant that it was eminently suitable for public reading.

In the 20th century many private translations, including one by J.B.Phillips, were made into modern English. The complete 'Revised Standard Version' was published in 1952. The 'Jerusalem Bible' appeared in 1966 and has been used by Catholics ever since. Evangelicals published their own versions, including the very popular 'Good News Bible', between 1966 and 1976. The New English Bible was published in 1970 and was replaced by the Revised English Bible in 1989.

The British and Foreign Bible Society (now just the 'Bible Society') and the Wycliffe Bible Translators have been labouring to translate the Bible into as many languages as possible. Parts of it are now to be found in over 500 languages although there are many more still to come.

ANSWER IN YOUR BOOK ...

1. What part did Hebrew, Greek and Latin play in the early versions of the Old and New Testaments?
2. Trace the various translations of the Bible from the pioneering work of William Tyndale through to the Authorised Version of King James 1.
3. Write two sentences on each of the following:
   ❖ The Septuagint
   ❖ The Vulgate
   ❖ The Authorised Version

IN YOUR OWN WORDS ...

Answer each of these questions in your own words:

a) What do you think was the importance of putting the Jewish Scriptures into the hands of Jews separated by circumstances from their homeland?
b) Why did the Bible need to be translated from Latin before the vast majority of people could understand it?
c) What prevented the widespread circulation of the Christian Scriptures before the 15th century?
d) Why did the Protestant Reformation give a great boost to the translation and printing of the Scriptures?
e) Why do you think there have been so many translations of the Bible?
f) What do you think are the main problems for those people who are still trying to translate the Bible into new languages?

WHAT DO YOU THINK?

The 'Good News' is a modern translation of the Bible.

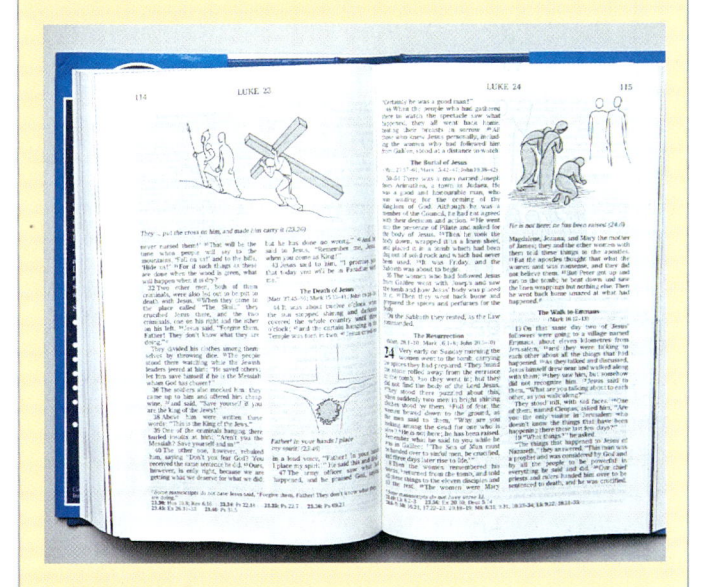

a) When you read the Bible, what do you find to be the main problems? What do you think that the Bible gains, or loses, by being put into modern English?
b) As a person reads the Bible, what do you think is most important – that they are excited by the beauty of the language or that they understand what they are reading?

IN THE GLOSSARY ...

Old Testament; New Testament; Bible; Authorised Version.

4.4 USING THE BIBLE

The Bible was brought together over a long period of time to provide a kind of 'inspirational warehouse' from which worshipping communities and individuals could draw. This they have done for centuries. The Bible shows the wide variety of ways in which God has been understood and the struggles which people have endured in trying to make sense of their religious experience.

The value of the Bible

While some Christians, most notably Evangelicals, would insist that the whole of the Bible was inspired, they would not maintain that all parts of it are of equal value. Few Christians, for example, would find the list of tribes that emerged from Egyptian slavery (Numbers 26) or the disreputable exploits of many Old Testament kings particularly interesting. More seriously, the Bible, because of its great antiquity, often reflects the standards and values of the time. To take just two examples:

a) It is assumed throughout the Bible that there will be slaves and slave-owners. The morality of slavery is never discussed. When an escaped slave, Onesimus, approached Paul in prison and asked for his advice, Paul recommended that he return to his Christian owner, Philemon. Elsewhere he tells slaves to:

> "... give single-minded obedience to your earthly masters with fear and trembling, as if to Christ ..." (Ephesians 6.5)

b) From the opening chapters of the Bible, which state that the woman was created from the rib of the man, women are given a secondary role. In the relationship between a husband and wife, Paul suggests that the woman should be subordinate and obey her husband. As he wrote:

> "Wives, be subject to your husbands as though to the Lord; for the man is head of the woman..." (Ephesians 5.22-23)

Yet, in contrast, many parts of the Bible contain insights into matters which are of timeless concern and interest. For example:

❖ The Ten Commandments (Exodus 20.1-17)
❖ The Beatitudes (Matthew 5.1-12)

These lay down principles which almost all Christians would agree are timeless. One of the main tasks of the Church today is to discover how much of the Biblical literature is meaningful for modern Christians.

A Can you think of one statement in the Bible which would not seem to apply to life today, and one that would?

B What do you think this group of Christians hope to gain from studying the Bible together?

The Church, the Bible and authority

The question of authority is one of the most important in the Christian Church. In the Roman Catholic and Orthodox Churches, authority has always resided in two places:

a) The traditions of the Church, and, for Roman Catholics, in the Pope;
b) The Scriptures.

The Reformation saw a widespread debate on the question of authority. When Martin Luther, the great Reformer, said 'Here I stand; I can do no other', he was referring to the authority of the Bible. The main principle of Protestants ever since has been to stand by the authority of the Bible. In practice, it has not been that easy. The Bible is a diverse collection of writings which do not present a systematic system of belief. There have been many arguments among Christians over just what the Bible does and does not say on crucial issues.

The Bible in use

The Bible is a source of inspiration for Christians. This is the way it is used in worship as passages are regularly read and used as the basis of sermons. Over a given period, most of the Bible is read in public. In most services there are two (Old Testament and New Testament) or three (Old Testament, New Testament and Epistles) readings.

Most Christians also read the Bible systematically and regularly in their own devotions. Study-notes are available to explain the various passages. Often Christians come together in groups to study the Bible with one another. In many churches this happens particularly during Lent, when Christians are preparing themselves spiritually for the great festival of Easter.

ANSWER IN YOUR BOOK ...

1. Why do you think that many Christians place such importance on personal Bible study?
2. What is the main difference in attitude between Roman Catholics and Orthodox believers on the one hand, and Protestants on the other, towards authority?
3. What use is made of the Bible in public worship?

WHAT DO YOU THINK?

The Bible is full of good and interesting advice. Make your own list of ten statements from the Bible which you think have relevance to the lives of people today. Can you then explain just what you think that relevance is?

FIND OUT AND NOTE ...

a) There are many different ways of approaching the Bible and these are reflected in the different Churches. Can you find out what is meant by 'fundamentalism'? What do you think might be the main attractions of taking this approach to the Bible? Why do many Christians find fundamentalism unattractive?

b) Invite two vicars, priests or ministers who have very different attitudes about the Bible in to your class. Try to find out what their attitudes are? On what do they base their attitudes to the Bible? What do they think of each other's attitudes? What do members of their congregations think about their attitudes?

IN THE GLOSSARY ...

Bible; Roman Catholic Church; Orthodox Church; Protestants; Old Testament; New Testament; Epistle; Easter.

5.1 INSIDE A CATHOLIC CHURCH

5 INSIDE THE CHRISTIAN CHURCHES

While Catholic churches were traditionally built in the shape of a cross, many newer ones are circular. This stresses the equality of all people in God's presence. The people either surround the altar or sit in a semi-circle in front of it. In both cases the intended symbolism is clear. The altar is the place where God meets with his people and so the most appropriate place for it is in the middle of the congregation.

Just inside the door of a Catholic church, worshippers find a small container of holy water. As they enter the building they dip their fingers into the water and make the 'sign of the cross' on their bodies. The water, which has already been blessed by a priest, is a symbol of cleansing and new life. The symbol in some churches is also reinforced by the position of the font just inside the door.

A What are these candles called? Why do you think that lighting candles and praying go together for many Christians?

This is the stone receptacle which holds the water when a baby is baptised. Its position is a reminder that everyone must be baptised before they can belong to the fellowship of the Church and share in the salvation it offers. For centuries the Catholic Church has taught that there is no salvation anywhere else. In some modern churches the font is placed in the middle of the congregation, again for important symbolic reasons. It is a reminder that baptism brings a baby into the warmth of the Church family, which then undertakes to cherish, love and care for it.

B This is the modern Cathedral in Clifton in Bristol. How is this different from a more traditional church?

The High Altar

In traditional churches the high altar stands, together with a crucifix and candles, at the end of the nave in the middle of the east wall. This location was originally chosen because the sun rises in the east.

A tabernacle (cupboard) stands behind the altar or in a side-chapel containing the Reserved Sacrament which is used every time that the Mass is celebrated. Originally, a rood screen blocked off most of the altar from the gaze of the people during Mass, the most solemn of all Catholic services, but most of these have been removed.

The crucifix always contains the figure of Jesus on the cross to help people to meditate on his death. Many Christians find it very moving to pray in front of a crucifix. Occasionally during the Church year, as at Easter, the crucifix is covered with a cloth.

Around the church

Around most Catholic buildings there are a number of side-chapels – one of which will be dedicated to Mary, the mother of Jesus. Confession cubicles are available to anyone who wants to confess their sins to a priest. On the walls are carved figures or pictures showing the fourteen 'Stations of the Cross'. They illustrate the different places where, according to the Scriptures and tradition, Jesus stopped on his way to be crucified. Statues of Mary and the saints are also a feature of Catholic churches. Candles are often lit in front of them by worshippers seeking some kind of spiritual help. So, also, is a candelabra containing Votive Candles, which can be lit by anyone who wants to pray in the church.

ANSWER IN YOUR BOOK ...

1. Why do you think that a crucifix is an important element in Catholic churches?
2. What is the symbolism behind the moving of the baptismal font and the altar into the middle of the congregation in many modern Catholic churches?
3. Explain, in your own words, the significance of the altar, the font and the rood screen in a Catholic church.

WHAT DO YOU THINK?

a) Why do you think that Catholics believe it is very important to bring a child up within the warmth and security of the Christian family of the church?
b) Why do you think that many Catholics find it very moving to pray in front of a crucifix?
c) Why do you think that the altar was placed in the east wall in old Catholic churches?
d) Why do you think that Roman Catholics often make the 'sign of the cross' on their bodies whilst performing acts of worship?
e) Why do you think that candles play an important part in Catholic worship?

IN YOUR OWN WORDS ...

'Stations of the Cross' are a feature of all Catholic churches.

a) What are the Stations of the Cross and where would you expect to find them?
b) What is happening in the Station shown in the photograph?
c) Can you discover what each of the fourteen Stations represent? Can you also find out what part these stations play in worship every Good Friday?
d) Why do you think that Roman Catholic worshippers are surrounded by so many reminders of the death of Jesus?

IN THE GLOSSARY ...

Altar; Sign of the Cross; Font; Crucifix; Nave; Reserved Sacrament; Mass; Easter; Stations of the Cross; Virgin Mary.

5.2 INSIDE AN ORTHODOX CHURCH

Of the three great Christian 'families', the one with which people in Great Britain are least familiar is the Orthodox Church. The reason for this is simple. While there may be 150 million Orthodox believers throughout the world, only a handful of them are found in this country. The majority are situated in Eastern Europe.

Orthodox churches and symbolism

Orthodox churches contain a lot of symbolism. The basic plan of most churches is that of a square with a dome above the centre. The square symbolises the belief that everything in God's world is orderly and correct. At the same time, it encourages everyone to feel that they are equal in God's presence. The four corners of the square represent the four Gospels while the dome above symbolises the heavens which stretch over the earth beneath. The floor represents the earth. An important feature of large Orthodox churches is a painting across the ceiling of Christ the Pantocreator (ruler of the heavens, the universe and the earth).

The interior of an Orthodox church is dominated by a large screen of wood or stone which separates the congregation from the altar. This screen, the iconostasis, is covered with icons (sacred paintings) of Jesus, Mary, the apostles and the saints. The screen symbolises the division, which can never be crossed, between heaven and hell, and also the gulf between God and humanity.

Icons

Orthodox Christians believe that God is all-powerful, and so beyond human understanding. Under normal circumstances, it would be quite impossible for any human being to worship God. Icons perform an important role as these religious 'pictures' bring God within human reach, and so make worship possible.

Examples of different icons can be found in many places, including the homes of Orthodox believers. Each icon is believed to be an earthly copy of a heavenly image, and so the painting of them is an exercise which requires a deep personal devotion from

A Why do you think that the people are separated from the altar in an Orthodox church?

the painter. They are usually painted in bright colours on wood, or can sometimes be mosaic, and have a distinct, formal style which makes them instantly recognisable. They are not intended to be portraits in any sense, but are devotional aids to prompt the worship of individuals and congregations. While they are treated with the greatest possible respect, they are not worshipped in themselves.

The Royal Doors

The iconostasis, then, is the screen which separates the congregation from the altar. Only ordained clergy may go through the central door (the Royal Door) of the iconostasis to the altar table although the people are not separated from the altar altogether. They are able to see it through the Royal Door. An icon on the left of the doors shows the Incarnation (Jesus born to Mary on earth) whilst the one on the right hand side shows the promised return of Jesus to the earth. During the Divine Liturgy, the communion bread and wine are brought through the doors to the congregation. The people are told that Christ is in the church through the communion elements, so linking the two icons on either side of the doors.

ANSWER IN YOUR BOOK ...

1. How does the architecture of an Orthodox church reflect the Orthodox belief in God?
2. Why is the iconostasis an important feature of an Orthodox church?
3. What message is proclaimed by the Royal Doors?

IN YOUR OWN WORDS ...

a) Look at the two photographs carefully. Explain what an icon is.
b) What makes an icon different from any other kind of painting?
c) How do people often show their respect for icons when they are in church?
d) Are icons themselves worshipped? If not, what is their function in religious worship?
e) How would you describe the symbolic importance of icons in Orthodox worship?

USE YOUR IMAGINATION ...

Imagine yourself to be an Orthodox Christian. Try to explain to a friend why you believe that the symbolism which surrounds you in church is so important. In particular:

a) Explain the importance of features in the church which are highly symbolic.
b) Explain why the iconostasis acts as a barrier to separate the people from the communion table. Try to explain why the priest alone is allowed to go through the Royal Doors to the altar.
c) Explain the significance of icons in your public and private devotions.
d) Explain why worshipping God would be very difficult, or impossible, without the symbolism which surrounds you.

IN THE GLOSSARY ...

Orthodox Church; Iconostasis; Icon.

5.3 INSIDE AN ANGLICAN CHURCH

The external appearance of most traditional parish churches is that of a cross-shaped building. In times past, most of these churches fulfilled two important social functions:

a) They provided ground for members of the parish to be buried. Although a few of these burial-grounds are still used, most of them are long since full.

b) The bells of the church not only called people to prayer and worship on Sundays, but also rang each hour to keep people informed of the time. They were used to announce important local, national and international events. In some parishes, groups of bell-ringers can still be heard on Sundays and on special occasions such as weddings.

A Can you identify some of the features inside this traditional parish church?

Inside the building

The older Anglican churches in this country were taken from the Roman Catholics during the Reformation. It is not surprising, therefore, to find a close similarity between the buildings of the two Churches. As in Catholic churches, the font is likely to be found just inside the door, and for the same reason. Many Anglicans consider baptism to be the door through which a child becomes a member of God's family.

The nave runs almost the length of the building, with the people seated in pews on either side. In between the end of the nave and the altar stands the choir-stalls as well as the lectern (from which the Bible is read) and the pulpit (from which the sermon is preached). The altar is situated in the east wall and a glance at this will tell us whether it is a High Church (Anglo-Catholic) or a Low Church (Evangelical) building. High Church altars resemble those in Catholic Churches, being ornate and containing several candles and a crucifix. Low Church altars are very simple, containing little more than an open Bible and some flowers. These obvious differences mask much deeper differences of belief between these two groups in the Church of England.

In traditional Church of England buildings the altar is often too far away, separated from the people by the choir stalls. When the priest is not close to his congregation, the communal aspect of modern worship is often destroyed. To bring the priest and people together, another table is often placed in front of the sanctuary, with the people gathering around it for worship. This is a much more common feature in Evangelical Churches.

The place of the Bible

Unlike Nonconformist chapels and churches, the altar, not the pulpit, is the focal-point in the building. This cannot be taken to suggest, however, that the Bible does not play an important and central role in Anglican worship. The Reformation, out of which the Church of England grew, was founded on the authority of the Bible as the Word of God. In most services there are three readings from the Bible – one from the Old Testament, the New Testament and the Epistles. Most of these take place from the lectern but, in High

Church worship, the Bible is passed down into the middle of the congregation for the Gospel reading. One of the passages usually forms the basis of the sermon.

It is interesting to note that in modern Roman Catholic and Anglican churches many of the traditional features have been dropped or changed. This is because the emphasis in modern worship is on participation by the people, and the breakdown of any distinction between the priest and people.

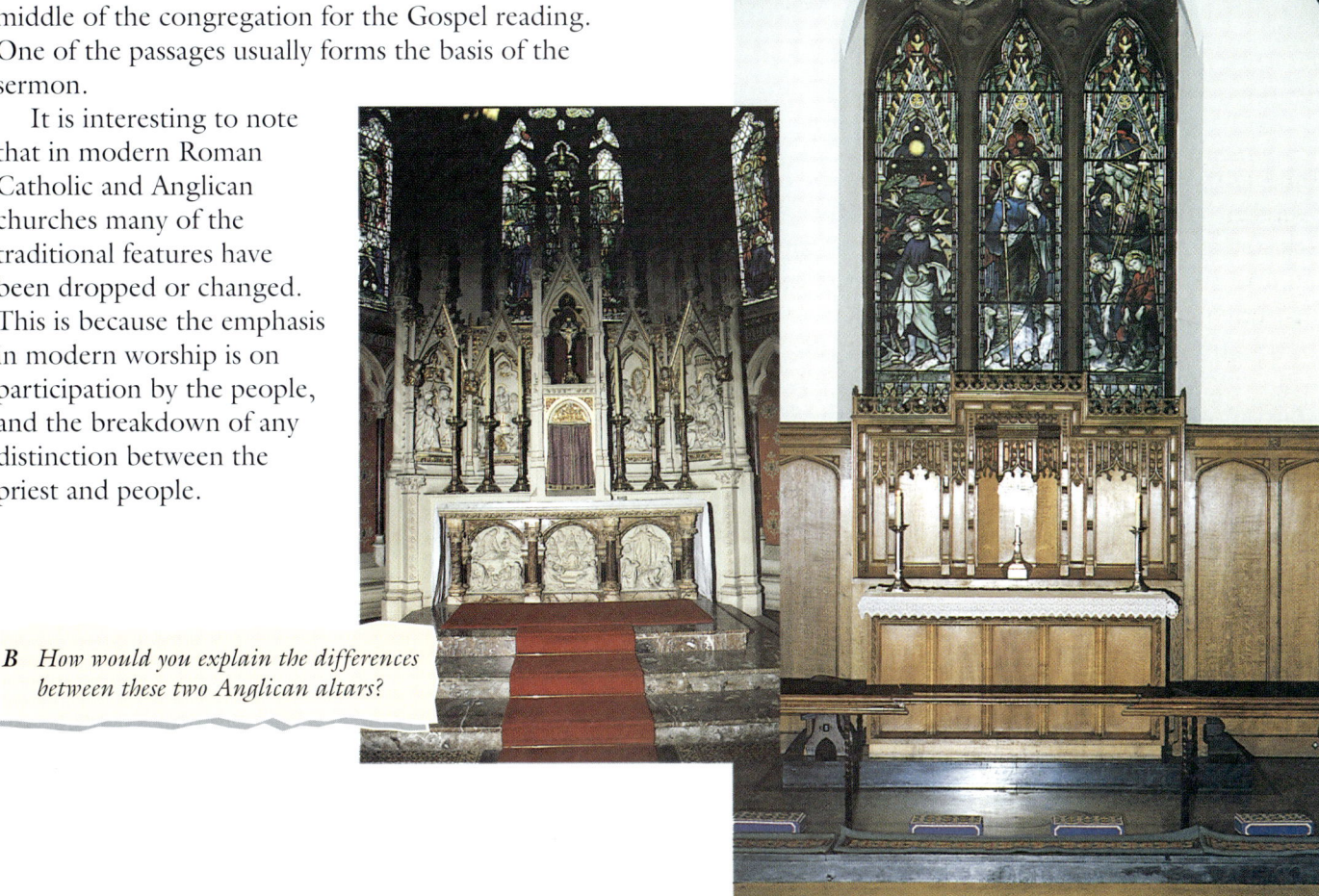

B How would you explain the differences between these two Anglican altars?

ANSWER IN YOUR BOOK ...

1. What changes might you find in a modern Anglican Church compared with its traditional counterpart?
2. How have many parish churches in the past served the community in which they stood?
3. What are the following: the lectern; the pulpit; the altar; the Gospel and the Epistles?

IN YOUR OWN WORDS ...

a) Why do you think that the early church builders usually constructed churches in the shape of a cross?
b) How would you describe the change in style between the older, traditional form of worship and the newer forms that worship often takes?
c) Why do you think that the altar is the focal-point in an Anglican church?
d) Why do you think that Holy Communion, the most important Anglican service, is always conducted from the altar?

FIND OUT AND NOTE ...

Try to find out more about the following:

a) The differences within the Church of England between those in the High Church and those who call themselves Evangelicals. You will need to discover those beliefs which separate the two groups and how these different beliefs are reflected in their styles of worship.

b) The ways in which modern Church of England buildings differ from their traditional predecessors. How do modern innovations in architecture reflect the way that beliefs in the Church of England have changed over the centuries?

IN THE GLOSSARY ...

Sunday; Nave; Altar; Bible; Pulpit; Church of England; Old Testament; New Testament; Epistle.

5.4 INSIDE A NONCONFORMIST CHURCH

Although some Nonconformist Churches, such as the Baptists, date their origins earlier, the great revival in Nonconformist faith took place in the 18th and 19th centuries. This was largely due to the effectiveness of the preaching of John Wesley and the huge contribution which his brother, Charles, made to hymn-singing in this country. Most of the Nonconformists places of worship (variously called churches, chapels, meeting-houses or citadels) were built during this time and so have many features in common, mainly influenced by the Methodist Church.

In recent years the newer denominations, such as the Pentecostal Church and the House Church Movement, have erected buildings which reflect their own styles of worship. They have a minimum of furniture and formality, and leave worshippers free to move around the building during services if they feel like doing so.

Features

The emphasis in Nonconformist worship is on the preaching of the Word of God (the Bible) and this is reflected in the design of the building. Unlike Catholic, Anglican and Orthodox churches, a Nonconformist church does not have an altar. This is because Nonconformist worship is not sacramental, although most Nonconformist churches do celebrate the Lord's Supper and baptism. The emphasis placed upon the Word of God is very much reflected in the fact that the pulpit, a raised platform at the front of the church, is the focal-point of such churches.

In many Nonconformist churches, such as Baptist and Methodist places of worship, there is a Communion table behind which the minister and church leaders sit for Holy Communion. During this service they take the elements of bread and wine to the people sitting in the pews.

Singing performs a very important role in Nonconformist worship. In many churches this is still led by an organ although a piano and a choir, or music-group, often play a prominent part in most services. In a Salvation Army citadel the singing is likely to be led by a brass band. In recent years much new music has been written and this is often designed to be performed by a small group of church members with the congregation joining in. The emphasis is very much upon the active participation of all the people in the service.

In Baptist churches, and some other denominations, there is a baptismal pool at the front which is opened up and filled with water when a service of adult baptism is held. At other times, the pool is emptied and covered.

Names

Many Nonconformist places of worship, especially in Wales, are called 'chapels'. Quakers, however, meet in 'Meeting-Houses'. These are essentially simple and bare rooms, with the chairs arranged in a square. A table with some flowers and a Bible is sometimes placed in the middle of the people.

A *This is a Methodist Church. Find out all that you can about the life of John Wesley and the subsequent development of the Methodist Church.*

5 · INSIDE THE CHRISTIAN CHURCHES

The Salvation Army calls its places of worship 'citadels'. These buildings are similar to other Nonconformist places of worship, but they do not have a communion table as the Salvation Army does not celebrate any of the sacraments. Instead, they have a 'mercy-seat', which is used by people who want to pray and by those who want to find out more about becoming a Christian. The Salvation Army flag is displayed prominently and in most citadels there is room for the band to lead the worship.

B How would you expect this Baptist church to reflect the style of worship that is conducted within it?

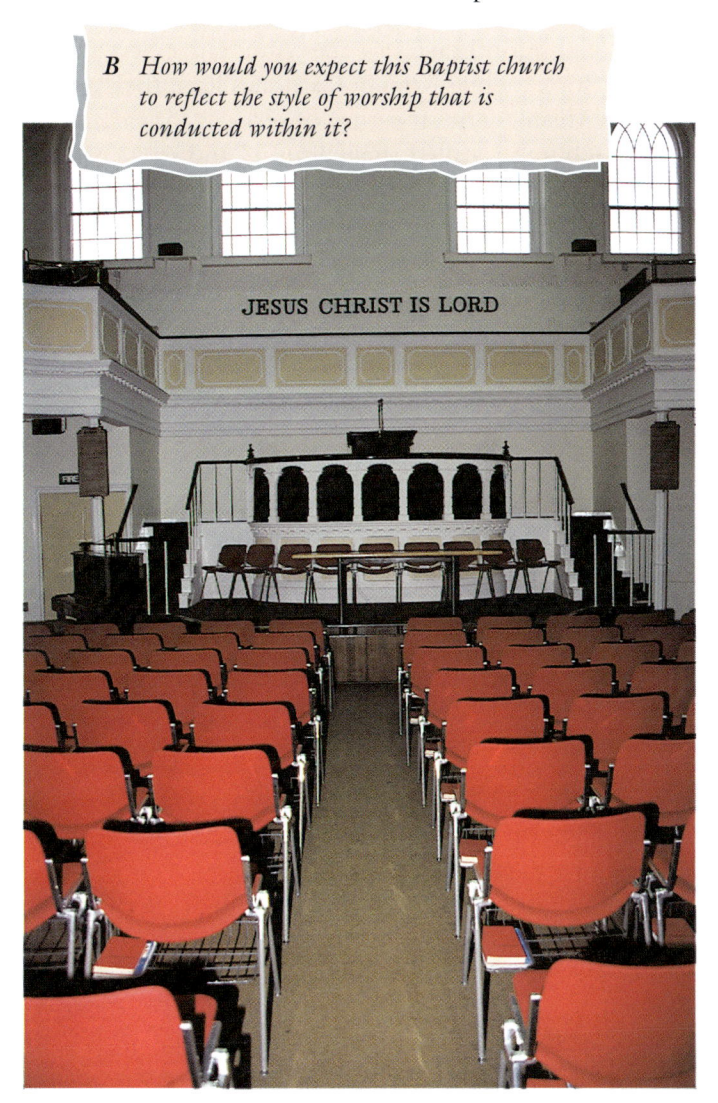

FIND OUT AND NOTE ...

a) Can you find out the meaning of the symbols on this Salvation Army flag? Why do you think that the Salvation Army alone, of all Nonconformist denominations, has a flag?

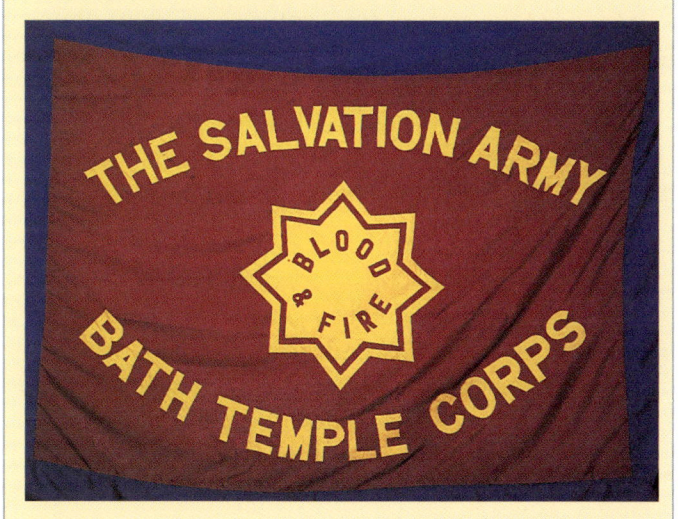

b) Can you find out how two of the Nonconformist Churches began?

c) Can you carry out a survey of Nonconformist Churches in your town or area? How many can you find? What are their names? How long have they been built? Draw a plan of one of them and write notes on the building, way of worship, and the part which the church plays in the community.

CAN YOU EXPLAIN?

a) Can you explain why music and singing play an important part in Nonconformist worship?

b) Can you explain why the preaching of the Bible rather than the celebration of sacraments plays a central role in Nonconformist worship?

c) Can you explain why Baptist churches, and some others, have a baptismal pool at the front of their buildings?

d) Can you explain why there is no Communion table at the front of Salvation Army citadels?

ANSWER IN YOUR BOOK ...

1. How do Nonconformist buildings reflect the practice which places the Bible at the centre of all worship?
2. What is the difference between a citadel and other Nonconformist places of worship?
3. Can you distinguish between a chapel, a meeting-house and a citadel?

IN THE GLOSSARY ...

Nonconformist; Methodist Church; House Church Movement; Bible; Roman Catholic Church; Orthodox Church; Salvation Army; Mercy-seat.

6.1 CHRISTIANS AND WORSHIP

At the start of this century a religious philosopher, Rudolf Otto, pointed out that God was 'Mysterium, Tremendum et Fascinans' – Mysterious, Tremendous yet Fascinating. These three elements are reflected in all genuine Christian worship, whether conducted in private or public.

a) There must be an element of 'awe' in all genuine Christian worship. God remains essentially unknowable and mysterious. It is God's transcendence (otherness) which always places him beyond human reach. God can never be really described since he will always be beyond the power of human language.

b) Worship must be designed to make God accessible: to bring him within reach. The language and the actions used in worship are means to that end. As frightening and remote as God is, the religious worshipper finds that he or she has mysteriously been drawn to him. That is the essence of Christian worship.

Patterns of worship

Broadly speaking, there are two styles of Christian worship:

1. Some Churches, including the Anglican, Catholic and Orthodox forms, follow strict patterns. Often these services are laid out clearly in a Prayer Book for the congregation to follow. The Anglicans use either the 'Book of Common Prayer' or the 'Alternative Service Book', while Roman Catholics have their 'Missal'. The structure of services for each Church is called their 'liturgy' and stress is laid on form, ritual and pattern. The hymns and some of the prayers are the only variety allowed in many church services.

2. The Nonconformist approach to worship is very different. To begin with they do not follow any strict liturgy because, they claim, it prevents the Holy Spirit from expressing himself through what is happening. In Nonconformist services the stress is placed on the following:
   - hymn and chorus singing with many new hymns having been written in recent years;
   - prayers which are 'extempore' – following no set form or content;
   - readings from the Bible;
   - the preaching of the Word (the sermon).

A *This is the interior of Bath Abbey. How do you think that the atmosphere of a place like this evokes the feelings that are associated with Christian worship?*

Underlying this, there is an important difference in approach to worship. The Anglican, Orthodox and Catholic Churches build their acts of worship around the sacraments. The emphasis in Nonconformist worship is very much on the spoken and written word. Often poetry, art, dance and other creative forms are also incorporated into the worship.

There are, of course, other Christian Churches which do not fit into either pattern. The most important of these are:

a) *The Quakers* – this group places a very high premium on silence in their worship, with this only being broken if someone feels prompted by the holy spirit to speak.

b) *Charismatic and Pentecostal churches* – their services have little, if any, formal pattern. These churches place a high degree of importance on modern music and the value of personal testimonies from members of the congregation.

B A small Catholic service takes place in a side-chapel of a large Cathedral. What do you think worshippers might gain from the size and intimacy of this service?

ANSWER IN YOUR BOOK ...

1 What was Rudolph Otto drawing attention to when he described God as 'Mysterium, Tremendum et Fascinans'?
2 Why do you think that the major Churches prefer to follow a set ritual in most of their services? What might this kind of familiarity offer worshippers?
3 What are the main ingredients of Nonconformist worship?

FIND OUT AND NOTE ...

Words and descriptions can only convey a certain amount about worship. It has to be experienced to be fully understood. Here is a list of different styles of worship:

a) A Church of England service
b) A Roman Catholic service
c) An Orthodox service
d) A Pentecostal or Charismatic service
e) A Baptist service
f) A Quaker service

Why not plan to attend one of these services? After you have been, record your impressions of the service. What did you like? What didn't you like? Would you go again?

IN THE GLOSSARY ...

Roman Catholic Church; Anglican Church; Book of Common Prayer; Alternative Service Book; Liturgy; Nonconformist; Holy Spirit; Free Church; Charismatic Movement; Orthodox Church.

6.2 CHRISTIAN LEADERS

Not all branches of the Christian Church have professional, full-time leaders. There are those, like the Quakers, who draw their leaders from among the local congregation. While this provides the opportunity for people who are not ordained to use their gifts, it is very much the exception in the Church. Although most churches make use of their members in worship there are certain services, most notably the Eucharist, which can only be performed by a priest. Having said that, the emphasis in almost all of the Churches in recent years has been placed upon more participation in church leadership. This is partly due to the increasing cost of maintaining full-time clergy. There is also, as the Second Vatican Council recognised, a desire to use the special gifts of all church members.

> **A** Why do you think that most Churches reserve certain functions that can only be performed by a minister?

Ordination

Each Church has its own way of training its priests or ministers. The training period is often a long one, with the Roman Catholic Church taking six years to train its priests. During this time the Church speaks of 'testing the vocation' of the ordinands. At the end of his training, a Roman Catholic priest takes a vow of celibacy at his ordination. No other Church requires this from its priests.

At the ordination ceremony, carried out by a bishop, hands are laid on the head of each person being ordained. This is to transmit God's Holy Spirit to them for the sacred task that lies ahead. As each priest is said to need a 'vocation' to enter the priesthood, it is also a recognition of the fact that the person being ordained has this.

Structure

The Roman Catholic, Anglican and Orthodox Churches have an 'episcopal' form of government, which simply means that they have bishops. Each bishop controls a large area (called a diocese) which contains many churches. In the Orthodox Church, the bishops of the five largest areas (sees) are called 'patriarchs'. Their equivalent in the Roman Catholic and Anglican Churches are Archbishops. In the Anglican Church there are just two of them, the Archbishops of Canterbury and York. The Archbishop of Canterbury is the overall leader of the Church of England, which is part of the worldwide Anglican Communion.

Women priests

There are no women priests in the Roman Catholic and Orthodox Churches. An episcopal letter written by Pope John Paul II in May 1994 ruled out the possibility of this ever happening, about the same time that women were being ordained into the Anglican Church. Most of the other Churches have been ordaining women to the priesthood for many years.

Within the Christian community the priest has two main functions:

a) To represent God in conducting the sacraments and preaching the Word.

b) To guide, lead and direct the Christian community for which he, or she, is responsible.

Within the community a minister's sphere of influence can cover many areas. These include dispensing the sacraments; conducting services; running youth activities; visiting the sick; preparing people for baptism, confirmation and marriage; helping the bereaved and conducting funerals; running the parish and organising fund-raising activities.

Some ministers do not have a parish, such as chaplains attached to a university, college or school, a hospital or a regiment in the forces.

B *Can you find out why some people are strongly opposed to having female priests?*

READ AND DECIDE ...

The Book of Common Prayer includes these words which are spoken by a bishop to a priest who is being ordained:

'A priest is called by God to work with the bishop and his fellow-priests, as servant and shepherd among the people to whom he is sent. He is to proclaim the word of the Lord, to call his hearers to repentance, and in Christ's name to absolve and to declare the forgiveness of sins. He is to baptise...He is to preside at the celebration of Holy Communion...He is to lead his people in prayer and worship...He is to minister to the sick and prepare the dying for death...'

a) The priest is described here as a 'servant and shepherd among the people to whom he is sent'. What is the significance of the words 'shepherd' and 'servant' for the work of the priest?

b) How do you understand the directive:
   'He is to proclaim the word of the Lord, to call his hearers to repentance, and in Christ's name to absolve and to declare the forgiveness of sins.'

   What are the four tasks of the priest?

c) Take each of the directives which begin 'He is...'. Explain, in your own words, what you understand by each of them.

ANSWER IN YOUR BOOK ...

1 What is an 'episcopal' form of Church government?
2 Try to invite a local priest in to speak to your class. Find out how priests spend their working week. What do they see as the most important part of their work?
3 Explain the meaning of the following: the Eucharist; celibacy; ordination; archbishop and chaplain.

IN THE GLOSSARY ...

Ordination; Roman Catholic Church; Celibacy; Bishop; Anglican Church; Orthodox Church; Diocese; Archbishop; Sacraments; Confirmation.

6.3 CHRISTIAN PRAYER

Although prayer is an important feature of Christian services of worship, many Christians prefer to pray in the privacy of their own homes. They find that it is in the silence of their own hearts that they encounter God most readily. 'Silence', in fact, is the key-word for understanding what prayer is all about. Jesus warned his disciples against using long prayers in the hope that they would be heard by God. Christians down the ages who have specialised in prayer, such as monks and nuns, have frequently indicated that silence lies at the heart of all genuine Christian prayer. This is reflected, as we shall see, in the use which many Christians make of meditation and contemplation.

The ingredients of prayer

Apart from the Lord's Prayer (Refer to READ AND DECIDE…), there are few prayers which are common to all Christian traditions. Most Christian prayers do, however, contain common ingredients:

a) *Offering praise to God* – this is the point at which prayer begins, with the worshipper thanking God for the world around, the blessings which they enjoy and for the people who are important to them.
b) *Confessing one's sins and seeking forgiveness* – coming into 'God's presence' the worshipper becomes aware of their own sinfulness and the need to find God's forgiveness.
c) *Requesting God's intervention* – in some way on behalf of the person praying, or others in need.
d) *Thanksgiving* – for all the blessings which have already been received from God's hand.

Times to pray

There are no set times for private or public prayer in the Christian tradition. The one exception to this is the monastic community where, traditionally, seven times have been set aside for prayer each day. Many Christians choose to start each day with a time of quiet for Bible reading, meditation and prayer. Many also like to look back with thanksgiving at the end of a day, and commit any problems that have arisen to God in prayer.

Meditation

Meditation is a way of praying in many faiths and some Christians choose to use it regularly. It brings together the two aspects of silent and vocal prayer although the emphasis is on silence. Some Christians try to imagine themselves in situations described in the Bible and this leads naturally into prayer and thought. A few employ 'contemplation': a silent form of prayer which relies on the promise of Jesus that the Holy Spirit will pray within each believer without words being necessary. Through contemplation, a kind of loving conversation takes place between God and the believer which any words would simply spoil.

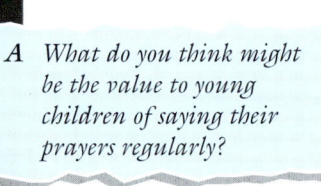

A What do you think might be the value to young children of saying their prayers regularly?

6 · CHRISTIANS AND WORSHIP

ANSWER IN YOUR BOOK ...

1. What do you understand by the description of people 'praying to God' in the silence of their own hearts'?
2. Take each of the ingredients for prayer and explain why you think that they are included in almost every Christian prayer.
3. What do you think the difference is between meditation and contemplation?

B The photograph shows a rosary. This is an aid for prayer which is particularly popular among older Roman Catholics. Can you find out what a rosary is and how it is used in prayer?

READ AND DECIDE ...

Jesus told his disciples that he was giving them a model prayer ("This is how you should pray..."). Most Christians call it 'The Lord's Prayer' although Catholics prefer to call it the 'Our Father'. As familiar as it might be, read it through carefully:
"Our Father in heaven,
may your name be hallowed;
your kingdom come,
your will be done,
on earth as it is in heaven.
Give us today our daily bread.
Forgive us the wrong we have done,
as we have forgiven those who have wronged us.
And do not put us to the test,
but save us from the evil one."
(Matthew 6.9-13)

What are the three 'ingredients' for all Christian prayer? Can you find examples of each of them in the Lord's Prayer?

FIND OUT AND NOTE ...

The 'Hail Mary' is a very important Catholic prayer:
"Hail Mary, full of grace,
The Lord is with thee.
Blessed art thou among women
and blessed is the fruit of thy womb, Jesus.
Holy Mary, mother of God
pray for us sinners now
and at the hour of our death. Amen."

Can you find out why Catholics often pray to God through the Virgin Mary? This prayer, the Hail Mary, says something important about the Virgin Mary. What is it?

IN THE GLOSSARY ...

Monk; Nun; Meditation; Holy Spirit; Hail Mary; Virgin Mary; Rosary.

6.4 HOLY COMMUNION

The clear link of Holy Communion with the life and death of Jesus has given the sacrament a unique place in the life of the Church. For most Christians it is the most important act of worship. Through its roots in the New Testament, Christians come into direct contact with the founder of their faith.

Back to the beginning

From the birth of the Early Church, Christians regularly met together to 'break bread'. They did so because they were convinced that Jesus had told them to – a belief that is underlined by the fact that all four Gospels and a letter of Paul's (1.Corinthians) reported his words. These accounts inform us that, on the night on which he was betrayed, Jesus took a loaf of bread, blessed and broke it, and gave a piece to each of his disciples with the words:

> 'Take this and eat. This is my body.'
> (Matthew 26.26)

Moments later he took a goblet of wine and passed it around among his friends saying to them:

> 'Drink from it all of you. For this is my blood, the blood of the covenant, shed for many for the forgiveness of sins.' (Matthew 26.27-28)

These words form the backbone of the modern service of Holy Communion. It is 'Holy' Communion since, in a unique way, the service brings together the human and the divine – God and humanity.

Different names

Ever since its inception, Christians have disagreed over the precise meaning of Holy Communion. These disagreements are reflected, to a large extent, in the different names that the service carries:

1. For Anglicans it is mainly the Eucharist (thanksgiving), although some prefer to call it Holy Communion.
2. In the Roman Catholic Church it is the 'Mass', from the final words of the old Latin Mass – 'Ita Missa Est' (Go, it is ended).
3. In Eastern Orthodox churches the service is called the 'Divine Liturgy' – a divine service of worship which follows a traditional pattern.

A What has brought these worshippers together to break bread and drink wine?

4. In Free Churches two terms are traditionally used – the 'Breaking of Bread' (as Jesus broke bread with his disciples at the Last Supper) and the 'Lord's Supper' (as Jesus shared his last meal with his friends).

The meaning

In understanding the service of Holy Communion, there is a basic difference between Catholic and Orthodox believers on the one hand and Protestants on the other:

a) The Catholic and the Orthodox Churches teach that Christ is actually 'present' in the bread and wine once they have been 'consecrated' (dedicated to God) by the priest in the Mass or the Divine Liturgy. This means that the bread and wine become the actual body and blood of Christ (transubstantiation) and the service becomes a sacrificial re-enactment of the actual death of Jesus at Calvary.

b) Protestants believe that Holy Communion is an act of remembrance through which they can arrive at a deeper understanding and appreciation of what the death of Jesus was all about. The bread and wine remain as symbols which are able to help and prompt them towards that deeper understanding.

READ AND DECIDE ...

The earliest written reference to Holy Communion is to be found in the letter that Paul sent to the Christians in Corinth:

> "...on the night of his arrest the Lord Jesus took bread and after giving thanks to God broke it and said: 'This is my body which is for you; do this in memory of me.' In the same way he took the cup after supper and said: 'This cup is the new covenant sealed by my blood. Whenever you drink it, do this in memory of me. For every time you eat this bread and drink the cup, you do proclaim the death of the Lord, until he comes.'"
> (1.Corinthians 11.23-26)

Copy this passage into your book and memorize it before answering these questions:

a) What is the link between the Last Supper that Jesus ate with his disciples and the Christian celebration of Holy Communion?

b) How would you explain the importance of the symbols of bread and wine?

c) How can the Eucharist be described as an act of 'Holy' Communion?

d) What do you think Paul meant by the words: 'For every time you eat this bread and drink the cup, you do proclaim the death of the Lord until he comes.' (v.26)

ANSWER IN YOUR BOOK ...

1) Can you explain why the service of Holy Communion occupies such a unique place in Christian worship?
2) Do you think that the different names for Holy Communion carry any real significance?
3) How does the belief of Roman Catholics and Orthodox Christians about Holy Communion differ from that held by Protestants?

B What was Jesus really trying to teach his disciples when he broke bread and shared wine with them before he was crucified?

IN THE GLOSSARY ...

Holy Communion; Sacrament; Eucharist; Mass; Roman Catholic Church; Eastern Orthodox Church; Divine Liturgy; Free Churches; Lord's Supper; Breaking of Bread; Transubstantiation; Last Supper.

6.5 THE EUCHARIST

In the Church of England, the service of Holy Communion is usually called 'The Eucharist'. The central theme of this service is one of thanksgiving although, over the centuries, the emphasis of the service has changed a great deal. In the old Book of Common Prayer, two aspects were emphasised:

a) The sufferings of Christ leading up to and during his death on the Cross.
b) The humble and penitent approach of the worshipper to receive the sacrament.

The Alternative Service Book, published in 1980, preferred to stress the importance of God's creation and the resurrection of Jesus from the dead. The change of emphasis draws attention to an even more fundamental change in approach that has taken place.

The Eucharist

Instead of re-creating the sacrifice of Jesus on the cross, as the Roman Mass does, the Anglican Communion has now become a community meal in which every worshipper shares on an equal basis. This community aspect is underlined in the modern service by the giving of the 'Peace' just before the bread and wine are shared. At this moment the people hug and kiss one another with the words 'The Peace of the Lord be with you'. The 'spiritual food' which the people then receive enables them to go out into the world to share the Gospel of Christ with others.

Once the priest has blessed the bread and the wine, the people come forward to kneel at the chancel steps. As they receive the bread the priest says to them:

'The body of our Lord Jesus Christ.'

Similarly, they take a sip of wine from the communal goblet accompanied by the words:

'The blood of our Lord Jesus Christ.'

Obviously, each church and worshipper attaches their own precise meaning to these words. In Anglo-Catholic churches, where the teaching of the Roman Catholic Church is accepted, people believe that some changes take place in the bread and wine as they become the body and blood of Christ. Low Church Anglicans, however, share the Protestant view that the service is a 'commemoration' of the Last Supper with the symbols remaining what they are. The bread and wine are living symbols of the sacrifice and suffering of Christ. This gives us a unique insight into the love that God has for the human race.

The frequency with which the Eucharist is celebrated is some guide to the importance that a particular church places on it. In Anglo-Catholic churches the Eucharist is firmly placed at the centre of their worship and it is celebrated several times a week. In other churches the usual practice is for the Eucharist to be held every Sunday and once during the week. In addition, special Eucharists are often held on Church festivals such as Ascension Day.

A *What is the significance of this worshipper receiving the bread during the Eucharist?*

6 · CHRISTIANS AND WORSHIP

B *Which event in the life of Jesus is this person celebrating?*

READ AND DECIDE ...

This prayer is taken from the Eucharist service in the Alternative Service Book:

'...Who in the same night that he was betrayed;
took bread and gave you thanks;
he broke it and gave to his disciples, saying:
Take, eat; this is my body which is given for you,
do this in remembrance of me.
In the same way, after supper
he took the cup and gave thanks;
he gave it to them, saying:
Drink this, all of you;
this is the blood of my new covenant,
which is shed for you, and for many, for the forgiveness of sin.
Do this, as often as you drink it,
in remembrance of me.'

a) Copy this prayer into your book.

b) Why do you think that this prayer, with its heavy reliance on Scripture, is recited in every Eucharist service?

c) Twice in this prayer the disciples of Jesus are told to 'Do this in remembrance of me'. What exactly are they being encouraged to do?

d) There are some reminders in this prayer that sharing in the Eucharist is both an individual and a collective experience. What do you think people might gain from both of these aspects in the Eucharist?

ANSWER IN YOUR BOOK ...

1. How has the emphasis of the Eucharist changed between the Book of Common Prayer and the Alternative Service Book?

2. Can you explain the difference between the High Church and the Low Church's approach to the Eucharist?

3. What do you understand by the following?
   ❖ 'The body of our Lord Jesus Christ'
   ❖ 'The blood of our Lord Jesus Christ'

IN THE GLOSSARY ...

Holy Communion; Eucharist; Book of Common Prayer; Sacrament; Alternative Service Book; Mass; Gospel; Anglo-Catholics; Roman Catholic Church; Low Church; High Church; Protestant; Last Supper; Ascension Day.

6.6 THE MASS

The Mass is celebrated frequently in every Roman Catholic church, and Catholics are under a strong obligation to attend regularly. Its liturgy underlines four basic beliefs:

1. That the service should mirror, as closely as possible, the Last Supper which Jesus ate with his disciples.
2. That the Mass is essentially a 'sacrifice' which is offered continually to God.
3. That the service itself is an act of thanksgiving offered up by a grateful people to God.
4. That the people are spiritually nourished through the Mass.

The liturgy of the Mass

In the Old Testament the Jews regularly offered sacrifices to God in the Temple at Jerusalem. Animal blood was spread over the altar to 'cover' the sins of the people. Only then could the people worship God. Similarly, the blood of Jesus was poured out on the cross so that everyone might find God's forgiveness. The priest, as God's representative, offers this same sacrifice to God during the Mass so that people might find the divine forgiveness. The celebration of the Mass falls into several parts:

a) The people are invited to repent of their sins and experience the forgiveness of God, pronounced through the priest. Three Bible passages are read – from the Old Testament, Gospels and Epistles – before the priest preaches his sermon. This part of the Mass is called 'The Liturgy of the Word'.
b) Turning towards the altar, the congregation recite the Nicene Creed, which sums up what the Church believes about God the Father, Jesus Christ, the Holy Spirit, the Church and the life to come. A series of prayers follow, seeking God's blessing on the world and the Church.
c) The people bring forward their gifts of bread and wine.
d) The prayer of consecration is then offered over the gifts of bread and wine. As the priest repeats the words of Jesus at the Last Supper, so the people believe that the elements become the body and blood of Christ.

They acclaim:

'Christ has died, Christ is risen, Christ will come again.'

By saying this they are declaring their confidence in the three beliefs which represent everything that the Church is committed to.

e) Before sharing the Mass together, the people say the 'Our Father' (the Lord's Prayer) and offer one another the 'sign of peace'. The priest receives the bread followed by the chalice of wine. All of the congregation eat the bread and sometimes drink the wine as well. When both bread and wine are offered to the congregation at the Mass, it emphasises that the Communion is for the nourishment of all God's people.

A Can you find out why Catholics are under a strong obligation to attend Mass regularly?

f) Everyone is finally sent out into the world to help their neighbour, especially if the neighbour is in need. By serving others they are not only helping those in need but serving God as well. They are also enhancing their own spiritual lives, something they had started to do by sharing the Mass together.

B Why is this banner appropriate for people taking Mass?

IN YOUR OWN WORDS ...

An extract from the Preface to the Holy Eucharist (Mass):

'He (Christ) is the true and eternal priest who establishes this unending sacrifice. He offered himself as a victim for our deliverance and taught us to make this offering in his memory. As we eat his body which he gave for us, we grow in strength. As we drink his blood which is poured out for us we are washed clean.'

a) What do you understand by the word 'sacrifice'?
b) What is the pattern in the Old Testament for understanding the 'sacrifice' of Jesus?
c) When did Jesus offer himself as a 'victim' for the deliverance of all believers?
d) What happens to each believer as they eat the body of Jesus in the Mass?
e) What is it that secures the cleansing of all who believe from their sins?

READ AND DECIDE ...

The Mass begins with the people confessing their sins to God:

'I confess to God Almighty, the Father, the Son and the Holy Spirit, in the sight of the whole company of heaven, and to you, Father, that I have sinned in thought, word and deed.'

a) What do Christians mean by 'the Trinity' and what part does it play in this confession?
b) Who are 'the whole company of heaven'?
c) How does this prayer of confession cover the whole area in which a person is likely to have sinned?
d) Whose fault is it that we have sinned?
e) Why do you think that the confession of sin is the point at which the Mass begins?

ANSWER IN YOUR BOOK ...

1 How do Catholics express their common faith and unity in the Mass?
2 What is the significance of the 'acclamation' of the people during the Mass?
3 Why do you think the service ends with the people being 'sent' out into the world to serve God and help other people?

IN THE GLOSSARY ...

Mass; Roman Catholic Church; Last Supper; Liturgy; Jerusalem; Old Testament; Gospels; Epistles; Eucharist; Nicene Creed; Holy Spirit; Lord's Prayer; Trinity.

6.7 THE DIVINE LITURGY

The 'liturgy' is literally any service which follows a prescribed and ancient ritual. It means 'the people's work of thanksgiving to God'. In this context, though, it refers to the service of Holy Communion. In the Eastern Orthodox Church, the Divine Liturgy is divided into two parts: the Liturgy of the Word and the Liturgy of the Faithful.

The Liturgy of the Word

This part of the service has its equivalent in both the Anglican Eucharist and the Catholic Mass – prayers, Bible readings and a sermon. The climax to the Liturgy of the Word comes when the priest, carrying the Book of the Gospels (which contains the stories of the life of Jesus) high above his head, comes through the Royal Doors into the nave of the church. Surrounded by attendants holding candles, the priest then reads a passage before returning through the iconostasis (the screen which separates the people in the congregation from the high altar).

The Liturgy of the Faithful

Most of the Liturgy of the Faithful is conducted behind the iconostasis, although the congregation can see enough to follow what is happening. The iconostasis has important symbolic significance in the Orthodox liturgy. It indicates that gulf which exists between God and humanity, brought about by sin. This gulf is so great that only the priest, consecrated to God by his ordination to the priesthood, is allowed to bridge it and enter God's presence, as symbolised by the High Altar. The people are allowed to glimpse that presence from a distance but they cannot draw near to it.

The Liturgy of the Faithful is the central part of Holy Communion and follows a clearly defined pattern:

a) It begins with the preparation of the bread and wine for communion. The priest stands at the altar and the Royal Doors are closed. This symbolises the holiness of the death of Jesus and the elements, bread and wine, by which it is represented.
b) After the bread and wine have been blessed and consecrated the priest brings them through the Royal Doors and the people kneel at the front of the church to receive them.
c) Each communicant waits to receive a piece of bread dipped in wine, which is placed at the back of his or her mouth on a long silver spoon.

A What do you think is the symbolic importance of the Book of the Gospels being carried high above the heads of the congregation?

6 · CHRISTIANS AND WORSHIP

The whole service is accompanied by a choir singing or chanting without any accompaniment.

The beauty of the Divine Liturgy is a very important element in its meaning. Orthodox Christians believe that they are celebrating an 'eternal liturgy', since everything on earth is a pattern of some kind of heavenly image. Through experiencing the liturgy they are able to imagine what life is going to be like in heaven. In particular, through the Divine Liturgy they can gain a glimpse of the members of the Trinity – God the Father, God the Son and God the Holy Spirit.

> **B** Can you think of three ways in which the Divine Liturgy is different from the service of Holy Communion in any other Church?

ANSWER IN YOUR BOOK ...

1. How does the Divine Liturgy express itself as the people's work of thanksgiving to God?
2. How is the element of 'mystery' preserved throughout the Divine Liturgy? Why do you think this element is particularly important?
3. What do you understand by the Orthodox belief that everything on earth has a perfect image in heaven? What are two implications of this belief?

WHAT DO YOU THINK?

a) Why do you think that in the Orthodox Church, as in the Roman Catholic Church, the priest takes communion before it is offered to the people?
b) What do you think is the symbolic importance of the bread being dipped in wine instead of the two elements being taken separately, as in the other Christian Churches?
c) Do you see any symbolic importance attached to the practice of placing the bread on a silver spoon and placing it directly into the mouths of worshippers?
d) Why do you think that Orthodox worshippers see the Divine Liturgy as a foretaste of heaven and what do they mean by this?

FIND OUT AND NOTE ...

a) Why is the service of Holy Communion in the Orthodox Church divided into two parts – the Liturgy of the Word and the Liturgy of the Faithful?
b) Why are the Gospels treated with particular respect during the Liturgy of the Word?
c) Why is the singing in an Orthodox church always unaccompanied?

IN THE GLOSSARY ...

Divine Liturgy; Liturgy; Holy Communion; Eastern Orthodox Church; Anglican Church; Roman Catholic Church; Trinity; Gospels; Holy Spirit; Nave; Iconostasis; High Altar; Priest.

6.8 THE LORD'S SUPPER

Nonconformists use two other titles for Holy Communion:

1 *The Breaking of Bread* – a term taken from the Acts of the Apostles:

> "On the Saturday night, when we gathered for the breaking of bread..." (Acts 20.7)

It describes the practice of the early Christians who came together frequently to share an ordinary meal. Quite apart from being an act of worship, this meal also served a very practical purpose – it fed those who were hungry and needy in the Christian community. Furthermore, by bringing together the wealthy and the needy, it emphasised the unity and the practicality of Christian fellowship.

2 *The Lord's Supper* – this expression was used by Paul in 1.Corinthians 11.20. The Lord's Supper, a time of sharing and fellowship, was always enjoyed in the light of Christ's return to earth.

The Lord's Supper

Wherever the Lord's Supper is celebrated by Nonconformists, there are four distinct parts to the service:

a) The people begin by confessing their sins to God before listening to a passage from the Bible. This passage might describe the last meal that Jesus ate with his disciples (Luke 22.7-13), or Paul's description of the meal in 1.Corinthians 11.17-34. The minister spends a short time explaining the meaning of the service and a collection is often taken up for the needy of the church. In Nonconformist churches the Bible is central to every act of worship and so it is natural that it should be there at the heart of the Lord's Supper.

b) Following this, the bread and wine are either placed on the Communion table (there is no altar in a Nonconformist church) or a cloth covering them will be removed. The bread and wine are consecrated to God as the minister, or leader, reads the words spoken by Jesus at the Last Supper (Mark 14.22-25).

c) In Methodist churches the people kneel at the rail in the front of the church to receive communion. In most Nonconformist services they remain seated whilst a loaf of bread, or wafers, are passed around. As each person takes the bread, they eat it at once. This symbolises the Protestant belief that Christ makes claims on each person individually.

d) The wine is then given to the people in tiny glasses on slotted trays by the elders or deacons of the church. The congregation waits until everyone has been served before drinking together 'as a mark of our oneness in Christ'. Protestants believe that the church fellowship is extremely important, and the act of drinking the wine together is a symbol of this. The glasses are then placed in special slots in the backs of the seats in front. They are collected up after the service has finished.

A In this Nonconformist church the deacons, seen here with the minister, are the elected leaders. Why do you think they play a leading part in the Lord's Supper?

Protestants do not believe that anything happens to the bread and wine during the Lord's Supper. The Catholic belief in transubstantiation (that the bread and wine become the body and blood of Christ) was emphatically rejected during the Protestant Reformation. The bread and wine simply act as important symbols of much deeper spiritual realities. As they are taken and consumed, they act as a stimulus to meditation and reflection on the death of Jesus. The minister advises the congregation before distributing the bread and wine:

'Feed on him (Christ) in your hearts by faith.'

B Why do the people in a Nonconformist church retain their glass and drink together?

ANSWER IN YOUR BOOK ...

1. Why do Nonconformists call this service 'The Breaking of Bread' or 'The Lord's Supper'?
2. The pulpit is the focal point in a Nonconformist church, drawing attention to the importance of the preached Word. How is this brought out in the Lord's Supper?
3. Protestant religion is built both on an individual response to God and collective responsibility. How is this reflected in the Lord's Supper?

READ AND DECIDE ...

In 1.Corinthians 11.23-26, Paul claims to have had a revelation from God about the Lord's Supper. This is what he writes:

> "For the tradition which I handed on to you came to me from the Lord himself; that on the night of his arrest the Lord Jesus took bread, and after giving thanks to God broke it and said: 'This is my body, which is for you; do this in memory of me.' In the same way he took the cup after supper and said: 'This cup is the new covenant sealed by my blood. Whenever you drink it, do this in memory of me. For every time you eat this bread and drink the cup, you proclaim the death of the Lord until he comes.'"

You should learn this passage.

a) What is Paul claiming to pass on to the Christians in Corinth?
b) What did Jesus say as he offered his disciples the bread and the wine?
c) What support does there seem to be for the Nonconformist belief that the Lord's Supper is essentially a time for remembering the death of Jesus?
d) What are the believers doing when they eat the bread and drink the wine?

IN THE GLOSSARY ...

Holy Communion; Lord's Supper; Breaking of Bread; Minister; Deacon; Nonconformist; Bible; Altar; Last Supper; Methodist Church; Protestant; Transubstantiation; Pulpit.

6.9 THE MONASTIC LIFE

Within a century or two of its birth, there were people in the Christian Church who felt the need to devote themselves entirely to God. Like Jesus before them, they too took themselves off into the desert areas to take up a life of prayer. St Antony of Egypt was probably the first but he was soon followed by others. A large number of monks and hermits were attracted to Mt. Athos, in northern Greece, and the many monasteries there became very influential in the development of Christianity in the east. Although the numbers living there have declined in recent years, there are still some twenty monasteries in the area, housing thousands of Orthodox monks.

In the centuries that followed, four great monastic Orders were established – the Benedictines; the Franciscans; the Dominicans and the Jesuits.

The Benedictines

St Benedict (480-547) was the most influential figure in the monastic movement because he laid down a series of 'Rules' (called The Rule) for those who joined him in the monastery at Monte Cassino, Italy. The Rule, later adopted by other monastic Orders, stipulated that all monks and nuns should do the following:

1. Live in absolute poverty with no earthly possessions. Possessions brought with them when they join the Order become the property of the monastery or convent.
2. Abstain from all sexual contact and intercourse – chastity. For nuns in many Orders, this came to take the form of being married to God. The wearing of a ring signified this.
3. Live in total obedience to the will of the community expressed through its leader. In a monastery this is the Abbot, and in a convent the Mother Superior. These leaders are chosen by the monks or nuns themselves, for the 'holiness' they display in living life.

A What do you think has been the great attraction down the centuries of the monastic life to men and women seeking God?

Ever since the first monasteries and convents were established a great emphasis was laid upon communal prayer. Traditionally, there were seven times during the day for such prayers:

- Morning prayers – Lauds (Praise)
- The first hour – Prime (6.00 a.m.)
- The third hour – Terce (9.00 a.m.)
- The sixth hour – Sext (Midday)
- The ninth hour – None (3.00 p.m.)
- Evening – Vespers (Early evening)
- Final Night Prayer – Compline (Complete)

Modern monastic communities follow a similar schedule although the number of times for communal prayer have been reduced.

The Franciscans

This Order of Roman Catholic and Anglican friars was founded by St Francis of Assisi in the 13th century. The Franciscans have always led a simple life spent in looking after the sick and, following the example of their founder, respecting nature, especially birds and animals.

The Dominicans

This is a Roman Catholic Order of friars and nuns founded in Toulouse in 1215. The founder, St Dominic, stressed the use of the intellect in the service of God. The aim of the Order is to teach truth, hence its motto 'Veritas' (truth). The order is divided into three branches:

a) Male preachers who teach.
b) Enclosed (living only within the confines of the convent) nuns who live a life of prayer and contemplation.
c) 'Tertiaries' – some of whom live in the community, while others simply share in the life of the community.

The Jesuits

Officially known as 'The Society of Jesus', the Jesuits are a Roman Catholic religious order founded by St Ignatius of Loyola in the 16th Century. Ignatius gathered a small community of men around him and they took vows of poverty, chastity and obedience to the pope as well as commiting themselves to missionary work throughout the world.

ANSWER IN YOUR BOOK ...

1. Why did the communal life and monasticism begin?
2. What was the great legacy that St Benedict bequeathed to the monastic tradition?
3. Explain the meaning of: a monk; a hermit; a monastery and celibacy.

FIND OUT AND NOTE ...

a) Four religious Orders are mentioned in the text – the Benedictines, the Franciscans, the Dominicans and the Jesuits. Carry out some research of your own into **one** of these Orders. Try to find out:
   - how, why and when it was founded;
   - any leaders who have had a considerable effect on the growth and development of the Order;
   - the main areas of work in which the Order operates – education, health etc;
   - the main beliefs of the Order.
b) Do you have a convent or a monastery nearby? If so, take the opportunity of inviting a monk or nun to answer your questions.

WHAT DO YOU THINK?

a) Why do you think that Christians who have wanted to dedicate themselves entirely to God have often made their way instinctively to the desert? What is thought to be so special about such areas?
b) Why do you think that monks and nuns have always put prayer at the centre of their communal lives?
c) Why do you think that St Benedict insisted on the three rules of poverty, chastity and obedience? Why were these rules considered essential for a communal life – and a life dedicated to God?

IN THE GLOSSARY ...

Monk; Monastery; Benedictines; Franciscans; Roman Catholic Church; Anglican Church; Dominicans; Nun; Jesuit.

6.10 TAIZÉ AND IONA

While the old monastic traditions and Orders still survive today, there are two modern communities which, for many Christians, sum up all that is beautiful and life-enhancing about the old tradition. The Taizé community was founded on the back of the Second World War while the Iona community was an ancient foundation which was revived in the 1930s.

A *This is part of the Taizé community worshipping. Find out as much as you can about the distinctive character of the worship in this community.*

In 1949 the first seven brothers in Taizé took monastic vows for life. Today there are over 80 brothers in the community from all religious backgrounds, with Roger Schulze, or Brother Roger as he is now known, as their Abbot. They are scattered worldwide as:

'…signs of the presence of Christ among men and the bearers of joy…'

In 1962 a group of German Christians were moving around Europe building signs of reconciliation in places where people had suffered at Nazi hands. They built the Church of Reconciliation in Taizé and this is visited each year by thousands of travellers, mostly young people, from all over the world. They are invited to spend a week with the community and to extend their stay with a further week of silence.

Taizé

Since 1949 young people from all faiths have travelled to Taizé, attracted by a growing community which places the theme of 'reconciliation' at the centre of its life and worship. When they arrive, visitors find Catholic, Anglican and Orthodox monks living and witnessing together to their common faith.

It all began in 1940 when Roger Schulze bought a house in Taizé, France, at the very time when Europe was beginning to feel the ravages of war. He intended to set up a religious community there but began by living alone and following the life of a monk, praying three times a day and living off the land. Soon he welcomed many refugees who were fleeing from the Nazis in occupied France. However, before long, he was forced to leave the country. After the war was over, Schulze returned to Taizé and began to offer food and shelter to German prisoners in a nearby camp. This was unpopular with many of Schulze's neighbours but the theme of the community – reconciliation – was in place from the very beginning.

Iona

It was in the 6th century that St Columba used the Scottish island of Iona as a base from which to carry the Christian message to the 'pagans' in northern England. He built a monastery there, although the community eventually died out. In 1938 the Rev. George Macleod decided to rebuild the monastery with unemployed people from Glasgow. He wanted them to learn about living in a community so that they could return to Glasgow and improve the quality of their lives there.

Today there are 200 full members and 800 associate members of the Iona community. None of them live on the island permanently, but they return to Iona for a week every year. They do not follow the old Rule of St Benedict but covenant (enter into an agreement) to spend time each day reading their Bible and praying. They give 10% of their money to the Church and work for peace and justice in their own community.

ANSWER IN YOUR BOOK ...

1. How did the dominant theme of Taizé, reconciliation, spring out of the time when the community was born?
2. The Iona community was first set up because George Macleod did not think that the Church was offering anything to people living in the inner cities. What do you think that time spent on the beautiful Scottish island of Iona might offer to people living in the middle of Glasgow?
3. Compare the covenant into which members of the Iona community enter with the traditional monastic vows. Which do you think is more realistic today?

WHAT DO YOU THINK?

Here is a short extract from the Rule at Taizé:
'That Christ may grow in me, I must know my own weakness and that of my brothers. For them I will become all things to all, and even give my life, for Christ's sake and the Gospel's...'

a) What do you think the Rule means by 'That Christ may grow in me...'?
b) Why do you think that it is vital for a person living in a community to be aware of his own weaknesses?
c) Why do you think that someone in a community needs to be aware of the weaknesses of others?
d) What do you think is meant by: 'For them I will become all things to all, and even give my life, for Christ's sake and the Gospel's...'?
e) What is the most striking difference between this Rule and the Rule of St Benedict?

DISCUSS AMONG YOURSELVES ...

a) Life in the Iona community is very basic. On the island, members only eat meat twice a week; do not eat red meat; eat only eggs from free-range chickens and only drink coffee from organisations where the profits go to the growers. What do you think is the link between these rules and the Christian basis of the Community?
b) What do you think are the advantages and disadvantages of having a community where members only come together once a year?

B *What is distinctive about the Iona Community?*

IN THE GLOSSARY ...

Monastery; Monk.

6.11 PILGRIMAGES

Although pilgrimages are a very strong and important tradition in many religions, this is not true of Christianity. There is no compulsion in Christianity, as there is in Islam and Hinduism, for anyone to go on a pilgrimage. Despite this, many Christians over the centuries have travelled to the 'holy places' which are associated with important people and events in Christianity, to seek forgiveness or healing. They have always been of more interest to Roman Catholics than to members of other denominations, and Protestants have always shown a marked lack of interest in them.

Christian pilgrimages

Christian pilgrimages do not seem to have started until the 4th century when St Helena, the mother of the Christian Roman Emperor Constantine, claimed to have discovered part of the cross of Christ in Jerusalem. As soon as the news spread, pilgrims made their way to the city. By the Middle Ages pilgrimages had become an important part of the Faith. Huge numbers of people were undertaking journeys fraught with danger to the Holy Land, and many died on the way. Many were making the journey because they had promised that they would do so if their prayers were answered. Others were seeking relief and healing for diseased bodies and minds.

There were also shrines much nearer home. In several places, stories circulated that visions or miracles had taken place there. These 'supernatural manifestations' were often associated with a saint who had been buried in the shrine or a supposed relic which had been brought to the place. During the Middle Ages there was a lively market in such relics although many of them turned out to be fakes. Some of the places which became pilgrimage centres achieved lasting recognition, like Walsingham in Norfolk. Others were never heard of again.

A *What do you think is the attraction of making a pilgrimage for some Christians today?*

> **ISRAEL**
> **IN THE STEPS OF CHRIST**
> An 8 day Holyland Pilgrimage
> from only £469
> Other Holy Land Tours £349–£655
>
> FOR COPIES OF OUR **1994** PROGRAMME DETAILS TELEPHONE PAX TRAVEL
>
> **PAX TRAVEL LTD**
>
> PAX TRAVEL
> 106 SEYMOUR PLACE
> LONDON
> W1H 5DG
> ☎
> 071-724 8206
> ABTA 85988
>
> **SHRINES OF EUROPE**
> Rome, Assisi, Bruges, Lourdes, Fatima, Santiago de Compostela & Vineyards and Saints Tour in France
>
> **PARISH AND SCHOOL GROUPS**
> We can offer a free 'tailor-made' quotation for the above destinations

Reasons for pilgrimages

Among the reasons for pilgrims to travel to holy places are the following:

a) To seek out or thank God for some kind of physical or spiritual healing. Perhaps the most well-known shrine to which pilgrims have gone for healing is Lourdes, in southern France – although few proven miracles have actually taken place there.

6 · CHRISTIANS AND WORSHIP

B *This shrine is at Walsingham, in Norfolk. Find out all that you can about this or another centre of pilgrimage.*

b) To visit a site where, it was believed, Jesus or the Virgin Mary had appeared to people in the past.
c) As an act of penance to seek forgiveness for sins.
d) To follow in the footsteps of Jesus, Paul and the early Christians in the Holy Land. Christians today still visit Israel in search of the roots of their Faith.

Many pilgrims return home disappointed. They have sought a blessing or healing which has not happened. Others, though, speak of having grown or developed in their spiritual lives as a result of the pilgrimage. Much of this comes from the experience of fellowship and friendship which they encounter from a 'spiritual journey' shared with others.

ANSWER IN YOUR BOOK ...

1. Why did many Christians undertake pilgrimages from the 4th century onwards?
2. What has traditionally marked out a site as holy and worthy of a pilgrimage?
3. What do you understand by a pilgrimage; a pilgrim; a shrine and a relic?

WHAT DO YOU THINK?

Here are two points for you to think about:

a) Do you think that miraculous healings can still take place? If so, do you think they can still be associated with the established pilgrimage sites – or is that just superstition?
b) If healings do not take place at the holy sites then could pilgrimages have other benefits? Do you think that people enjoying the fellowship of a shared journey or pilgrimage is important?

DISCUSS AMONG YOURSELVES ...

Here are three comments from Christians who have recently been on pilgrimages:

a) **Alan, 27:** 'My reason for undertaking a pilgrimage was quite simple. I believe that the Christian life itself is a journey, a pilgrimage if you like. That journey will continue for the rest of my life. My pilgrimage to Walsingham was part of that journey...'
   ❖ What do you think Alan means when he describes his Christian life as a 'journey, a pilgrimage'?

b) **Anne, 22:** 'I have suffered from a debilitating illness since I was five years old. I didn't think that going to Lourdes would cure me of that illness – and it didn't. However, I did find the love of God at Lourdes, in the faces of those that took me, in the care of those who looked after me and in almost everyone I met on the way.'
   ❖ Would you describe Anne's experience as being, in any way, a miracle?

c) **John, 24:** 'Through undertaking a pilgrimage with other members of my church I found great strength in the sense of community we had with each other. We were all very different kinds of people but we learned to live together and love each other's failings. Barriers came down. I was a much stronger Christian when I returned home.'
   ❖ Is this a rather unexpected benefit of a pilgrimage which people might overlook?

IN THE GLOSSARY ...

Protestant; Jerusalem; Shrine; Relic; Virgin Mary.

6.12 HOLY PLACES

There are many 'holy places' in Great Britain and throughout Europe. Apart from the Holy Land, where Jesus lived and died, most of these places are either associated with the burial of a saint or a supposed 'vision' of the Virgin Mary. They can be divided into three categories, according to whether they are associated with saints, the Virgin Mary or Jesus in the Holy Land.

Holy places associated with saints

An old belief that James, one of the original disciples of Jesus, had visited Spain seemed to have been confirmed in the 9th century with the discovery of some bones. These were thought to have been those of the apostle. Unfortunately, in 1589, the Bishop of Compostella, believing that the bones were about to be stolen, hid them – and then promptly died without telling anyone where they were! They were not rediscovered until 1879, by which time Santiago de Compostella had become a major pilgrimage destination.

In the 12th century Thomas Becket, Archbishop of Canterbury, fought for the authority and independence of the Church against King Henry II. Four of Henry's knights murdered Becket on the steps of the altar of his cathedral. Within three years he had been declared a saint because of numerous miracles associated with his tomb. The spot where Becket died became extremely holy, as did three other locations in the cathedral bearing parts of his body – the altar and two shrines.

Holy places associated with the Virgin Mary

We have already mentioned Lourdes, in France, in Unit 6.11. It was there, in 1858, that Bernadette Soubirous, a fourteen year old girl, claimed to have had a series of visions of the Virgin Mary. A spring of water mysteriously appeared and 'miraculous healings' were claimed from 1873 onwards. Since then, Lourdes has become the most popular of all the pilgrimage sites, attracting over 2,000,000 pilgrims a year. The Roman Catholic Church, however, is reluctant to claim that more than a mere handful of miracles have taken place there.

A Apart from the desire to be healed, can you think of anything else that might draw pilgrims to Lourdes?

Holy places associated with Jesus in the Holy Land (Israel)

The Church of the Nativity in Bethlehem is built on the supposed site of the stable in which Jesus was born. Along with other sites, this one is shared among different Christian traditions. The church has altars tended by Greek, Serbian and Egyptian Orthodox priests, together with those from the Roman Catholic Church. Two other churches in Nazareth claim to be standing on the exact place where the Angel Gabriel announced to Mary that she was going to become pregnant and bear God's Son.

The two most important holy sites can be found in Jerusalem. Golgotha, where Jesus died, and the Garden tomb, in which his body was laid, are both covered by churches. Many pilgrims choose to walk along the Via Dolorosa (Way of Grief), following the path that Jesus took from the Judgement Hall of Pilate to Calvary, the place of his execution. Many Christians make a devotional pilgrimage along the route, especially on Good Friday, when they walk behind a wooden cross. They stop to pray at 'Stations of the Cross' which are marked along the way – places where, according to tradition and the Scriptures, Jesus stopped on the way to his death. There are fourteen such places altogether.

B *These pilgrims are retracing the route which is thought to have been taken by Jesus on the way to his execution. What spiritual benefits do you think these pilgrims might hope to gain from doing this?*

ANSWER IN YOUR BOOK ...

1. What do you understand by a 'Christian pilgrimage'?
2. Why do you think that sites where healings or visions were believed to have taken place were so highly valued in the Middle Ages and beyond?
3. Very few sites in the Holy Land can be identified with any certainty. Do you think that such doubt ruins the effectiveness of a pilgrimage to them?

WHAT DO YOU THINK?

Does it strike you as being strange that places associated with the life and death of Jesus in the Holy Land have to be shared out among the different Christian Churches? What does this say to the outside world? Why do you think that the different Churches cannot unite in the very place where their faith was born?

CAN YOU EXPLAIN?

a) Why are Bethelehem, Nazareth and Jerusalem centres of Christian pilgrimage?
b) Why were the bones of James missing from Santiago de Compostella for almost 300 years?
c) Why did pilgrims start coming to Canterbury Cathedral in the 12th century?
d) Why did Christians in the past greatly value the bones of saints who had died?
e) Why did certain tombs become centres of Christian devotion?

IN THE GLOSSARY ...

Virgin Mary; Apostle; Altar; Shrine; Roman Catholic Church; Stations of the Cross.

7.1 INFANT BAPTISM

From Matthew's Gospel we learn that when Jesus emerged from obscurity at the start of his ministry he presented himself to John the Baptist to be baptised (Matthew 3.1-17). Jesus, we think, was about thirty years old when this happened, so we are clearly talking here about adult baptism. Like any other Jewish boy, he had been circumcised and dedicated to God in the Temple when he was just a few days old (Luke 2.21-35).

No reference there, or anywhere else in the New Testament, is made to infant baptism. This ritual did not begin until the 4th century when Christian families began to have their babies baptised as soon as possible after birth. What was the reason for this ritual? The ritual began when people started to believe that unbaptised babies, many of whom died in infancy, would not enter heaven.

Infant baptism

Originally the term 'baptism' was applied to sheep who were dipped beneath the water to kill any parasites attached to their bodies. When the term was applied to the baptism of people in the Christian Church the same idea was carried forward and given a spiritual meaning – the dipping of people under the water to cleanse them from their sins.

For most Christian Churches baptism has become the means by which a baby becomes a member of Christ's Church. Not surprisingly, there are variations among the Orthodox, Roman Catholic and Anglican ways of carrying out the service:

a) In an Orthodox church, baptism and confirmation follow each other in the service, which is carried out when the baby is eight days old. This service, called Chrismation, begins with prayers that the baby may come to know God and his commandments. The child's clothes are then removed to symbolise the leaving behind of the old life.

A Why do you think that this baby's parents have brought him to church to be baptised?

The service which follows falls into three parts:
❖ The priest blesses the baptismal water with a prayer and breathes on the water in the shape of a cross.
❖ A pre-baptism anointing with the 'oil of gladness' takes place.
❖ The baptism itself, for which the baby is held in the font – facing east (a symbol of resurrection) – and submerged beneath the water three times as the priest says:

'The servant of God (giving the child its name) is baptised in the name of the Father, Amen. And of the Son, Amen. And of the Holy Spirit, Amen.'

The baby is then dressed in a new robe (the robe of righteousness) showing that he or she has become a new person, and anointed with oil (chrism) to demonstrate that the Holy Spirit has been received.

7 BETWEEN BIRTH AND DEATH

7 · BETWEEN BIRTH AND DEATH

b) The Roman Catholic and Anglican services of infant baptism follow the same broad pattern. The essential elements are the following:
- The child is presented for baptism by its parents and god-parents. The god-parents promise to watch over the child to see that he or she is brought up in the Christian faith.
- Parents and god-parents are asked by the priest to indicate their own belief in the Christian faith.
- A passage from the Bible is read which underlines the importance of baptism.
- The child is baptised with water poured over him or her by the priest with the words:

"I baptise you in the name of the Father and of the Son and of the Holy Spirit."

c) After the baby has been baptised in an Anglican service, a lighted candle is often handed to the parents to symbolise the moving of the child from darkness to light. The whole congregation then tells the child:

'We welcome you into the Lord's family. We are members together of the body of Christ: we are children of the same Heavenly Father; we are inheritors together of the Kingdom of God.'

B *Why do you think that thousands of couples still bring their babies to be baptised in church?*

ANSWER IN YOUR BOOK ...

1. What is meant by 'baptism'?
2. Why did infant baptism come to be a popular practice in the Christian Church?
3. Write a description of the part that infant baptism plays in most churches.

FIND OUT AND NOTE ...

The water for infant baptism is kept in a font. Can you find out the following?

a) Where has the font always traditionally stood in a church – and why?
b) Where is the font often found in modern churches – and why?
c) What does the change imply for an understanding of baptism, which has also changed over the passage of time?

WHAT DO YOU THINK?

During the infant baptism service three questions are directed at the baby's parents and godparents. They are:
Priest: Do you turn to Christ?
Answer: I turn to Christ.
Priest: Do you repent of your sins?
Answer: I repent of my sins.
Priest: Do you renounce evil?
Answer: I renounce evil.

Why do you think that these questions are directed at the parents and godparents before a baby is baptised? What do you think their significance is intended to be?

IN THE GLOSSARY ...

Infant Baptism; Confirmation; Chrismation; Font; Roman Catholic Church; Anglican Church; Holy Spirit; Bible; Priest.

7.2 CONFIRMATION

In the period which the New Testament describes it seems that baptism and the 'laying on of hands' (to bestow the gift of the Holy Spirit) were rituals performed on adult converts to Christianity at the same time. As the Church began to accept the baptism of infants, Confirmation (the laying on of hands) was retained as a sacrament to be performed later.

The Eastern Orthodox Church, however, retained the old practice with Confirmation following baptism in the same service. In the Anglican and Roman Catholic Churches, those who were baptised as babies have the opportunity to return to church to be confirmed. This happens when they have reached an age of 'spiritual responsibility'. In the Catholic Church, where Confirmation is a sacrament, children are normally confirmed at the age of fourteen – although converts to Roman Catholicism can be confirmed much later.

The Confirmation Service

The same three questions directed at parents and godparents in baptism are now asked of the person being confirmed. This is deliberate. Now the person can respond to those questions for him/herself. By so doing, they demonstrate that they have reached an age at which they can take spiritual responsibility for themselves.

The importance of Confirmation in the life of the Church is reinforced by the fact that the service, unlike baptism, is always taken by a bishop. When the questions have been answered, the bishop lays his hands upon the head of each candidate. This part of the ceremony, the 'laying on of hands', is an old traditional symbol which goes back to the earliest days of Christianity. Then, as now, it is the means by which the Holy Spirit is passed on.

Two further features of the Roman Catholic Confirmation service are worth noting:

a) The candidates are anointed with oil. From earliest times, oil has been rubbed into wounds to help them heal. Here, though, it is the healing of the soul and not the body which is being symbolised.
b) The bishop lightly slaps the face of each candidate with two fingers. This is a symbolic gesture of the suffering, persecution and contempt the candidate may have to endure for his/her faith. For them, the service represents a new beginning – with all the peace of mind that comes from having one's sins forgiven.

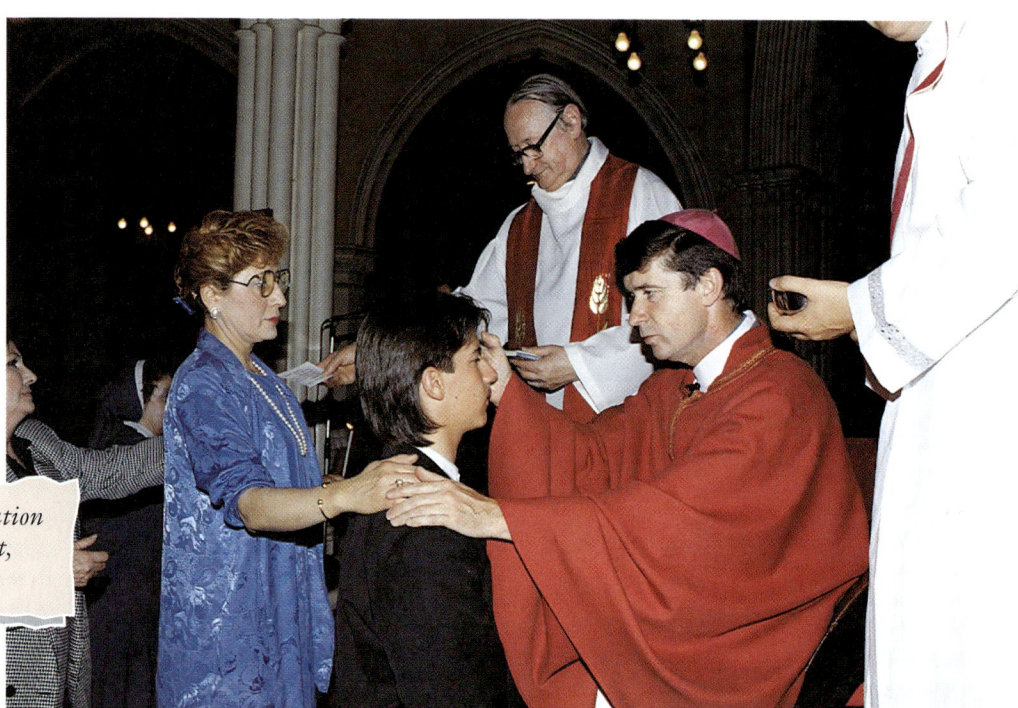

A When people speak of confirmation as being an act of commitment, what do you think they mean?

Methodist Confirmation

The Methodist Church has its own service of 'Public Reception into Full Membership or Confirmation'. This involves the person promising that they will be faithful to the Christian way of life. The minister lays his hands upon them in blessing. In this way the person is admitted to full membership of the Christian Church.

In one sense, Confirmation marks a completion. It completes the promises that were made for the person when they were baptised. They have now expressed their personal commitment to Christ and signalled their determination to follow a Christian way of life. Through Confirmation they have been made a member of Christ's Church, and they will now be expected to play a full part in its life and witness. The process is completed soon afterwards when the person shares in the body and blood of Jesus by taking Communion.

CAN YOU EXPLAIN?

The photograph shows the membership ticket of those who belong to the Methodist Church.

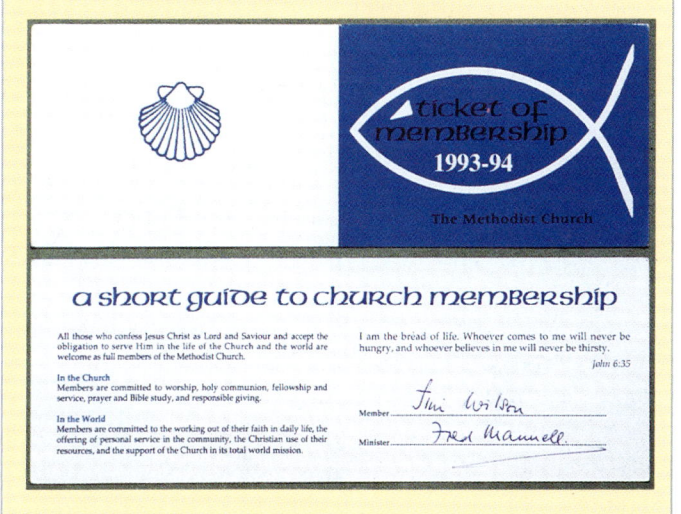

a) The ticket contains the symbols of the shell and the fish. Can you find out the significance of these two symbols on the Methodist membership ticket?

b) Describe those people who are welcome to become full members of the Methodist Church.

c) Members are commited to seven activities within the Church. What are they?

d) Which four activities are members commited to in the outside world?

e) Can you explain the relationship between Paul's words in Romans 12.5 and Church membership?

ANSWER IN YOUR BOOK ...

1. What is the link between the services of infant baptism and Confirmation?
2. Look up Acts 8.17 and 9.16 and then explain why the bishop lays his hands on the head of each Confirmation candidate.
3. Describe, in your own words, two features of a Confirmation service in a Catholic church.

IN YOUR OWN WORDS ...

Look at the photograph on page 92. Can you:

a) List three Churches in which this ceremony could be taking place?

b) Explain why this ceremony is always conducted by a bishop?

c) Describe what happens during a Confirmation service?

d) Decide at which age you think someone is old enough to 'confirm' their commitment to Christ and the Church? Explain the reasoning behind your answer.

IN THE GLOSSARY ...

Confirmation; Roman Catholic Church; Orthodox Church; Sacrament; Anglican Church; Holy Communion; Bishop; Laying on of hands; Holy Spirit; Methodist Church.

7.3 ADULT BAPTISM

From the beginning of its history, in the 17th century, the Baptist Church has strenuously argued that there is only one form of baptism known in the New Testament – adult baptism. They point out the following:

1. Jesus was baptised by John the Baptist in the River Jordan when he was an adult and just about to begin his public ministry.

2. The Apostle Peter, in his sermon on the Day of Pentecost, told converts to:

    'Repent and be baptised, every one of you, in the name of Jesus the Messiah; then your sins will be forgiven…' (Acts 2.38)

3. Paul used the symbolism of adult baptism to express what had happened to those beginning the Christian life:

    'By that baptism into his death we were buried with him, in order that, as Christ was raised from the dead by the glorious power of the Father, so also we might set out on a new life.' (Romans 6.4)

Who baptises adults?

A small and persecuted group in the 16th century, the Anabaptists, insisted that the only people who could be baptised were those who had commited their lives to Christ. Even those who had been baptised as children needed to be 're-baptised' as adult believers. These were the forerunners for the modern Baptist Church.

A group of Baptists met for the first time in Amsterdam in 1609 and opened their first church in London three years later. Today the Baptist Church is particularly strong in the USA, where it has over 25 million members. A sizeable number (200,000) belong to it in Great Britain. There is also a very strong Baptist Church in Russia.

Believer's baptism

When it comes to being baptised many Christians want to follow the example of Jesus as closely as possible. Some actually travel to the River Jordan but others settle for any sea, river or lake. The majority are baptised in their local church, where a pool is sunk into the floor at the front. Although baptisms were only carried out in the early Church at Easter and Whitsun, they are now performed at any time. The custom of wearing white – the colour of purity – largely remains. Women wear a simple white dress and men a white shirt and grey flannel trousers.

The service of adult baptism involves the whole church. Each person to be baptised makes a public declaration of their own faith in Christ. Three important symbolic acts then take place:

a) The person goes down into the pool so leaving their old, sinful life behind them for ever.

b) The person's body is immersed totally beneath the water. In this way, the person dies to that old life and is buried with Christ.

A These pilgrims have come to the River Jordan to be baptised by a Greek Orthodox priest. A palm frond is used to sprinkle the water over them. Why do you think that they want to be baptised in this particular river?

c) The person comes up out of the water to share with Christ in the new life that he had after his resurrection.

Nothing actually takes place as a result of adult baptism. The service is full of symbolism which points to spiritual changes which have already taken place in the believer, or are continuing to do so. The next step is for the believer to be received into a full and active membership of the church. This takes place at the first Lord's Supper after baptism, when the person is given 'the right hand of fellowship' by the minister and welcomed as a full church member by the congregation. He or she is now expected to play a full part in the church's ministry by proclaiming the Christian Gospel to those outside the church.

B What reasons do you think a person might have for wanting to be baptised?

READ AND DECIDE ...

Here are two quotations from the Acts of the Apostles – the book in the New Testament which describes the exploits of the early Christians:

❖ "Then Peter said, Can anyone keep these people from being baptised with water? They have received the Holy Spirit just as we have. So he ordered that they be baptised in the name of Jesus Christ." (Acts 10.48)

❖ 'Crispus, the synagogue ruler, and his entire household believed in the Lord; and many of the Corinthians who heard him believed and were baptised.' (Acts 18.8)

a) What seems to be the link in these two quotations between believing in Jesus Christ and being baptised?
b) How is this link stressed in the modern service of adult baptism?

ANSWER IN YOUR BOOK ...

1 How do Baptists justify the restriction of baptism to adults alone?
2 Religious symbolism plays a very important part in adult baptism. Describe and comment on three such pieces of symbolism.
3 Explain how Baptists link adult baptism with the death and resurrection of Jesus.

CAN YOU EXPLAIN?

The service of adult baptism contains a lot of symbolism. Can you explain the symbolic importance and meaning of each of the following:

a) The waters of baptism.
b) The wearing of white clothes for baptism.
c) The lowering into the water to be baptised.
d) The baptism itself.
e) The coming up out of the water after baptism.

IN THE GLOSSARY ...

Messiah; Adult Baptism; Easter; Whitsun; New Testament; Lord's Supper; Gospel.

7.4 A WEDDING

In the Preface to the Wedding Mass in the Roman Catholic Church we find these words:

> 'The love of man and woman is made holy in the Sacrament of Marriage, and becomes the mirror of your everlasting love'.

While the Anglican and Nonconformist Churches do not agree that marriage is a sacrament, they do accept it as a solemn agreement made between a man and a woman who love each other in the sight of God. The love that the two have for each other reflects, as Paul tells us, the love that Christ has for the Church:

> 'Husbands, love your wives, as Christ loved the Church and gave himself up for it.'
> (Ephesians 5.25)

Although the actual form that the Wedding Service takes varies from Church to Church, several common themes run through all the services. Among them are the following:

1. The wedding is taking place in the sight of God and before gathered relatives and friends. While there must be at least two human witnesses to all weddings, the most important witness to the new relationship is God. It is this element, more than any other, which distinguishes between a church and a registry office wedding.

2. The marriage is a lifelong commitment between a man and a woman, although all of the Churches, except the Roman Catholic Church, felt it necessary to come to terms with divorce. In all church weddings, however, the man and the woman are required to promise that they will be faithful to each other: "... until death us do part...".

3. Every marriage can expect to be blessed by the gift of children – although it is a sad fact that 1 in every 10 couples are unable to have children of their own.

4. The marriage is a powerful symbol of that close and intimate link between Christ and his Church. In the Bible, Christ is described as a 'bridegroom' and the Church as his 'pure, spotless bride'.

The Wedding Service

In the Anglican Church service the priest provides three reasons for marriage to be important:

a) So that the two people can love and comfort one another. The vows which they make to one another spell out what loving and caring mean in practice.
b) To provide the most secure and loving environment in which sexual intercourse can take place.
c) To provide a loving and caring home into which children can be born and brought up.

This is the order of reasons laid down in the recent Alternative Service Book of the Church of England. The order is slightly different in the old Book of Common Prayer.

The priest then asks the two people individually:

'N, will you take N to be your husband (wife)? Will you love him (her); comfort him (her); honour and protect him (her) and forsaking all others be faithful to him (her) as long as you both shall live?'

The couple then make their vows or promises to each other before the groom places a ring on the bride's finger. In modern weddings, the couple often exchange rings.

A What do you think are realistic promises for this couple to make to each other as they set out on their married life?

The ring, a perfect and unending circle, is taken as a beautiful symbol of a love which, it is hoped, will last for eternity. In the Catholic Church, as we have seen, marriage is a sacrament. In the other sacraments the blessing is bestowed by the priest on the people. In marriage, however, the couple uniquely bestow the sacrament, and its blessings, on one another.

There is a rather beautiful variation in the Orthodox wedding service. The priest crowns the couple with 'wreaths', indicating that they will become 'king' and 'queen' over their own small kingdom (the house they will set up together). To symbolise their unity together the couple then share a glass of wine and walk three times, hand in hand, around a table in the centre of the church.

B What does the wedding ring symbolise? Do you think that it is an effective symbol?

ANSWER IN YOUR BOOK ...

1. Can you explain three important pieces of symbolism which are included in the Anglican wedding service?
2. How do the reasons given in the Marriage Service for marriage compare with your own reasons for two people getting married?
3. Why do you think that Wedding Services stress that a church marriage takes place:
   ❖ in the sight of God;
   ❖ in front of witnesses.

   What important points do you think are being made?

WHAT DO YOU THINK?

The vows and the signing of the marriage register are the only parts of the wedding service which are legally required. In the vows the man and woman promise to:

'I, N, take you, N, to be my wife (husband), to have and to hold, from this day forward; for better, for worse, for richer, for poorer, in sickness and in health, to love and to cherish, till death us do part, according to God's holy law; and this is my solemn vow.'

a) What do you think is the point of the couple making solemn vows (promises) to each other?
b) What do you think are the practical implications of the promises they make to one another?
c) In the old service a woman also promises a man that she will:

   '...love, cherish and obey.'

   What do you think is the significance of omitting any reference to obedience in the modern service?

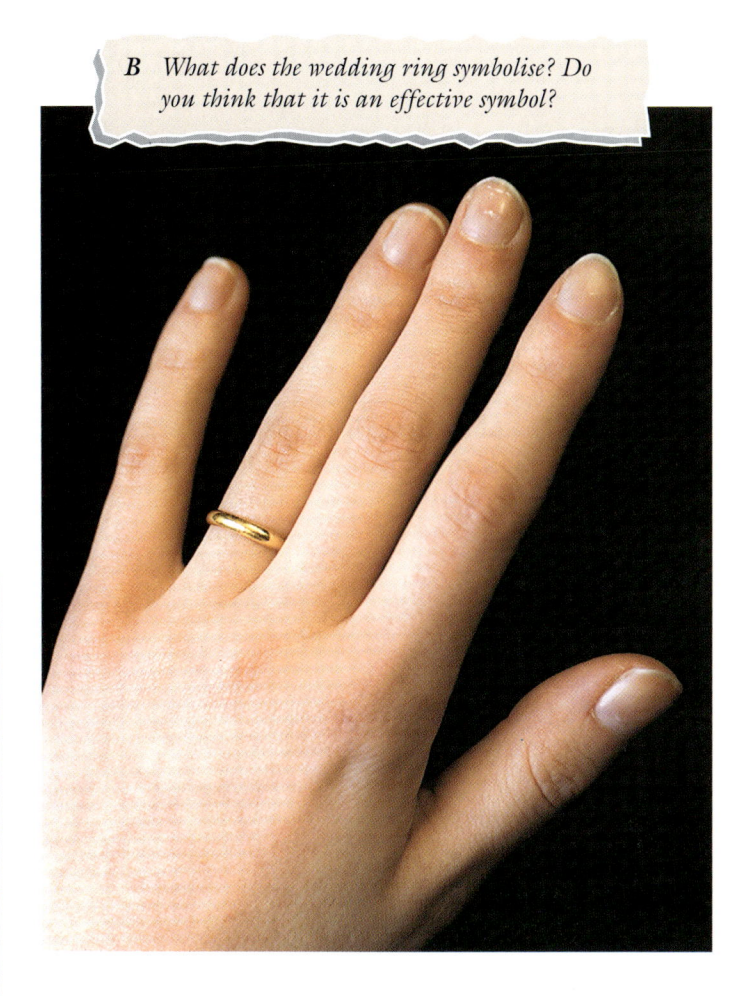

READ AND DECIDE ...

As the man places the ring on the finger of the woman he says:

'I give you this ring as a sign of our marriage. With my body I honour you, all that I am I give to you, and all that I have I share with you, within the love of God the Father, the Son and Holy Spirit.'

a) What do you think is meant by the statement that the ring is a 'sign of our marriage'?
b) What is the symbolism behind the giving of a ring? Is that symbolism made more meaningful if rings are exchanged?
c) Why is a ring a particularly appropriate symbol to use in this situation?

IN THE GLOSSARY ...

Sacrament; Roman Catholic Church; Anglican Church; Book of Common Prayer; Alternative Service Book; Mass

7.5 A FUNERAL

The Christian Church has always held clearly defined beliefs about life after death, and these are reflected in the various funeral services of the different denominations. Underlying all other beliefs is the conviction that death is the gateway to everlasting, or eternal, life. The physical body of the person decays and returns to dust, but the essential part of that person, their soul or spirit, lives on for ever.

Roman Catholic and Protestant funerals

The traditional arrangements for a Roman Catholic funeral include prayers in the home. Traditionally, this took the form of an all-night vigil or 'wake', with the coffin in the home on the night before the funeral. Nowadays, the coffin is taken to the church the night before the funeral and prayers are said for the soul of the dead person there.

The priest is dressed in white robes. White is the colour associated with life after death and the resurrection of the body – both essential Christian beliefs. In fact, they are the twin themes that form the basis for a Christian funeral. They are announced by the priest as he meets the coffin at the door of the church, sprinkles it with holy water and recites the words from John's Gospel:

> 'I am the resurrection and the life; he who believes in me, though he die, yet shall he live, and whoever lives and believes in me shall never die.' (John 11.25)

In the prayers which follow, the hope is expressed that the soul of the dead person will be eternally happy and will rise to meet with Christ on Judgement Day. Roman Catholics believe that the soul does not immediately go to heaven but spends time in purgatory. It is natural, therefore, to pray for the soul while it is there. The Requiem Prayer is said at every Mass:

> 'Eternal rest grant unto them, O Lord, and let light perpetual rest upon them.'

A This memorial bears witness to many martyrs who lost their lives in Uganda in 1886. Why do you think the memorial adds the words 'Glory be to Almighty God'?

The same themes of purgatory and the eternal rest of the soul are also stressed in Anglo-Catholic Anglican churches. Among Protestants, though, Anglo-Catholics are very much the exception. Most Protestants do not believe in purgatory. They do, however, strongly believe in a life after death. When a person has died they commit his or her soul to God's safe keeping through a series of Bible readings and prayers. This, they maintain, is the only appropriate thing to do. Once a person has died, Protestants believe that their soul is with God in heaven. Everyone then looks forward to the 'end of time' when all Christian believers will be given 'a new body' similar to the one that Christ had when he returned from the dead.

Orthodox funerals

One of the most important beliefs of the Orthodox Church is that there is no difference between the living and the dead. Just as we pray for those who are alive, then we must pray for those who have died.

The Orthodox Church tries to take the mystery and fear out of death. As soon as someone has died their body is washed, dressed in new clothes and placed in an open coffin. A strip of material containing icons of John the Baptist, Mary and Jesus is placed across the forehead of the corpse and an icon placed in the hand. The body is then covered with a linen cloth to symbolise the protection that Christ offers to all, whether dead or alive. The coffin lid is only closed for the last time when the service is over.

Everything in the service combines to remind those present that death is a tragedy; a direct result of the sin which separates God and the human race. Yet even in grief and bereavement there is real hope for the believer. This hope is expressed by the burning candles and the incense which is freely wafted over the coffin. The Bible readings encourage this by urging everyone to look forward to the time in the future when Christ will return to the earth and all will be raised from the dead.

ANSWER IN YOUR BOOK ...

1. The Christian funeral service reflects the beliefs that Christians hold about life after death. How would you sum up those beliefs?
2. What is purgatory and how do Roman Catholics express their belief in it?
3. How is the Orthodox belief that nothing separates the living and the dead expressed in their burial service?

READ AND DECIDE ...

As an Anglican vicar commits the body of a dead person to the earth he says:
   'We have entrusted (John) to God's merciful keeping and we now commit his body to the ground: earth to earth, ashes to ashes, dust to dust in sure and certain hope of the resurrection to eternal life through our Lord Jesus Christ.'

a) What do you think is meant by the words: 'We have entrusted John to God's merciful keeping'?

b) In Genesis 3.19 God is said to have told the first man:
   '...and only by the sweat of your brow will you win your bread
   until you return to the earth;
   for from it you were taken.
   Dust you are and to dust you shall return.'

   What point is being made here and how is this idea reinforced by the words of the priest?

c) Is it possible to have a 'sure and certain' hope? What do you think the words mean?

WHAT DO YOU THINK?

The Kantachion is a beautiful hymn which is included in Orthodox burial services. It contains these words:
   'Give rest, O Christ, to all thy servants with thy saints.
   Where sorrow and pain are no more, neither sighing but life everlasting.
   Thou only art immortal, the creator and maker of man,
   And we are mortal born of the earth, and unto earth will we return, all we go down to the dust.'

a) How is the Orthodox belief that living and dead are united expressed here?

b) Who, alone, is untouched by death?

c) Is the promise that all human beings return to dust intended to comfort? What is its purpose?

IN THE GLOSSARY ...

Sacrament; Roman Catholic Church; Anglican Church; Book of Common Prayer; Alternative Service Book; Protestant; Orthodox Church; Icon; Purgatory; Mass; Anglo Catholic; Bible.

8.1 THE CHRISTIAN YEAR

The 'Christian Year' (sometimes called the Liturgical Year) is a pattern of festivals which is observed by the Anglican, Catholic and Orthodox Churches. In addition, there are smaller festivals which some of the Churches celebrate and others ignore. Nonconformist Churches observe the main festivals, such as Christmas and Easter, but not the secondary ones like Advent and Lent.

The chart below shows how the 'Christian Year' falls into three 'cycles'.

The Christmas Cycle

The 'Christian Year' begins with the first Sunday of Advent at the end of November. There are four Sundays in Advent, culminating in the festival of Christmas on December 25th, celebrating the birth of Jesus. Epiphany then follows on January 6th, recalling the time when the Wise Men visited the infant Jesus (Matthew 2.1-12), becoming the first non-Jews (Gentiles) to play a part in the life of Jesus.

The Easter Cycle

The second cycle in the Christian Year, the Easter cycle, is the most important since it leads up to the festivals commemorating the death and resurrection of Jesus. It starts some six weeks after Epiphany with Ash Wednesday, the beginning of Lent, and ends on Easter Sunday. During the 40 days of Lent, Christians prepare themselves by reading their Bibles and praying, to celebrate the two events which stand at the very centre of the Christian faith.

Easter is described as a 'moveable feast'. Whereas Christmas Day falls on the same day each year, the dates in the Easter cycle vary.

THE CHRISTIAN YEAR

SEASON	DATE	SPECIAL DAY	EVENT	MEANING
Advent	Sunday nearest November 30th	Advent Sunday		Preparing for the coming of Jesus
Christmas	December 25th	Christmas Day	Birth of Jesus	God sends his Son into the world
Epiphany	January 6th		Visit of Wise Men to Jesus	Wise Men were Gentiles and not Jews Jesus, Saviour of all
Lent	$6\frac{1}{2}$ week period	Ash Wednesday	Jesus in desert	Repentance before God
	Week before Easter Day	Palm Sunday	Jesus enters Jerusalem on donkey	Humility of Jesus
	Thursday	Maundy Thursday	Jesus washes feet of disciples	Loving and serving one another
	Friday	Good Friday	Jesus crucified	Jesus died to save everyone
Easter	Sunday	Easter Day	Resurrection of Jesus	God brings Jesus back to life
	$5\frac{1}{2}$ week period	Ascension Day	Jesus returns to heaven	The end of the life of Jesus
Pentecost	10 days after Ascension	Whitsunday	The Holy Spirit given to disciples	Jesus gives power to his followers

For centuries, Easter was the time in the Christian calendar when new converts to Christianity were baptised, 'alms' were distributed to the poor and many prisoners were released from prison.

Obviously, a time of preparation is needed for such an important festival and this has traditionally been the important contribution of Lent. This starts on Ash Wednesday and ends on Good Friday. On that day, which is the most solemn in the whole Christian year, Christians spend much time in church meditating on the death of Jesus. Two days later they celebrate the resurrection of Jesus from the dead on Easter Day. In the Western Church this always falls on the Sunday following the first full moon on or after March 21st. The 'Easter cycle' is then complete.

Whitsun or Pentecost

The third cycle, less important than the other two, is based on the days set apart for remembering the birth of the Christian Church. The Roman Catholic Church also has days dedicated to certain saints and the Virgin Mary around this time. Finally, Harvest is celebrated at the beginning of Autumn.

In addition to these festivals, there are other minor festivals which some Churches celebrate. Among these are Trinity Sunday (a week after Pentecost) and All Saints Day (November 1st).

ANSWER IN YOUR BOOK ...

1 What are the main events in the Christian Year?
2 What are the three 'cycles' of the Christian Year?
3 What is celebrated at each of these festivals – Advent, Christmas, Epiphany, Lent and Easter?

IN YOUR OWN WORDS ...

a) Why is Advent the beginning of the Christian Year, and why is it so called?
b) How would you explain the link between Christmas and Epiphany?
c) Why is Ash Wednesday a suitable day to mark the beginning of Lent?
d) What is the link between the time of Lent and the festival of Easter?
e) Why do you think that 'Good' Friday is so-called, even though it commemorates the death of Jesus?

FIND OUT AND NOTE ...

Pictured here is one of the many symbols associated with the Christian year. Carry out some research to discover its meaning. Why do you think that symbols play a very important role throughout the Christian year? Make your own list of symbols, and their meanings, which play an important part in the different Christian festivals.

IN THE GLOSSARY ...

Anglican Church; Roman Catholic Church; Orthodox Church; Nonconformist; Christmas; Easter; Advent; Lent; Epiphany; Ash Wednesday; Good Friday; Whitsun; Pentecost; Virgin Mary; Maundy Thursday; Ascension Day; Holy Spirit.

8.2 ADVENT

As we have already discovered, Advent marks the beginning of the Christian Year. The early Christians did not celebrate Advent or the birth of Jesus at Christmas. It was not until the 6th century that Christians began to set time aside to prepare themselves for the coming of Jesus the Messiah into a stable in Bethlehem. Advent Sunday always falls on the Sunday nearest to November 30th and is the first of four Sundays in the season. It ends on December 24th, Christmas Eve.

Advent within the Church

The sense of anticipation at the approach of Christmas is built up during Advent (the time of 'comings'). Three 'comings' are remembered at this time through the hymns that are sung and the readings from the Bible in church. They are:

1 *The coming of John the Baptist* – as told in Luke's Gospel. John played a very important role in the early life of Jesus. He is presented in the Gospels as God's messenger, sent to prepare the people for the coming of the Messiah. John was the cousin of Jesus whose parents, Zechariah and Elizabeth, were much too old to have children. The birth of John, therefore, was considered to be a miracle. Zechariah was a prophet and he had some prophetic words to say about his son's role in the future ministry of Jesus:

   'And you, my child, will be called a prophet of the Most High, for you will go on before the Lord to prepare a way for him.' (Luke 1.76)

2 *The coming of the Messiah* – which was promised through the prophets in the Old Testament. The prophet who 'foresaw' this event most clearly was Isaiah and readings from his book figure prominently during Advent. Then there is the announcement to Mary and Joseph that they are going to become the parents of Jesus. Luke records the announcement to Mary, and Matthew the words of the Angel to Joseph.

3 *The 'Second Coming' of Jesus back to the earth* Ever since Jesus left the earth Christians have been expecting him to return to set up his earthly kingdom. The original disciples of Jesus expected it to happen in their lifetime. Christians have been waiting for it ever since, and they are reminded of this during Advent.

Through the readings during Advent, two important Christian truths are emphasised:
- That Jesus was the Son of God – a truth underlined by the story that he was born to a virgin mother and conceived by the Holy Spirit.
- That Jesus was the long-awaited Messiah.

The Church during Advent

In many churches, Advent is still used as a time of preparation for Christmas, with believers setting aside time for fasting and prayer. The church altar is covered with a purple or violet cloth, the colour of repentance.

In church, there is also likely to be an evergreen wreath containing four candles: three of them being purple while the fourth is pink. At the beginning of Advent one of them is lit for prayer, during the second week another candle, and this continues until the final candle is lit on the fourth Sunday of Advent.

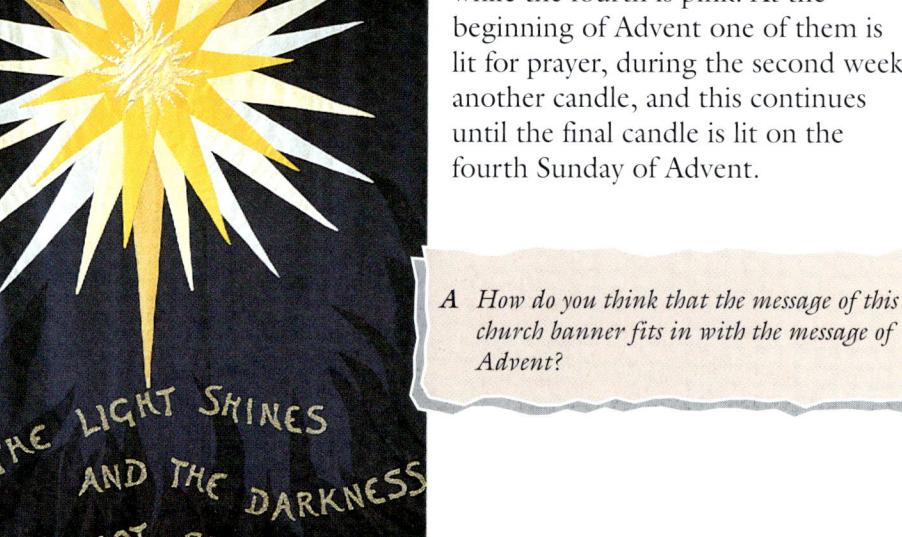

THE LIGHT SHINES AND THE DARKNESS CANNOT CONSUME IT

> A How do you think that the message of this church banner fits in with the message of Advent?

8 · CHRISTIAN CELEBRATIONS

The Advent Candle is an excellent example of the use of religious symbolism:

a) The evergreen wreath symbolises eternal life.
b) The flame of each candle is a reminder of Christ, who is described in John's Gospel as being the 'light of the world'.
c) The purple candle and ribbons act as a reminder that Advent is a time for personal preparation.
d) The pink candle, which is lit on the third Sunday, reminds worshippers that in the hardship of penitence there is joy and happiness.

ANSWER IN YOUR BOOK ...

1 Who was the Messiah, and how is Advent a time of preparation for his birth?
2 Why do you think that John the Baptist plays a prominent part in Advent?
3 How is a sense of spiritual anticipation built up in church during Advent?

B Can you find out other situations in which candles play a very important part in Christian worship? Why do you think that candles and religious worship often go hand in hand?

IN YOUR OWN WORDS ...

a) Explain what the word 'Advent' means.
b) Outline the three different 'comings' which are remembered during Advent.
c) Explain the link between John the Baptist and the coming of Jesus.
d) Describe the two fundamental Christian beliefs which are behind the celebrations of Advent. Explain the beliefs.

CAN YOU EXPLAIN?

a) What is the significance of the candles in the Advent Crown, pictured above, being set in an evergreen wreath?
b) What do the flames of the candles signify?
c) How do the colours of the candles fit in with the overall purpose of the season of Advent? What is their purpose?

IN THE GLOSSARY ...

Advent; Messiah; Lent; Christmas; Gospels; Old Testament; Holy Spirit; Fasting; Altar.

8.3 CHRISTMAS AND EPIPHANY

While Easter is the most important Christian festival, Christmas is the most widely celebrated. The name for this festival came originally from the Old English 'Christes Masse', or 'Christ's Mass'. The festival was not celebrated by the early Christians. The date of Christmas was only fixed after the conversion of the Roman Emperor Constantine to Christianity in the 4th century. It seems to have had previous links with both the Yule feast of the Norsemen and the Roman festival which commemorated the birth of Mithras, the sun-god, on December 25th. The date was widely accepted by most Christians since no-one knew the actual date on which Jesus had been born. The Eastern Orthodox Churches, however, originally celebrated the birth of Jesus on January 6th, and some still do.

The story of a birth

As we have discovered, a Creed is a statement of Christian belief. One of the oldest of all Creeds, the Apostles, contains these words:

> 'I believe in Jesus Christ, his only Son, our Lord. He was conceived by the power of the Holy Spirit and born of the Virgin Mary...'

From the very beginning Christians believed that Jesus, the Son of God, became a human being – an event known as the 'Incarnation' ('in the flesh'). Both Matthew and Luke tell the story of the birth of Jesus while, strangely, Mark and John do not mention it at all. Even Matthew and Luke look at the event from very different perspectives:

1 In Matthew's account (1.18-2.12) an Angel announces the birth of Jesus to Joseph in a dream, informing him that the baby has been conceived in the womb of Mary by supernatural means:

> "It is through the Holy Spirit that she has conceived." (1.20)

A Can you decide from these two crib scenes how our own background, and culture, determine how we see the birth of Jesus?

After the birth takes place in Bethlehem, Herod tries to discover from some Wise Men where the baby was born. The Wise Men leave Herod, follow a star to the stable, and then return home another way.

2. In Luke's description the story is told from Mary's viewpoint (Chapters 1 and 2). In her encounter with the Angel (called the 'Annunciation') she is told that she is going to bear God's Son. The baby is born in Bethlehem, after which she is visited by some shepherds.

All of these different elements feature prominently in the carols (hymns), Bible readings and symbols of Christmas. Yet the idea of God being born as a human being and to a virgin is very difficult to understand. To help them absorb the deeper meaning of Christmas, Orthodox Christians use icons of the Virgin and Child in their prayers. Statues of the Madonna (Mary) and child are also common in Roman Catholic Churches.

Epiphany

The word 'Epiphany' means 'to show forth.' In the Eastern Orthodox Church, Epiphany has come to celebrate three manifestations (showings forth) of Christ:

a) *The birth of Jesus* – when Jesus was 'shown' as the Saviour of the world.
b) *The baptism of Jesus* – when Jesus was shown to be God's Son and God gave him his blessing.
c) *The first miracle of Jesus* – when he changed water into wine (John 2) and announced to the world that he had come to usher in God's kingdom.

In Roman Catholic and Protestant churches, however, Epiphany, which is held on January 6th, is connected with the coming of the Wise Men to visit Jesus and the showing of Jesus to them – the first non-Jews (Gentiles) to recognise Jesus as the Saviour of the world. Throughout his ministry, Jesus made it clear that he had been sent by God first to the Jews, but also to the Gentiles.

ANSWER IN YOUR BOOK ...

1. What do Christians mean when they speak of the 'Virgin Birth'?
2. How do the Eastern and Western Churches differ in their understanding of Epiphany?
3. Explain what is meant by: a Creed; the Incarnation of Jesus and the Annunciation to Mary.

READ AND DECIDE ...

This is how Luke described the birth of Jesus:
'In those days Caesar Augustus issued a decree that a census should be taken on the entire Roman world…And everyone went to his home town to be registered. So Joseph also went up from the town in Nazareth in Galilee to Bethlehem, in Judea, the town of David, because he belonged to the house and line of David. He went there to register with Mary, who was pledged to be married to him, and was expecting a child. While they were there, the time came for the baby to be born and she gave birth to her first-born, a son. She wrapped him in cloths and placed him in a manger, because there was no room for them in the inn.' (Luke 2.1-7)

a) How would you describe the relationship between Joseph and Mary?
b) Why did Joseph and Mary travel together to Bethlehem?
c) When we speak of this event being the 'Incarnation' what do we mean?
d) Why do Christians believe that the birth of Jesus is of the greatest possible significance?

IN THE GLOSSARY ...

Christmas; Epiphany; Eastern Orthodox Church; Creed; Holy Spirit; Virgin Mary; Incarnation; Icon; Roman Catholic Church; Gentile.

8.4 LENT

There is no festival in the Church between the end of Epiphany, in early January, and Ash Wednesday. The period of Lent begins on that day and runs all the way through to Good Friday. Holy Week begins on Palm Sunday and runs through until Easter Sunday.

What is Lent?

Lent, a time of fasting and spiritual preparation, provides a lengthy run-up to Easter. It is based on a Biblical precedent. According to Matthew (4.1-11), Jesus had just been baptised by John the Baptist in the River Jordan when he was:

> "...led by the Spirit into the wilderness..."

For forty days he was tempted by the Devil. During this time he fasted and this is why 'abstinence from food' has been a common ingredient in Christian worship ever since. During Lent, Christians seek to follow the same path of self-denial as Jesus before living through the events leading up to his crucifixion.

In preparation for the fast of Lent, people would eat up all the fat in the house on Shrove Tuesday, the day before Ash Wednesday. The fat was often used to make pancakes and this provided a last opportunity for people to enjoy a feast before the fast of Lent began.

Lent begins with Ash Wednesday, when a special Eucharist is held in most Catholic, Orthodox and Anglican churches. This service marks the beginning of the time of self-denial and penitence which only ends with the forgiveness of Easter Day itself. During this ceremony ash, a traditional symbol of penitence, is smeared on the foreheads of worshippers. The ash is made by burning the previous year's palm crosses.

Fasting is rarely practised today in the Christian Church although some believers try to give something up for Lent. In recent years, many churches have felt that this approach is too negative. They try to encourage their members to act positively by spending more time than usual reading the Bible and praying.

This makes Lent a real time of spiritual preparation for the coming meditation which will centre on the death and resurrection of Jesus.

Mothering Sunday

The 4th Sunday of Lent in the Western Church calendar is 'Mothering Sunday'. The term 'mothering' here refers to three separate things:

a) The old Bible reading set aside for the day which refers to heaven as 'mother'.
b) The practice in the Middle Ages of the congregations of small chapels and churches visiting either their 'mother' or parish church, or the 'mother church' of their diocese, the cathedral, for spiritual refreshment.
c) The old practice of people visiting their mothers with presents on this day.

For this one day, the fast of Lent was suspended and special simnel cakes were eaten. After the day was over, however, the fast was imposed again all the way through to Good Friday.

Nowadays, people in church give God thanks for their mothers and families on this day.

A Why do you think that Jesus spent forty days in this barren place? How did this time end?

8 · CHRISTIAN CELEBRATIONS

B There was an old tradition of people wearing sackcloth and ashes. Can you find out what the wearing of this indicated? How do you think it might link up with the ash cross that the priest makes on the foreheads of worshippers at the beginning of Lent?

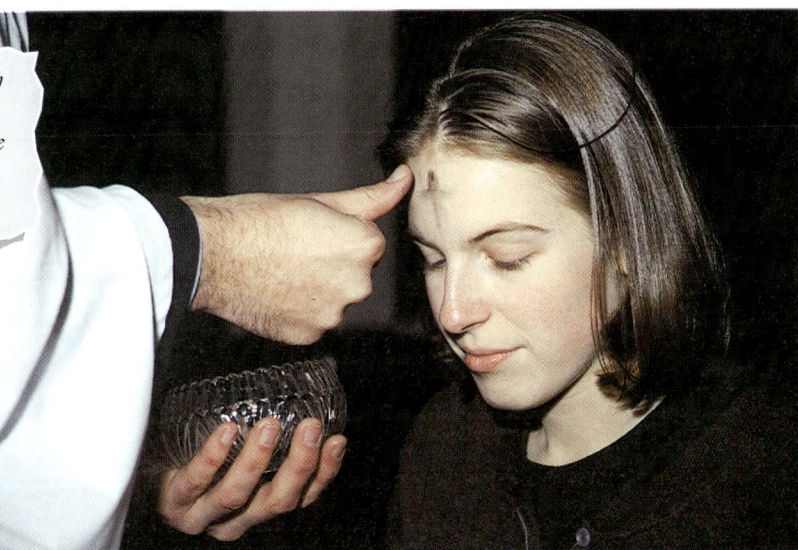

READ AND DECIDE ...

According to the Synoptic Gospels, Jesus spent forty days in the desert being tempted by Satan. Read Luke's account of this event, 4.1-13, before going on to answer these questions:

a) Why did Jesus go to the desert in the first place?

b) What were the three temptations directed at Jesus? Why do you think they were particularly attractive?

c) Lent begins with remembering the temptations of Jesus and ends by celebrating the death of Jesus. Do you see any link between these two events?

IN YOUR OWN WORDS ...

a) What does the priest burn to make the ash which he or she uses on Ash Wednesday?

b) What does ash symbolise?

c) Why do you think that Ash Wednesday is an important day in the calendar of the Christian Church?

d) Read Genesis 3.19 and Job 42.6. On the basis of these two verses, can you explain why the sign of the cross is made from ash at the beginning of Lent?

e) If you were to ask a Church worshipper why they were going to church on Ash Wednesday, what do you think they might say?

ANSWER IN YOUR BOOK ...

1 What is the link between the time that Jesus spent in the wilderness being tempted by the Devil and the Christian fast of Lent?

2 Given that Easter is the most sacred time of the year for Christians, why do you think that a time of fasting and preparation was thought to be necessary beforehand?

3 Fasting has played a comparatively important role in the history of Christianity. Find out all that you can about it – in particular, the spiritual benefits that it is believed to bring about.

IN THE GLOSSARY ...

Epiphany; Ash Wednesday; Lent; Good Friday; Holy Week; Palm Sunday; Fasting; Easter; Eucharist; Anglican Church; Roman Catholic Church; Orthodox Church; Satan.

8.5 PALM SUNDAY AND MAUNDY THURSDAY

The long period of preparation for Easter is almost over. Events in the Church move rapidly towards their climax on Good Friday, just as they did in the life of Jesus centuries ago. Holy Week begins with Palm Sunday.

Palm Sunday

On Palm, or Passion, Sunday the minds of Christians go back to the time when Jesus rode into the city of Jerusalem on a donkey (Luke 19.28-44). Welcoming him with great enthusiasm, the crowd spread their coats on the road in front of him and laid out palm branches. The welcome was one normally reserved for a king.

Christian services on this day usually end with a procession led out of church by a donkey, often carrying a small child, to testify to the community that Jesus is king. Small palm crosses are distributed to members of the congregation to remind them of the beginning of Holy Week and what lay ahead of Jesus in Jerusalem. Next year, the same palm crosses will be used to supply the ash for Ash Wednesday.

The meaning of Palm Sunday

What is the significance of Palm Sunday? Why did Jesus enter the city of Jerusalem on a donkey? It was primarily to fulfill a prophecy from the Jewish Scriptures which would have been familiar to most people in the crowd:

> 'Daughter of Sion (Jerusalem), rejoice with all your heart;
> Shout in triumph, daughter of Jerusalem!
> See, your king is coming to you,
> his cause won, his victory gained,
> humble and mounted on a donkey,
> on a colt, the foal of a donkey.'
> (Zechariah 9.9)

A What do you think Christians today might get from the re-enactment of events in the life of Jesus like this Palm Sunday procession?

At the same time, Jesus was making a public declaration about the nature of his future ministry and work. While horses were associated by the public with war, donkeys were always thought of as animals of peace. Jesus was telling the people in no uncertain terms that their Messiah, the one for whom their ancestors had been waiting for centuries to lead the Jewish people in a successful uprising against the Romans, was the bringer of peace, not violence. If they were expecting something else, they had closed their eyes to the clear message of their Scriptures. One of their most important prophets, Isaiah, had spoken eloquently of a future kingdom in which a lion would lie down peacefully with a lamb.

Maundy Thursday

On the Thursday of Holy Week, Jesus performed two important acts. They have had a considerable effect on the life and worship of the Church ever since:

a) He washed the feet of his disciples. In any Eastern household this was the task of the lowest servant. Jesus wanted to teach his disciples a very important lesson about the kingdom of God, so he acted out a parable in front of them by washing their feet. In this way he reinforced his message that anyone who wanted to become a disciple must place himself at the service of others – without reservation!

b) He changed the traditional Jewish Passover meal by instructing his followers to break bread and drink wine in memory of his forthcoming death. This is the origin of the Holy Communion service which stands at the heart of most Christian worship. In Roman Catholic churches a special Mass is held on Maundy morning. The bishop consecrates the oils which will be used in the sacraments during the forthcoming year.

B What is the link between the verse in Isaiah, illustrated by this banner, and the events of Palm Sunday?

ANSWER IN YOUR BOOK ...

1. How was Jesus making an important statement about his life and ministry when he entered Jerusalem on a donkey?
2. Throughout his ministry Jesus saw himself as fulfilling prophecies in the Old Testament. How did he do so in the events of Palm Sunday?
3. Why is Maundy Thursday a particularly important day in the Church calendar?

READ AND DECIDE ...

On Palm Sunday, Christians often re-enact the entry of Jesus into Jerusalem. Read Matthew's account of this event in 21.1-11.

a) How did Matthew see a donkey as suitable for Jesus to ride into Jerusalem as the fulfilment of prophecy?
b) Describe, in your own words, the reaction of the people as Jesus entered the city. How do you account for their behaviour?
c) Why is Palm Sunday an important day in the Church calendar?
d) What do you think is the message of Palm Sunday for Christians in the modern world?

IN YOUR OWN WORDS ...

Before Jesus ate his last meal with his disciples he washed their feet. You can read about this event, one of those commemorated on Maundy Thursday, in John 13.2-11.

a) Why did Simon Peter initially object to having his feet washed by Jesus?
b) What did Jesus say in return? What did he mean by it?
c) How did Jesus use the occasion to point out who it was who would betray him?
d) What other important event in the life of Jesus is also commemorated on Maundy Thursday?
e) Carry out some research to discover how Maundy Thursday is celebrated in the Christian Church today.

IN THE GLOSSARY ...

Easter; Good Friday; Holy Week; Palm Sunday; Jerusalem; Ash Wednesday; Maundy Thursday; Holy Communion; Roman Catholic Church; Mass; Sacraments; Old Testament.

8.6 GOOD FRIDAY

Easter is the time when Christians of all denominations seek to gain a deeper understanding of the suffering, death and resurrection of Jesus. During the events of Holy Week, and particularly on Good Friday and Easter Sunday, they experience all kinds of emotions, ranging from intense sadness to overwhelming joy.

Good Friday

The Easter weekend begins with 'Good Friday'. This is the most solemn day in the whole Christian calendar, and in the past was often called 'Black Friday' – the day on which God's Son, the Messiah, was crucified. Special services are held in many churches on this day to meditate on the crucifixion of Jesus, often running from midday through to three o'clock in the afternoon. During this time, sombre hymns about the crucifixion are sung, the story of the crucifixion from the four Gospels is read and time is spent in silent or guided meditation. There is no act of Holy Communion on Good Friday – that must wait for Easter Sunday. The decor of many churches displays the sombre mood, with the church emptied of moveable items and the permanent ones covered. There are no flowers in church on Good Friday.

Each Church has its own distinctive way of celebrating this day. Among the most interesting traditions are the following:

a) In Roman Catholic churches permanent drawings or paintings mark out the fourteen Stations of the Cross. These illustrate places where Jesus is thought to have stopped on his way from Pilate's Judgement-Hall to the cross. As they visit each of these Stations on Good Friday, the worshippers stop, kneel and recite appropriate prayers. At three o'clock in the afternoon, the time when Jesus is thought to have died, the veneration of the cross takes place. A covered cross is placed in the middle of the church, and this is slowly unveiled as members of the congregation prostrate themselves in front of it. Then they listen again to the story of the Passion of Jesus from one of the Gospels.

b) In Orthodox churches, where Good Friday is known as 'Great Friday', the priest carries an icon of the dead Christ and lowers it into a stand in the middle of the church. The people gather around with candles as if they were attending a funeral. Later, the icon is carried around the outside of the church in a 'funeral procession' as the church bells toll.

c) In Great Britain, churches of different denominations often join together on Good Friday to walk behind someone carrying a cross. They describe this as an 'act of witness', showing others that Christians are strongly united in bearing witness to the death of Jesus.

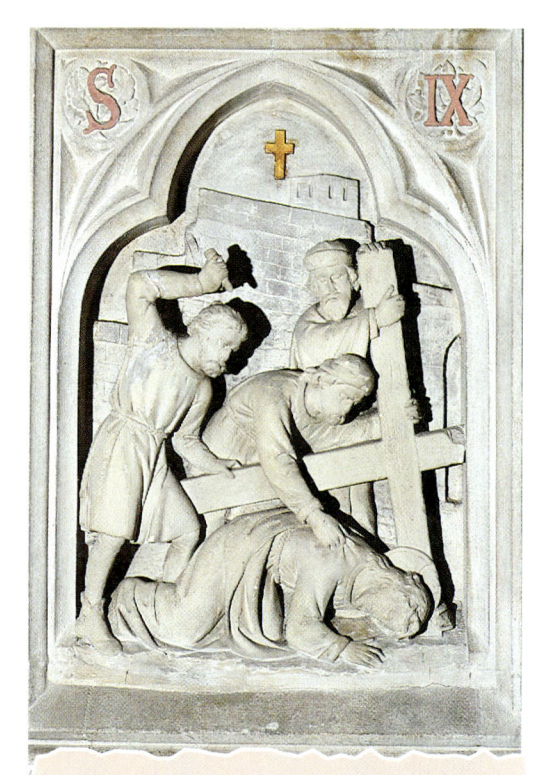

A These two Stations of the Cross illustrate two incidents in the journey of Jesus to the cross. Can you identify them?

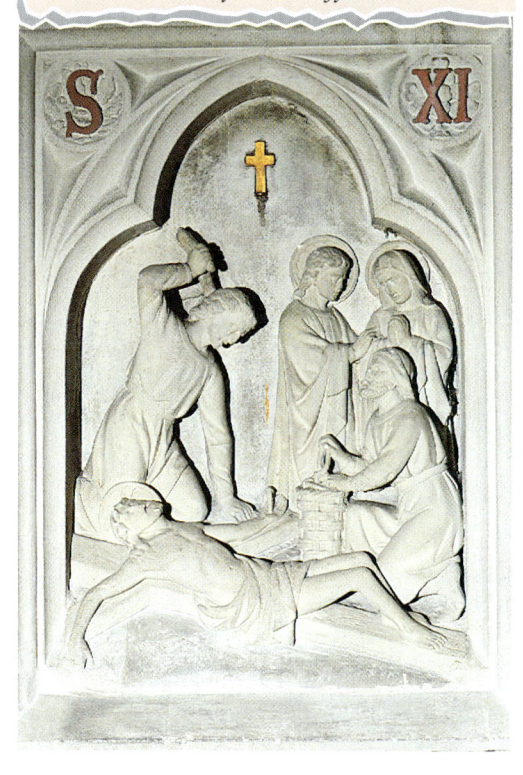

8 · CHRISTIAN CELEBRATIONS

Why is Good Friday important to all Christian believers?

❖ The crucifixion is part of the 'Good News' on which the whole of the Christian Gospel is based. The crucifixion, followed by the resurrection, ensures that humanity's sins can be forgiven.

❖ The crucifixion was the last attempt by all the powers of evil and darkness to thwart the purposes of God. It is a little ironic for Christians to call this day 'Good Friday', but the message is plain – for Christians, all kinds of good have come from what appears, on the surface, to be the blackest day in history.

B *Christians all over the world carry out marches of witness on Good Friday. What do you think these believers are 'bearing witness' to?*

READ AND DECIDE ...

This is how Mark describes the crucifixion of Jesus in his Gospel:

> 'They brought Jesus to the place called Golgotha, which means 'Place of the skull', and they offered him drugged wine, but he did not take it. Then they fastened him to the cross. They shared out his clothes, casting lots to decide what each should have.
> It was nine in the morning when they crucified him; and the inscription giving the charge against him read: 'The King of the Jews'. Two robbers were crucified with him, one on his right and the other on his left.' (Mark 15.22-27)

a) At what time of the day was Jesus crucified? How does this link up with the way that many Christians celebrate Good Friday?

b) Pilate dictated the message placed on the cross. Can you detect a note of irony or sarcasm in the title 'King of the Jews'? Who do you think this sarcasm was directed against?

c) Why do you think that Mark thought it important to comment that Jesus had been crucified between two thieves? How do you think that later Christians may have made use of this fact in their preaching?

d) Read Mark 14.53 – 15.41 for yourself. Make a list of all the things that happened to Jesus in the last hours of his life. How do Christians try to re-enact some of these events on Good Friday?

ANSWER IN YOUR BOOK ...

1. How do the various churches reflect the sombre mood behind events remembered on Good Friday?

2. How would you answer someone who questioned whether this particular day should be called 'Good' Friday?

3. What do many churches do on Good Friday to show that they are united? What do you think of such public demonstrations?

IN THE GLOSSARY ...

Easter; Holy Week; Good Friday; Messiah; Holy Communion; Roman Catholic Church; Stations of the Cross; Orthodox Church; Priest; Icon.

8.7 EASTER SUNDAY

Between Good Friday, which is the most serious day in the Christian year, and Easter Sunday, the most joyful, there is Holy Saturday.

Holy Saturday

This day is forgotten in the celebrations of most churches, yet for some it is a day of quiet anticipation. After Jesus died his body was removed quickly from the cross as the Sabbath Day began at nightfall. It was laid in a borrowed and unused tomb belonging to Joseph of Arithmathea. Joseph was a prominent Jew of the time, a member of the Sanhedrin and, according to the Gospels, a secret disciple of Jesus.

On Holy Saturday, in most churches, the buildings are thoroughly cleaned and the best furnishings and vessels brought out in preparation for Easter Day. Flowers are a very important symbol in church over this weekend, especially daffodils, since they remind everyone of Spring and the new life which is apparent all around in the world of nature. It is also, of course, a potent symbol for that new life which is to become apparent when Jesus rises from the dead.

Easter Day

Some Churches have very distinctive ways of announcing the news that the body of Jesus is no longer in the tomb:

a) In Orthodox churches, on Holy Saturday, there is a coffin decorated with flowers to remind worshippers of the dead body of Jesus. Late in the evening, all worshippers leave while the church is plunged into darkness. On the stroke of midnight the Paschal Candle is lit, the priest shouts out 'Christ is risen', and the people reply 'He is risen indeed'. The candle is then carried into the darkened church, with the people following close behind. Three pieces of symbolism are being enacted:

❖ When the doors of the church are thrown wide open at midnight this symbolises the rolling away of the stone from the door of the tomb.

❖ As the candle is carried through the darkened church the darkness is gradually dispelled, symbolising the light of the resurrection of Jesus which gradually overcomes the powers of darkness in the world.

A Can you explain the symbolism behind the carrying of the Paschal Candle into a darkened church?

- ❖ As the light is passed from person to person, everyone is reminded that the Good News of the Light of the world (Jesus) is similarly passed from believer to non-believer. This tall candle is lit for every service until Ascension Day or Pentecost.
- b) The Roman Catholics also hold their main Easter service at midnight with the Easter Vigil. They too carry a Paschal candle into a darkened church to symbolise the new light brought into the world by Christ's resurrection. The worshippers light their candles from each other. The Bible readings recount the rising of Jesus from the dead and a baby, a sign of new life, is baptised. A Eucharist is celebrated later, and church bells ring out for the first time since Good Friday.
- c) Many Christians in Anglican and Free churches are up early on Easter morning to join in 'sunrise services'. This was the time when the women went to the tomb to anoint the body of Jesus after the Sabbath Day had ended. These services often end with Holy Communion in church or in the open-air.

Easter Day sets the tone for the coming year. The Church year reaches its climax with this event. The return of Jesus to life by the power of God is the foundation of the Christian Gospel. The Church still has to wait for the coming of the Holy Spirit at Pentecost but the essential elements of its message are now in place. Jesus has died so that the sins of the world can be forgiven and God has set his seal on everything by raising Jesus from the dead.

B For many churches, banners are rather like icons – the conveyors of deeply important spiritual truths. What is this banner trying to say to members of the congregation?

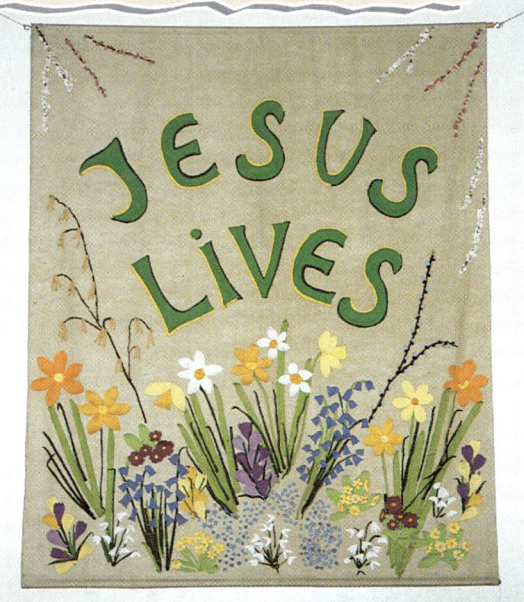

ANSWER IN YOUR BOOK ...

1. How do the Orthodox and Catholic Churches use the symbols of light and darkness to convey the basic realities of Easter?
2. What are 'sunrise services'?
3. Why do you think that Easter Day is the most important day of all in the Christian calendar?

READ AND DECIDE ...

This is how Mark, in his Gospel, describes the resurrection of Jesus:

> "When the sabbath was over, Mary of Magdala, Mary the mother of James and Salome brought aromatic oils, intending to go and anoint him; and very early on the first day of the week, just after sunrise, they came to the tomb. They were wondering among themselves who would roll away the stone for them from the entrance to the tomb, when they looked up and saw that the stone, huge as it was, had been rolled back already. They went into the tomb, where they saw a young man sitting on the right-hand side, wearing a white robe…he said to them, 'Do not be alarmed; you are looking for Jesus of Nazareth, who was crucified. He has been raised…" (Mark 16.1-6)

Now read the other two descriptions in the Synoptic Gospels of this event – Matthew 28 and Luke 24.

a) Make a list of the 'events' on which the three Gospel writers agree.
b) Make a list of those 'events' which are to be found in two of the three Gospels.
c) Are there any 'events' which are only found in one of the Gospels?
d) How do Christians commemorate this 'event'?

IN THE GLOSSARY ...

Good Friday; Paschal Candle; Orthodox Church; Roman Catholic Church; Easter; Eucharist; Anglican Church; Free Church; Sabbath Day; Synoptic Gospels.

8.8 ASCENSION DAY AND PENTECOST

After his resurrection from the dead, the Gospels tell us that Jesus spent forty days making 'appearances' to various individuals and groups. He then left the earth altogether and this event is called the 'Ascension'. Shortly after this happened, the Holy Spirit was given to the first Christian believers and the Church was born. The first of these events is celebrated by Christians on Ascension Day, and the second on Pentecost or Whitsunday.

Ascension Day

Ascension Day is, therefore, celebrated forty days after Easter Day and always falls on a Thursday. You can read about the 'ascension' of Jesus into heaven in Luke 24.48-53 and Acts 1.3-14. As you do so, you will soon become aware of the reason why many Christians have difficulties with this event and are reluctant to celebrate it. The accounts in the New Testament suggest that Jesus was taken 'upwards' into heaven, so locating heaven 'above' the earth – an idea that Christians no longer accept.

Those who do celebrate the day leave the precise details of what happened to one side. They concentrate on the fact that Jesus told his disciples to wait in Jerusalem until they received the promise of the Holy Spirit. This Spirit would give them the strength to give witness to Jesus to the ends of the earth. That promise, and its subsequent fulfilment on the Day of Pentecost (from the Greek word meaning fiftieth day), is what really matters about Ascension Day.

Pentecost

Pentecost, or Shavuot ('The Feast of Weeks'), was an old Jewish festival which commemorated the giving of the Ten Commandments to Moses on Mount Sinai.

A This modern stained glass window comes from Clifton Cathedral in Bristol. Look at it carefully and try to decide what it is saying about the Holy Spirit.

It always fell fifty days after the great Jewish festival of Passover at which the deliverance of the Jews from slavery in Egypt (an event known as the Exodus) was commemorated.

The early Christians were Jews and so it was natural for them to celebrate the Jewish festival of Pentecost shortly after Jesus had been crucified. On this occasion, though, something dramatic happened when the Holy Spirit fell upon the assembled gathering and the Church was born. This is why Pentecost is such an important day in the Church calendar. Without the gift of God's spirit, the Church would not have come into being and the Christian message would almost certainly have died out within a generation or two.

Why call this particular festival 'Whitsun'? In the early Church there were two occasions during the year when new Christians were baptised – Easter and Pentecost. Those who were baptised at Easter wore white clothes which they continued to wear through to Pentecost – hence 'Whit' or 'White' Sunday.

Whitsunday is no longer used for that purpose. Baptisms now take place throughout the Christian year. It is marked, however, in many places by special walks, when members of different churches go together through towns and villages as an act of unity and witness.

B Carry out some research of your own to discover why a dove came to be the most widely used symbol for the Holy Spirit.

ANSWER IN YOUR BOOK ...

1. What can we learn from the Acts of the Apostles about the giving of the Holy Spirit to the first disciples? You may need to look back to Unit 2.1 to answer this question.
2. What do Christians celebrate on Ascension Day?
3. What makes Whitsun a particularly important Christian festival?

USE YOUR IMAGINATION ...

Read Luke 24.48-53 and Acts 1.3-14.

Imagine that you are a priest preparing a sermon for Ascension Day.

a) Why do you think that Ascension Day presents more than one problem to Christians who read these passages in the Bible?

b) Can you think of **three** things to say in your sermon which would make the reasons for celebrating the day clearer?

WHAT DO YOU THINK?

a) The Holy Spirit is often associated with the symbols of wind, fire and a dove in the Bible. What characteristics of the Holy Spirit do these symbols suggest to you?

b) The banner above was erected in a church to make people aware of Whitsun. How do you think it does this?

c) Do you think that we still need to use symbols when we talk about God? If a symbol proves to be useful at one time in history, does this mean that it will always be useful?

IN THE GLOSSARY ...

Ascension Day; Whitsun; Pentecost; Holy Spirit; Gospels; Jerusalem; Passover; Easter; Roman Catholic Church; Mass; Eucharist; Confirmation.

8.9 HARVEST

Most religions have deep roots in the soil, the land and nature. Christianity is no exception. Even before Christianity arrived in Great Britain there were many agricultural festivals. The first Christians came over with the Romans and, by the time that Pope Gregory the Great sent Augustine to 'Christianise' the English in the 6th century, there was already a form of Christianity here. That form, Celtic Christianity, stayed very close to the earth and the seasons. Although Augustine's Roman form of Christianity prevailed, the Celtic form remained in many remote parts of the country.

Before long, the different agricultural festivals were Christianised. 'Harvest' is the best-known of these agricultural festivals although, strangely, it is the most recent. It was celebrated for the first time in this country in 1862. Other agricultural festivals, however, are much older and are still celebrated in many country areas. As you read about them you might like to reflect on what each has to say about the Christian understanding of God.

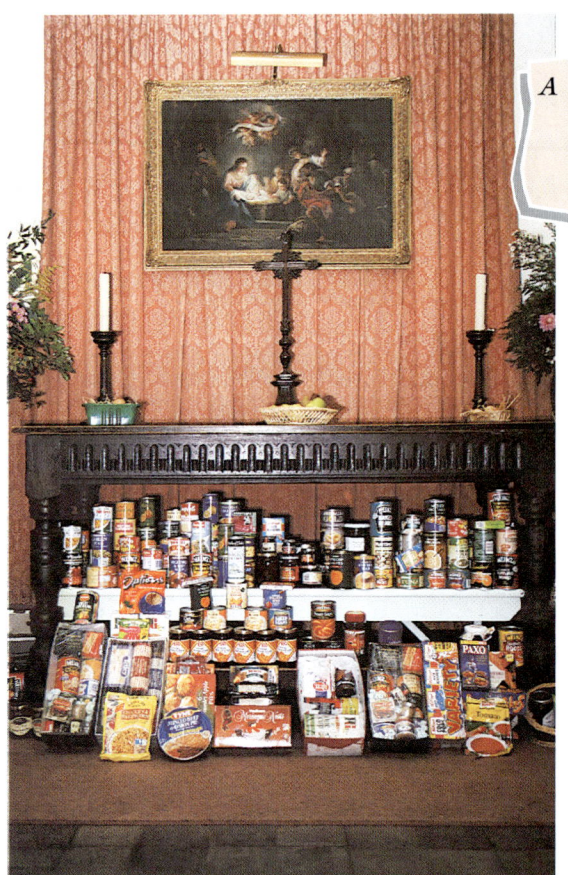

> **A** Why do you think that harvest festival services tend to have much more meaning in country rather than town areas?

Plough Sunday

Farmers begin to plough the land in February ready for a spring sowing of their seed. Plough Sunday allows local farmers to bring a plough into church so that it can be blessed by the priest.

Rogationtide

Early spring sees a very old tradition which is still carried out in many parishes in the country. On Rogation Sunday, in early spring, Christians of all denominations walk around local fields as the vicar or minister blesses them. The natural processes which will lead to the harvest are just beginning to take place beneath the soil and the priest is seeking God's blessing on them.

Lammas and Harvest

Lammas (loaf-mass) was the earliest form that the Harvest festival took. Around the beginning of August, farmers brought a loaf of bread, made from the first grains of the wheat that had been harvested, to church. This was then replaced by the Harvest Festival, held some time in late September or early October. In rural communities the festival is one of the most important during the whole year since farmers are aware that their whole livelihood depends on the fertility of the soil and the weather.

In the Harvest festival service readings are chosen from the Bible which praise and thank God for the fruits of the earth. Extracts from the book of Psalms and the story of the seed and sower told by Jesus (Mark 4.3-12) are familiar Harvest readings. The church is decorated with a wide selection of agricultural produce, making this one of the most colourful occasions in the Church year. It is important that the produce has been brought in by the people themselves since this is a time for thanking God for all his gifts personally. As the Apostles Creed states:

> "I believe in God, the Father Almighty, Maker of heaven and earth..."

Familiar hymns, such as 'We plough the fields and scatter' and 'Come, ye thankful people, come', are sung before the gifts are distributed to needy people in the area.

Harvest is a festival of thankfulness and praise. It obviously carried more importance in an age when the lives of people depended more directly on the earth and the fullness of the harvest it produced. Even today it seems to take on more meaning when celebrated in a country church surrounded by the very fields whose produce and harvest are on display.

> **B** Why do you think that bread often forms the centre-point of a harvest display?

ANSWER IN YOUR BOOK ...

1. Why were Rogationtide and Plough Sunday services held?
2. What is the link between Lammas and the Harvest festival?
3. What do you think is at the heart of the Harvest Festival?

WHAT DO YOU THINK?

For many people the Harvest festival does not seem to have any real meaning.

a) Why do you think that many people both inside and outside the church do not find it possible to relate to the Harvest Festival service?

b) Can you think of any ways by which the service could be made more meaningful for those people who do not come into regular touch with the earth and nature?

COMPLETE A CHART ...

With Harvest completed the last annual Christian festival is over. It is time then to summarise using the table below. Copy it into your book and complete it.

FESTIVAL	BACKGROUND EVENT	HOW CELEBRATED
ADVENT		
CHRISTMAS		
EPIPHANY		
LENT		
PALM SUNDAY		
MAUNDY THURSDAY		
GOOD FRIDAY		
EASTER SUNDAY		
ASCENSION DAY		
WHITSUN		
HARVEST		

IN THE GLOSSARY ...

Apostles Creed; Bible.

8.10 SUNDAY

> **A** Do you think it is important to have one day a week when families can be together?

As most of the early Christians were Jews, it was natural for them to continue to worship in their local synagogue on the Sabbath Day. Two factors eventually persuaded the Church to abandon this practice:

a) More and more Gentiles became Christians, and they had little allegiance to the old Jewish traditions, including worshipping on the Sabbath Day.
b) The Jewish authorities began to forbid Christians from taking part in synagogue services since they were using them to preach that Jesus was the Messiah. The Jews did not accept this.

The Church began to detach itself both from the synagogue as its spiritual home and the Sabbath Day. Matters finally came to a head around 90 CE when the Christians were forced to leave the synagogues altogether. The practice of worshipping on the Sabbath Day died at the same time.

The Lord's Day

The most natural time for Christians to worship was Saturday evening, as the Sabbath drew to a close. Under the Emperor Trajan in the 3rd century, these Christian meetings became illegal and so the Lord's Supper was moved to Sunday mornings. This move cut the last Christian tie with the old Sabbath and linked it naturally to the resurrection of Jesus, an event which had also taken place on a Sunday. Sunday became the 'Lord's Day', and the Russian Orthodox Church still calls it 'Voskresnie' ('Resurrection Day'). Under the Christian Roman Emperor, Constantine, all public work was stopped on Sundays and the law courts were closed. However, agricultural work was exempt from all restrictions. It is interesting that the name 'Sunday' was retained even though it was linked directly to the worship of the sun-god in pre-Christian times.

A day of re-creation

The early Christians not only linked the Lord's Day with the resurrection of Jesus but also with the activity of God in creating the world. The two accounts of this in the Jewish Scriptures (Genesis 1 and 2) inform us that after God spent six days creating the whole of life he 'rested' – having expressed his satisfaction with his six days of work.

This became the model for the Church's approach to Sunday. Just as God stopped all creative activity on that day, so Christians began to set aside the Lord's Day for rest, relaxation and worship. That same link remains unbroken today although, in practice, its meaning is variously interpreted. In countries such as Spain, where the Roman Catholic Church is dominant, church services are confined to Saturday evening and Sunday morning.

In the recent Catechism of the Catholic Church, published in 1994, Catholics are placed under a strong obligation to take part in the Mass every Sunday.

8 · CHRISTIAN CELEBRATIONS

Countries dominated by Protestantism have tried to restrict activities on the Sunday. In Great Britain, until 1994, when the law was changed, people could legally buy a pornographic magazine in a newsagent but not a Bible from a Cathedral or church. Under the new laws almost all restrictions have been removed although large shops are only allowed to open for a maximum of six hours.

This change in the law was a surprisingly controversial move for Parliament to make. The opposition came from an alliance of those who wanted Sunday to remain special (they formed a Keep Sunday Special Campaign) and those who represented shop workers. A further Bill allowed betting on Sundays, making it possible for horse-racing to take place on that day. In the opinion of most people in the UK, Sunday has now become just like any other day of the week.

B Find out all that you can about the synagogue and the Jewish way of worship. Are there any Jewish practices which the Christian Church has taken over. Have they been adapted or changed?

ANSWER IN YOUR BOOK ...

1 Why do you think that the earliest Christians were reluctant to leave the Jewish synagogues in which they worshipped?
2 Why was the Lord's Day linked with the resurrection of Jesus and re-creation?
3 Are you happy about the recent changes in the law concerning Sunday? Does it matter that all the days of the week are now going to be almost identical?

WHAT DO YOU THINK?

The word 'Sunday' is older than the Christian religion, going back to the ancient day dedicated to the sun-god, Mithras. This was celebrated in the Roman Empire on the first day of the week. Bearing this in mind, here are two quotations which you need to read carefully:

❖ 'My saving power will rise on you like the sun and bring healing like the sun's rays...' (Malachi 4.2)
❖ 'And on the day which is called the day of the sun there is an assembly...' (Justin Martyr, 2nd century Christian leader)

a) Why do you think that the early Christians were content to take over a festival previously dedicated to a pagan sun-god?
b) What do the two quotations suggest to you about the meaning that the early Christians attached to this weekly festival?
c) Why is every Sunday of the year a Christian festival?

FIND OUT AND NOTE ...

Brainstorming is a way of collecting contributions from everyone in a group. Appoint one member of your class to be the recorder and to keep the time. Block everything else out of your mind for five minutes and ask each person to call out the things that first come into their head when they think of Sunday. The recorder must write down everything that people say. Then make lists in your book under two headings:

a) Negative things about Sunday
b) Positive things about Sunday

Now write, in about 500 words, what you think Sunday should be like. Try to be as positive as possible.

IN THE GLOSSARY ...

Sunday; Sabbath Day; Synagogue; Lord's Supper; Roman Catholic Church; Gentile; Messiah; Mass; Protestants; Bible.

9.1 THE FAMILY

In every country the family is the smallest and most important social unit. The exact form that the family arrangement takes may vary from place to place and age to age, but there are just two basic arrangements in the modern world:

The extended family

In the extended family three generations live together or very close to one another. While this kind of arrangement died out in Britain in the 1950's, it is still the unit upon which society in India, Africa and other parts of the world is built.

The nuclear family

In Western industrialised countries the typical family now has just parents and children living together.

The real situation is, of course, much more complex than this. In Britain, as elsewhere, there are many other kinds of family arrangement – only 45% of the population live in a nuclear family. Among the other kinds of groupings are:

1 *Single parent families* – over 1,000,000 children live with just one parent – 200,000 with their fathers and 900,000 with their mothers. Divorce, the death of one parent and unmarried mothers are the most common causes of single-parent families.
2 *The 'expanded' family* – old people, the disabled and the mentally handicapped often live together as a 'family'.
3 *The 'community'* – some people choose to live together in a community, such as a monastery or a convent, where a common faith binds them together.
4 *The 'reconstituted' family* – 70% of people who divorce re-marry, often bringing their own children into the new relationship.
5 *The childless family* – many couples nowadays make a conscious decision not to have children. In addition, 1 in 10 couples in this country cannot have children because either the man or the woman is infertile.

Then, of course, there are single people. 25% of the nation's adults are unmarried.

The importance of the family

In our society the family is expected to play a crucial role in the well-being of the community. Let us look at some important features of family life:

a) It gives people their sense of identity as well as instilling into them their first values and opinions.
b) It teaches a growing child how he or she is expected to behave (a process called socialisation) and his/her future role in society.

A A Nepalese extended family. Why do you think that Western countries have moved away from this kind of family arrangement?

9 Christianity in Today's World

c) It provides the first close bond that we have with others. From members of our family we learn how to give and take; how to deal with anger and frustration; how to share and how to treat others with care and consideration.

Of course, all families have their shortcomings – some more than others! The Gospels make it clear that Jesus did not always see eye to eye with his own family. Modern psychiatry has taught us that many problems in adult life can be traced back to a person's earliest years. The family is very important.

ANSWER IN YOUR BOOK ...

1. What are the main differences between a nuclear and an extended family?
2. What are: an expanded family, a community and a reconstituted family?
3. Why do most people think that family life is very important?

B Do you think that there is such a thing as a 'typical' British family? If so, how would you describe it?

READ AND DECIDE ...

We do not hear a great deal about the family of Jesus in the Gospels. On one occasion, though, he had some sharp words to say to them:

> "Then his mother and brothers arrived: they stayed outside and sent in a message asking him to come out to them. A crowd was sitting round him when the word was brought out that his mother and brothers were outside asking for him. 'Who are my mother and brothers,' he replied. And looking round at those who were sitting in the circle about him he said, 'Here are my mother and brothers. Whoever does the will of God is my mother and sister and brother." (Mark 3.31-33)

a) Does this look as if Jesus was rejecting his family?
b) Could there have been a purpose in the life of Jesus which overrode his family ties? If so, what do you think it was?
c) What point do you think Jesus was trying to make in this difference of opinion?

COMPLETE A CHART ...

Draw up a chart, like the one below, listing the advantages and disadvantages of belonging to each kind of family:

	ADVANTAGES	DISADVANTAGES
Extended family		
Nuclear family		
One-parent family		

WHAT DO YOU THINK?

a) Why do you think that some couples today choose not to have children? Does this particular idea appeal to you? What do you think that couples gain or lose by not having children? If you discovered that you, or your partner, were infertile, what would your reaction be?
b) What do you think are the most important features of family life? What would be missed most if family life was to be abolished?

9.2 MARRIAGE

Over the centuries the Christian Church has put itself forward as the main supporter and upholder of 'traditional family values'. Such values begin with marriage and the Church has always attached a considerable degree of importance to this institution. In the Catholic and Orthodox Churches this importance is underlined by calling marriage a sacrament – a divinely appointed channel through which God's grace can be experienced. Protestants do not regard marriage as a sacrament but they do take it to be a unique symbol of the intimate relationship that exists between Christ and his Church.

Why marry?

98% of all adults in Great Britain will marry at some time. Even among those who divorce over 75% return to another marriage. Why, though, marry? In our society there are many reasons for marriage:

1. To provide a suitable relationship in which two people can express their love and commitment for each other. The notion that marriage lasts "...until death us do part" expresses just how most people feel about it. Most people who get married view it as a life-long commitment. This does not mean to say, of course, that such love and commitment cannot thrive in an unmarried relationship.
2. To allow two people to live together with the full approval of their family, friends and society. This is not only important to the two people concerned but also to society. Even today, society does not treat a couple who have not gone through a marriage ceremony in the same way as a couple who have.
3. To provide the couple with that sense of security which only a permanent and stable relationship can bring.
4. To create a suitable environment in which two people can express their sexual feelings for one another.
5. To create a suitable relationship into which children can be born and brought up.

In Great Britain just over 50% of weddings take place in a religious building – a church, a mosque, a synagogue etc. – where the ceremony is conducted 'in the presence of God'. The remainder are carried out in a Registry Office with a secular (non-religious) ceremony.

Sex and marriage

Recent surveys have shown that only about 20% of the population are virgins when they marry. About 50%

> A What do you think are the main reasons for choosing to be married in a) a church; b) a Registry Office?

have lost their virginity by the time they reach their 18th birthday. Statistics like these alarm many Christians. They point out the personal and social consequences of widespread sexual activity outside marriage. The surveys draw particular attention to the following:

a) The number of marriages which break down because one or both partners have been unfaithful. A married person who has sex with someone who is not their marriage partner commits adultery. Adultery breaks one of the Ten Commandments (Exodus 20.14), and Paul tells us that it excludes a person from the kingdom of God. The new Catechism of the Catholic Church expresses the belief that:

> 'Adultery, divorce, polygamy and free union (sex outside marriage) are grave offences against the dignity of marriage.'

b) The risk of an unwanted pregnancy – and the increasing number of abortions and one-parent families.

c) The danger of contracting a sexually transmitted disease – including AIDS.

The Catechism of the Roman Catholic Church would win almost unanimous support from the rest of the Christian community in condemning casual sex. It sees such sex as being destructive, damaging and degrading. Some Christians, though, accept that two people can have a truly committed and loving relationship outside marriage. Others condemn such a relationship as 'fornication' or 'living in sin'.

READ AND DECIDE ...

Here are three quotations from the Bible about marriage:

a) 'Who can find a good wife?
Her worth is far beyond red coral.
Her husband's whole trust is in her,
and children are not lacking.
She works to bring him good, not evil,
all the days of her life.' (Proverbs 31.10-12)

b) "Then the Lord God said, It is not good for man to be alone; I shall make a partner suited for him." (Genesis 2.18)

c) 'That is why a man leaves his father and mother, and is united to his wife and the two become one flesh. It follows that they are no longer two individuals: they are one flesh. Therefore what God has joined together, man must not separate.' (Matthew 19.4-6)

As you can see, each of these quotations looks at marriage from a male point of view. Bearing this in mind, do you think that they say anything valuable on the relationship between a husband and a wife?

ANSWER IN YOUR BOOK ...

1. Given that marriage is so important do you think that some kind of training should be given for it? What kind of training do you think would be most appropriate?
2. Do you agree with the view expressed by many Christians that adultery is the ultimate sin of betrayal in a marriage? Need adultery, in your opinion, always lead to the break-up of a marriage?
3. What do you think are the most damaging consequences of sex outside of marriage?

WHAT DO YOU THINK?

a) Make your own list of reasons for people marrying. Remember that people of all ages marry – it is not just something that young people do. Are the reasons why older people marry likely to be different from those for younger people?

b) Now put the reasons that you have produced in your own order of importance. How do they compare with the reasons given in the Anglican Marriage Service (see Unit 7.4).

IN THE GLOSSARY ...

Roman Catholic Church; Orthodox Church; Sacrament; Anglican Church; Fornication.

9.3 Divorce

Before 1857 every divorce in this country required a separate Act of Parliament, making it a very lengthy and costly business. Then the law was changed:

1 A woman could obtain a divorce if she demonstrated that her husband had committed adultery and another matrimonial offence, such as cruelty or desertion.
2 A husband could divorce his wife if she had committed adultery alone.

This blatant discrimination between the sexes remained until 1923. A law was then passed allowing both men and women to obtain a divorce on the ground of adultery alone – with insanity, desertion and cruelty being added in 1937. When many marriages broke down under the strain of the Second World War, Legal Aid (the payment of legal expenses) was extended to cover divorce in 1949.

The Divorce Reform Act, 1969

Divorce remained an exceedingly unpleasant business. Private detectives had to be hired to provide evidence of adultery. Then, in 1971, the Divorce Reform Act became law and people now had to provide evidence that their marriage had '…irretrievably broken down…'. To show this a person can demonstrate that their partner has committed adultery, been cruel or deserted them. If both partners agree to a divorce then a separation of two years is necessary. However, if only one of them wants a divorce, a five year separation is required. This Act marked a considerable departure from the old divorce laws which demanded the agreement of both people before a divorce could be granted. As a consequence, many couples lived apart for a long time without being able to divorce each other.

When the Act became law there was an immediate upsurge in the number of couples seeking a divorce. Many had been trapped in a loveless marriage for years. The total climbed to around 180,000 divorces a year and it has stayed around that figure ever since. Now, one in every three marriages in this country ends in divorce.

The Churches and divorce

When discussions took place in the 1960s about changes in the law, the Churches, like many other interested bodies, put forward their opinions. Those opinions were so influential that many of them were incorporated into the new Act. Yet the Churches can hardly be said to have come to terms with divorce:

A As all marriages start out with high hopes, what do you think causes most marriages to break up?

9 · CHRISTIANITY IN TODAY'S WORLD

B This one-parent family was created through divorce. What do you think are the main problems likely to be faced by this mother in bringing up her three children?

a) The Roman Catholic Church remains implacably opposed to divorce. In just a few cases, though, it is prepared to 'annul' a marriage. To 'annul' a marriage means that the church considers that the marriage had never really taken place. An annulment can be granted if, for instance, it can be shown that the couple did not fully understand what they were doing when they married or if the marriage has not been 'consummated' (i.e. sexual intercourse has not taken place).

b) While the Church of England accepts that divorce is necessary in certain situations, most priests will not re-marry divorced people in their churches. They can do so legally as long as they have the permission of their bishop but his rarely happens. At best, they will offer a church blessing on a marriage which has already taken place in a Registry Office.

c) Most Free Churches have a more tolerant attitude towards divorce and will re-marry divorced people. At the same time, the Nonconformist Churches preach strongly that marriage should be for all time.

Among the groups of people with the highest divorce rates are the clergy. Recent reports have suggested that they are so busy advising others on how their marriages can be saved that they tend to ignore their own. Poor pay, long hours and a lack of structure in their daily lives all contribute to this state of affairs.

ANSWER IN YOUR BOOK...

1 What changes took place in the divorce laws in the 19th and 20th centuries?
2 How many people now pass through the divorce courts?
3 Do you think that it is realistic for the Roman Catholic and Anglican Churches to maintain a very strong attitude towards divorce at the end of the 20th century?

CAN YOU EXPLAIN?

a) Why did the number of people seeking a divorce increase so dramatically after 1971?
b) Why is the Roman Catholic Church's practice of granting occasional annulments not the same as divorce?
c) Why do many churches still retain a strong position against divorce?

READ AND DECIDE...

Here are three quotations from the New Testament about divorce:

a) '…what God has joined together man must not separate…' (Matthew 19.6)
   ❖ How would you describe the grounds on which divorce is rejected here?
b) 'I tell you, if a man divorces his wife for any cause other than unchastity, and marries another, he commits adultery.' (Matthew 19.9)
   ❖ Does this seem to contradict the previous quotation?
c) '…a wife must not separate herself from her husband – if she does, she must either remain unmarried or be reconciled to her husband – and the husband must not divorce his wife.' (1.Corinthians 7.10,11)
   ❖ How would you sum up the Bible's attitude towards divorce?

IN THE GLOSSARY...

Roman Catholic Church; Church of England; Free Churches.

9.4 SEX

Sexual activity plays an important part in the lives of most people. Everyone is a sexual being and even the youngest babies appear to have sexual sensations. Questions about sexual behaviour, however, only begin to arise when a person reaches puberty, which normally takes place between the ages of 12 and 18. During this time there are profound changes in a person's body as well as deep emotional changes. In many young people these far-reaching changes can bring about an 'identity crisis'. Many of the doubts and upheavals connected with this time (adolescence) are to do with one's sexuality. The problem is that a young person's body usually matures more quickly than his/her emotions. As a result, while the law allows that person to have sexual intercourse at the age of 16, few young people are ready for a deep sexual relationship at this stage.

A *Do you think that sex before marriage is wrong? If so, why? If not, then what rules do you think apply to sexual behaviour?*

Sex and marriage

A person who has never had a sexual relationship is a virgin. A person who takes a definite decision not to be involved in a sexual relationship is celibate. Some people, such as monks and nuns, take a life-long vow of celibacy when they join their religious order. Roman Catholic priests are expected to be celibate although no other Church makes the same demand.

For most people sex is a special and precious part of their lives. At its best it is a unique symbol of the love and commitment which two people feel for each other. As such, it is something to be enjoyed at the deepest level but always within the context of responsibility towards each other. For most Christians this kind of relationship can only be found in marriage.

Both sex before marriage (pre-marital sex) and sex outside marriage (extra-marital sex) have become much more common in recent years.

There are several reasons for this:

a) Contraception is more widely available – both for married and unmarried couples.
b) If contraception fails, then abortion is always there as a last resort.
c) Fewer people expect their partners to be virgins when they marry.
d) Fewer people accept the teachings of the Church which has always been strongly against sex before marriage (fornication).

There is a price to be paid for this change in attitude. Sexually transmitted diseases, such as gonorrhea and herpes, are on the increase, AIDS is spreading, more unwanted children are being born, and thousands of families break up each year because one partner has been unfaithful. So, what is the Christian teaching about sex? Broadly speaking, there are two opinions in the Christian community:

- The Bible condemns fornication and adultery frequently. Both the Bible and the teaching of the Church emphasise that marriage is the only proper place for sex.

- What really matters is the quality of the relationship between two people, not whether they are actually married. If they love each other, and intend to set up a home together, then sexual intercourse is perfectly acceptable. Times have changed and the Church must make sure that its teaching stays up-to-date.

B What responsibility do you think this couple have to each other? If you were in their situation, how would you carry this responsibility out?

ANSWER IN YOUR BOOK ...

1. What is the split between Christians on the question of sex outside marriage?
2. In 1994 a vicar in Hampshire publicly exposed two members of his congregation who had left their married partners to live together. He claimed that he was doing it to try and save them from the error of their ways. What do you think of his action?
3. Write an essay of about 500 words with the title 'Sex, inside or outside marriage – the great dilemma'.

WHAT DO YOU THINK?

Write a paragraph on each of the following:
a) Puberty and adolescence
b) The age of consent
c) Celibacy
d) Pre-marital sex
e) Extra-marital sex

READ AND DECIDE ...

Here are two controversial opinions about sex. Read them carefully.

a) 'If they (the unmarried and widowed) do not have sufficient self-control they should marry. It is better to be married than to burn with (sexual) desire.' (1.Corinthians 7.9)
- Does the fact that Paul was unmarried seem to affect his judgement about sexual desire and marriage?

b) 'A girl plays at sex, for which she is not ready, because fundamentally what she wants is love: and a boy plays at love, for which he is not ready, because what he wants is sex.' (Mary Calderone)
- This quotation suggests strongly that the two sexes look at love and sex very differently. Do you think this is true? If so, how do they differ?
- Do you think that love and sex should always go together? How would you seek to justify your response to this question – whatever it was?

IN THE GLOSSARY ...

Virgin; Celibacy; Monk; Nun; Priest; Fornication; Bible.

9.5 CONTRACEPTION

A contraceptive is any device which effectively prevents conception after sexual intercourse. Not very long ago choice in contraceptives was almost non-existent. Now couples are faced with a bewildering array of devices – each with its own advantages and disadvantages.

Why use contraceptives?

There are many possible reasons:

a) To space out the birth of children or to limit the overall number of children in a family. When it is used for these reasons contraception is called 'Family Planning'.
b) So that a couple can enjoy their love-making without worrying about an unwanted pregnancy.
c) A couple may decide not to have any children.

The choices include the two most popular methods of birth-control – the Pill and the condom. The former is almost totally reliable while the latter is not only very effective but offers real protection against sexually transmitted diseases, including AIDS. The Intra-Uterine Device is often fitted to women who have had children already, but Catholics maintain that it works by inducing an abortion shortly after conception has taken place. For Catholics the only choice is Natural Family Planning. This depends on a woman discovering when she is fertile each month – and then avoiding sexual intercourse at that time. For couples who do not want any more children there is sterilisation – an operation which is called a 'vasectomy' in a man.

The Church and contraception

In the early part of the 20th century, contraception was a very controversial issue in the Christian Church. Most Churches were strongly opposed to the idea of 'birth prevention'. Surrounded by the poverty of the 1930s, however, most of them came to realise that birth-control could be of enormous benefit to men, women and their families.

The Roman Catholic church has strongly maintained its opposition to all artificial forms of birth-control. In 1968 Pope Paul VI issued a declaration called 'Humanae Vitae' in which he laid down two principles about sexual intercourse:

❖ That it should strengthen the bond between a husband and a wife.
❖ That it should always be open to the possibility of creating new life.

The Pope argued that artificial means of contraception broke the second of these principles and so outlawed them for all Roman Catholics. Despite this ban many Roman Catholic couples have decided that there are occasions when birth-control is right for them.

A Contraceptives are now readily available from chemists, doctors and clinics. Can you suggest why many couples still do not use them when they are making love?

9 · CHRISTIANITY IN TODAY'S WORLD

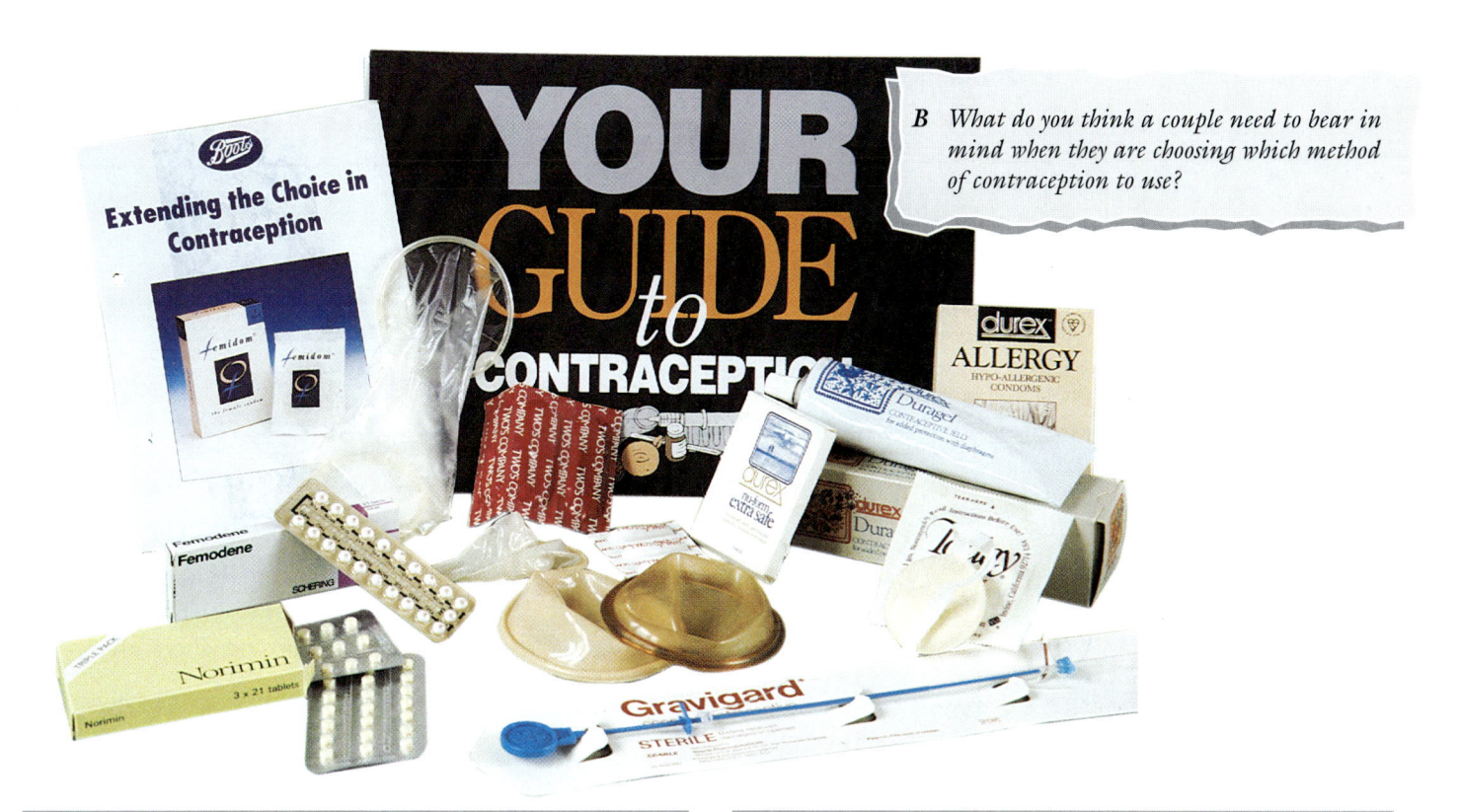

B What do you think a couple need to bear in mind when they are choosing which method of contraception to use?

ANSWER IN YOUR BOOK ...

1. What different emphases are conveyed by the terms contraception; birth-control and family planning?
2. What are the main reasons why a couple might decide to use contraception?
3. What, in your opinion, are the most acceptable forms of birth-control? Do you think that young people should be better educated in the use of contraception? Why do you think that so many women become pregnant when contraception is so readily available?

READ AND DECIDE ...

Here are two statements by different Popes:

❖ **Humanae Vitae. Pope Pius VI**
'...condemned is any action, which either before, or at the moment of, or after sexual intercourse is specifically intended to prevent procreation – whether as an end or as a means – it is never lawful, even for the gravest of reasons, to do evil that good may come of it.'

❖ **Pope John Paul II**
'Only natural forms of birth-control do not offend the moral order established by God.'

a) What does the pope means by 'natural forms of birth-control'?
b) What do you think is meant by 'the moral order established by God'? (You may need some help with this one.)
c) What do you think is meant by the argument, used by many Roman Catholics, that artificial means of birth-control are 'unnatural'?

WHAT DO YOU THINK?

Here are two quotations from the Bible for you to think about:

a) "God blessed them and said to them, Be fruitful and increase, fill the earth and subdue it." (Genesis 1.28)
b) 'Like arrows in the hand of a warrior are the sons of one's youth. Happy is he who has his quiver full of them.' (Psalm 127.4-5)

What would you say to someone who claimed that these verses gave everyone total freedom to have as many children as they wanted? Do you think that all children are a blessing from God? Can you give reasons for your answer?

IN THE GLOSSARY ...

Roman Catholic Church; Pope.

9.6 HOMOSEXUALITY

Although the word 'homosexual' was not coined until 1869, homosexuals have been a prominent feature in most societies going back to the ancient Greeks. The word itself comes from the Greek word meaning 'same', not from the identical Latin word meaning 'man'. It refers to any man or woman who has a sexual preference for members of their own rather than the opposite sex. Female homosexuals usually prefer to be called 'lesbians' while most homosexual men nowadays would rather be called 'gay'.

The law and homosexuality

The Kinsey Report, published in America in 1948 and 1953, was the first serious investigation into human sexual behaviour. It discovered the following:

a) Approximately 10% of the population are homosexual although the majority of these prefer to keep their sexual preference secret.
b) There are three male homosexuals for every lesbian.

This would suggest that there are about 1,900,000 gays and 600,000 lesbians in Great Britain. While later studies have suggested that the total number of homosexuals may be rather lower than Kinsey suggested, the balance of males to females is about right.

Before 1967 it was illegal for any man to be a practising homosexual in Great Britain while lesbianism has never been illegal. If detected, a man faced a heavy fine or a spell in prison. Undetected, he was easy prey for an unscrupulous blackmailer – especially if he was a family man.

This state of affairs could not continue. The Wolfenden Committee suggested changes that needed to be made in the 1950s but successive Governments were unwilling to act. Then, in 1967, homosexual behaviour became legal as long as:

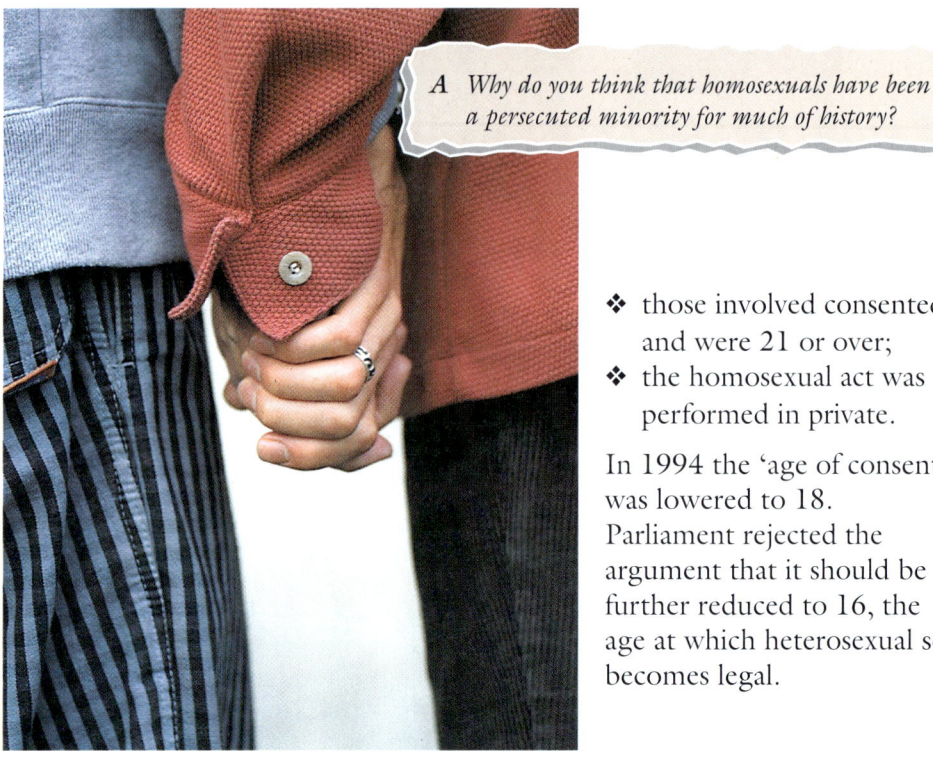

A Why do you think that homosexuals have been a persecuted minority for much of history?

- those involved consented and were 21 or over;
- the homosexual act was performed in private.

In 1994 the 'age of consent' was lowered to 18. Parliament rejected the argument that it should be further reduced to 16, the age at which heterosexual sex becomes legal.

The Church and homosexuality

Ever since biblical times the Church has condemned homosexuality – even though many Christians, including clergy and bishops, are practising homosexuals. The reason for the Church's attitude is that the Bible condemns homosexuals and homosexuality. It begins with the Jewish Book of Leviticus. This laid down rules for a nomadic community and condemned the practice outright. It was also part of the folklore that the divine judgement which fell on the two cities of Sodom and Gomorrah (Genesis 19) was mainly inspired by the homosexual behaviour which was tolerated there. This was not true. The main sin of the inhabitants was that they refused to practise the old Jewish laws of hospitality to strangers.

Jesus had nothing to say about homosexuality. This is somewhat strange since Paul, writing some 20 years after the death of Jesus, condemned it out of hand. He said that homosexuals, along with adulterers and others, had no place in God's Kingdom. You can find out what he had to say in 1.Corinthians 6.9-10.

Both St Augustine (354 – 430) and St Thomas Aquinas (1224 – 1274) taught that homosexuality was wrong because it could not lead to conception. Their influence has been considerable in the Catholic Church, which continues to maintain that homosexual behaviour is both 'unnatural' and 'sinful'. The General Synod of the Church of England has debated homosexuality twice in recent years and came to the conclusion that homosexuality was unacceptable for the clergy. A similar conclusion has been reached by the Methodist Church. Evangelical Free Churches have always maintained that homosexuality is a totally unacceptable form of sexual behaviour.

ANSWER IN YOUR BOOK ...

1. How would you define homosexuality?
2. What changes in the law about homosexuality came about in 1967? Why do you think that the law continues to discriminate over the 'age of consent' between heterosexuals and homosexuals?
3. Why do you think that the Christian Church has always struggled to come to terms with homosexuality?

READ AND DECIDE ...

Here are three quotations about homosexuality:

a) 'If a man has intercourse with a man as with a woman, both commit an abomination. They must be put to death; their blood be on their own hands.' (Leviticus 20.13)
   - Bearing in mind that Israel was a wandering, nomadic community, can you think of any justification for this sweeping law?

b) 'Make no mistake: no fornicator or idolator, no adulterer or sexual pervert (homosexual), no thief, extortioner, drunkard, slanderer or swindler will possess the kingdom of God.' (1.Corinthians 6.9-10)
   - Why do you think that Paul excluded these people from the kingdom of God?

c) 'It is the nature and quality of a relationship that matters... one must not judge it by its outward appearance but by its inner worth.' (Towards a Quaker View of Sex)
   - What is this quotation suggesting about both heterosexual and homosexual behaviour?

WHAT DO YOU THINK?

The new Catechism of the Roman Catholic Church states:
> 'Tradition has always declared that 'homosexual acts are intrinsically disordered' ...Under no circumstances can they be approved...Homosexual persons are called to chastity...'

a) What do you think the phrase, '...homosexual acts are intrinsically disordered' means?
b) Is it realistic to expect homosexual men and women to live chaste lives when the same demand is not made of heterosexual people?

IN THE GLOSSARY ...

Roman Catholic Church; Methodist Church; Free Churches; Bishop; Bible; Church of England; Evangelical.

B Why do you think that, while homosexuality was illegal for a long time in this country, no law has ever been passed against lesbianism?

9.7 ABORTION

Before 1967 abortion was illegal in the UK although it is thought that some 200,000 'back-street abortions' were carried out every year. These abortions were very risky since they often led to serious injury or worse (about 70 women died each year from their injuries). The need to deal with this situation was the motivation behind the Abortion Act of 1967 which allowed the legal 'termination of a pregnancy'. There are certain conditions:

a) It has to be carried out before the 'time of viability', i.e. before a foetus is capable of surviving outside the womb on its own. Viability was said to be after 28 weeks of pregnancy. This made little difference in practice since very few abortions were carried out between 24 and 28 weeks.
b) An abortion could proceed if:
   ❖ to continue with it would endanger the physical or psychological health of a mother – or that of her family;
   ❖ there is a substantial risk that the baby might be born physically or mentally handicapped.
c) Two doctors agree that an abortion is legal and desirable.

Abortion – pro-choice

The movement to legalise abortion in this country began in the 1930s and was boosted in 1936 with the setting up of the Abortion Law Reform Society. It achieved most of its objectives in 1967. Some Christians accept that abortion, though always regrettable, might be the only answer in certain situations. In favour of the current abortion situation the following arguments have been put forward:

1. Every woman has the right to decide what happens to her own body. No woman should be forced to give birth against her will.
2. There are far too many unwanted children in today's world without increasing the number unnecessarily.
3. Every baby has the right to be born into a loving, caring family – one that is able to provide the basic necessities of food, shelter and clothing.
4. Other members of the family have the right to be taken into account since they will be greatly affected by the birth of a new baby.
5. If a woman discovers that her baby is likely to be born handicapped, she must decide whether she can cope or not.
6. A woman who is raped should not, under any circumstances, be expected to carry the baby of her attacker.

Abortion – pro-life

The Society for the Protection of the Unborn Child (SPUC) and LIFE are two organisations who campaign vigorously against abortion. They draw much of their support from Roman Catholics and the Evangelical wing of the Anglican Church. Among the arguments they use are the following:

a) Every child is a unique and precious gift from God. We have no authority to destroy that gift – even if the child is handicapped or the mother has been raped.
b) An unborn baby needs special protection since it cannot defend itself. The rights of an unborn child are at least as great as those of the mother. Roman Catholics believe that they are greater.

9 · CHRISTIANITY IN TODAY'S WORLD

A What do you think are the main arguments against abortion?

B What do you think are the main arguments in favour of making abortion legal?

c) The foetus is a human being from the moment of conception – so abortion is legalised murder.

d) A physically or mentally handicapped child can lead a full and rewarding life – and be a great blessing to others.

e) Abortion places an intolerable burden on the doctors and nurses who carry it out – they are trained to save life, not to destroy it.

ANSWER IN YOUR BOOK ...

1 Why was it important to do something about the abortion situation in 1967?

2 Why do you think that the debate about abortion generates so much deep feeling? What is there about the subject that causes people to feel so deeply?

3 What are your own feelings about abortion? Set them down as clearly as you can. Remember – as important as your feelings are, you must always support them by argument if you want to be taken seriously!

FIND OUT AND NOTE ...

Try to find out as much as you can about the 1967 Abortion Act and the subsequent abortion situation in the UK.

a) What was the situation about abortion in the UK before 1967?

b) What were the main provisions of the Act?

c) Do you think that the provisions of the Act are too strict, too lenient or just about right? Do you think that there is scope for them to be interpreted in different ways?

d) Around 140,000 abortions are now carried out in the UK every year. Some 90% of them are carried out under one of the provisions of the 1967 Act. Can you say what that provision might be?

IN THE GLOSSARY ...

Abortion; Roman Catholic Church; Evangelical; Anglican Church.

9.8 AIDS

During the early 1980s a new and terrifying disease hit the headlines for the first time – AIDS (Acquired Immune Deficiency Syndrome). This disease is caused by a virus, Human Immunodeficiency Virus (HIV), which enters the bloodstream of an infected person and attacks the cells which maintain the body's normal defence mechanisms, thus weakening the body and making it vulnerable to illness. Once inside the cell, the virus multiplies until it eventually destroys the host cell. The person's defence mechanism begins to fail and they are unable to recover from diseases which are not normally fatal. There is no cure for AIDS, yet AIDS does not kill. Victims succumb to a variety of illnesses and infections. Not everyone, however, who is HIV positive goes on to develop full-blown AIDS and no-one yet knows why.

A *Recently this poster was used to alert people to the danger of AIDS. What do you think is the best way of informing and educating people about this particular disease?*

Who is most at risk?

The HIV virus seems to have originated in Africa but it is now firmly established in over 100 countries. No-one knows how many people have died as a result but the death-toll in the USA alone now exceeds 30,000, with thousands testing HIV positive. In the UK over 3000 people have died and over 70,000 are thought to be HIV positive.

As fear about AIDS spread in the 1980s, so did rumours about how it could be caught. To begin with AIDS was thought to be an exclusively homosexual problem and some Christian leaders declared that it was God's judgement on homosexual behaviour. Thankfully, few people would make such a judgement today as AIDS strikes down both homosexuals and heterosexuals. In the UK, 70% of those affected are homosexual although this figure is rapidly changing. In most African countries well over 50% of those affected are heterosexual. Unlike other viruses, AIDS cannot be carried in the air, consumed in food or picked up from ordinary contact. It is, in fact, only transmitted in one of three ways:

a) Through contaminated blood.
b) Through contaminated needles.
c) Through the exchange of body fluids – especially semen and vaginal secretions. All unprotected sexual intercourse carries a real risk but anal intercourse (where the penis enters the anus) seems to carry a particularly high risk.

The groups most at risk are:

1 Practising homosexual and bisexual men. In Western countries 80% of those with HIV are homosexuals, but in African countries the majority are heterosexual.
2 Drug addicts who use and share needles.
3 Babies who are born to infected mothers.
4 Haemophiliacs and other people who received contaminated blood from transfusions. All blood was screened for the virus from 1987 onwards and so this is no longer a problem.
5 Both homosexuals and heterosexuals who have many sexual partners and do not practise safer sex.

Any answers?

There is no vaccine against AIDS in sight. Instead, attention has switched to helping people come to terms with HIV and caring for those who are dying. Some of the charities which work in this area have a strong Christian motivation but the majority do not. The most well-known is the Terence Higgins Trust which was named after the first person known to have died of AIDS in this country. The Trust sets out to:

a) offer all the necessary support for those suffering from AIDS, their families and friends;
b) produce material and engage speakers to educate the general public about AIDS;
c) support, in every possible way, research into AIDS.

There are also a handful of hospices which specialise in looking after AIDS patients in the last few weeks of their lives.

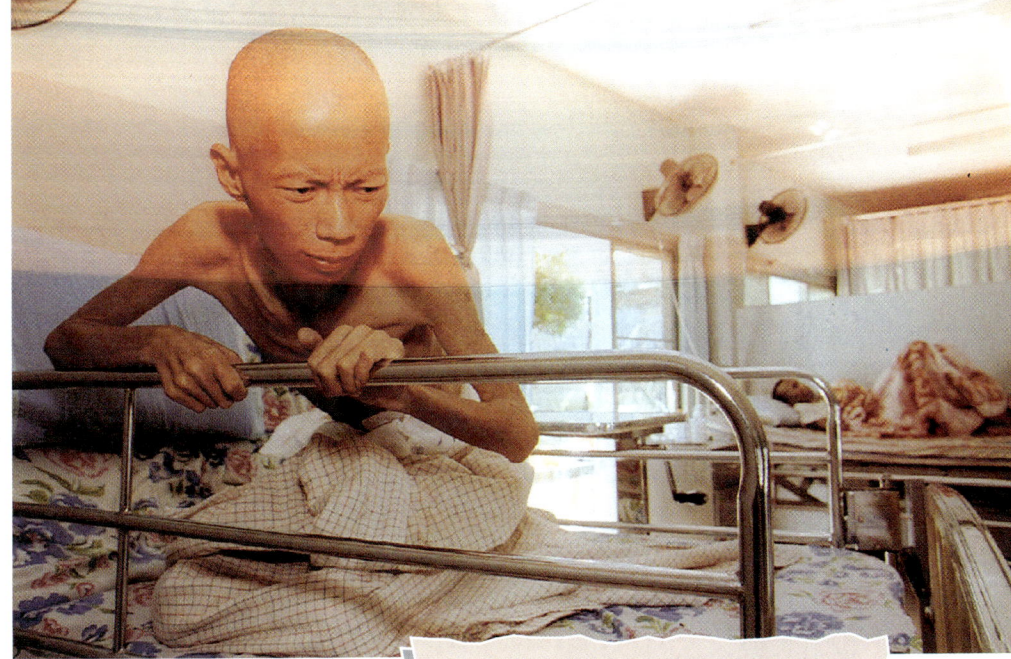

B Can you find out about the work of a charity or hospice which specialises in caring for those dying from AIDS?

ANSWER IN YOUR BOOK ...

1 What is AIDS?
2 What is HIV?
3 Why, when it was first discovered, did AIDS increase the opposition which has always been directed towards homosexuals?

WHAT DO YOU THINK?

Opening a conference of Health Ministers in London in 1988 the Princess Royal, Princess Anne, said:
  'The AIDS epidemic is a classic own-goal by the human race, a self-inflicted wound that serves to remind homo sapiens of its own fallibility.'
This remark enraged many AIDS sufferers and their carers. Why do you think they were so upset? Do you think that the remark would help to combat, or reinforce, prejudice against AIDS victims?

DISCUSS AMONG YOURSELVES ...

The whole question of AIDS, and how society responds to it, raises many important personal, social and religious questions. Debate some of these issues with others in your class and record any important conclusions. Here are some questions to begin with:

a) Should there be some kind of compulsory testing programme in this country for HIV – at least of those people known to be in high risk groups?
b) Should people known to be HIV positive be banned from leaving the country in which they are living?
c) Should a campaign be launched to discourage people who know that they are HIV positive from having sexual relationships with other people? Should people who are HIV positive be forcibly isolated?
d) Should expectant mothers known to be HIV positive be encouraged to have their babies aborted and then be sterilised?
e) Should condoms be freely available for everyone in schools, colleges and shops?

9.9 DRUGS

Headlines:
- illicit trade in steroids
- Pupils expelled
- Seven-year-olds to get lessons in drugs
- A pill to stop you popping down to the shops
- 10 ways to spot if YOUR kid is on drugs
- COCAINE: ON THE INCREASE
- ECSTASY: THE RAVE EFFECT
- Danger warning to five-year-olds
- Cocaine makes a comeback
- £9m drugs on stricken boat
- Ministers abandon shock tactics in fight against drugs
- Schools told not to expel drug pupils automatically

> **A** Why do you think there is such a ready market for drugs, especially among young people, today?

Few social problems have received such widespread publicity in recent years as that of illegal drug-taking. The problem is world-wide with drugs being grown and manufactured in South America and the Far East before being exported into countries such as Britain. In the UK, as in most Western countries, there is a ready and eager market. The drug market has now become a billion dollar business. Despite increased vigilance from the authorities, this market is growing all the time.

Why take drugs?

There are a whole range of factors which might lead a person to take drugs which have not been medically prescribed, either for the first time or to keep taking them. Among them are likely to be:

a) *pressure from one's friends* – drug-taking is usually a social activity and it is not easy to resist the pressure that a group of people can exert;
b) *anxiety and tension* – certain drugs such as cannabis (hash) have a calming, tranquilising effect on those who smoke it, which is why drugs appeal to people who find themselves suddenly under great pressure. Certain states of mind, such as depression, make a person more susceptible if they are offered drugs;
c) *boredom* – nothing else to do;
d) *personal problems and pressures* – such as exams or work;
e) *the pleasure that they give* – at least, in the short-term.

Of course, few people are aware of the long term risks of drug-taking when they participate for the first time. Nor is it true to say that everyone who takes part in drug-taking on a casual basis will become dependent or addicted. The consequences for those who do, however, are little short of catastrophic.

Drug dependence

'Drug abuse' occurs whenever a person takes a drug for a non-medical reason. If they continue to take drugs for a length of time they may become dependent on them. Such dependence takes two forms although they are closely related:

1. *A physical dependence* – this means that a person experiences physical cravings for a drug and suffers unpleasant symptoms if the drug is withheld. As a person's body becomes more used to a drug, so they will need to take more of it to feel the same physical sensations.
2. *A psychological dependence* – by becoming psychologically dependent on a drug a person feels that they cannot cope without it.

Most drug dependence has a physical and a psychological aspect. Any attempt to break a person's dependency must take both aspects into account and that makes the process very difficult.

The dangers of drug-taking

It obviously makes a considerable difference whether a person is taking hard or soft drugs. Hard drugs are those substances which have a considerable effect on the metabolism of the body and usually need to be sniffed or injected. Soft drugs are usually taken orally (by mouth) and their effect on the body is far less damaging. Among the long-term consequences of taking hard drugs might be the following:

a) Addiction – using drugs regularly can lead to abuse, dependency or addiction.
b) Very unpleasant side effects – including depression, hallucinations and paranoia.
c) Frightening mental and emotional effects – not only do the emotions become unbalanced but there is a more serious link between serious drug-taking and schizophrenia.
d) Constipation and the total disruption of a woman's menstrual cycle.
e) Injecting drugs opens up the real risk of suffering from abscesses, blood poisoning and AIDS.
f) A disastrous impact on personal relationships with a decline into theft and, in the end, possible death.

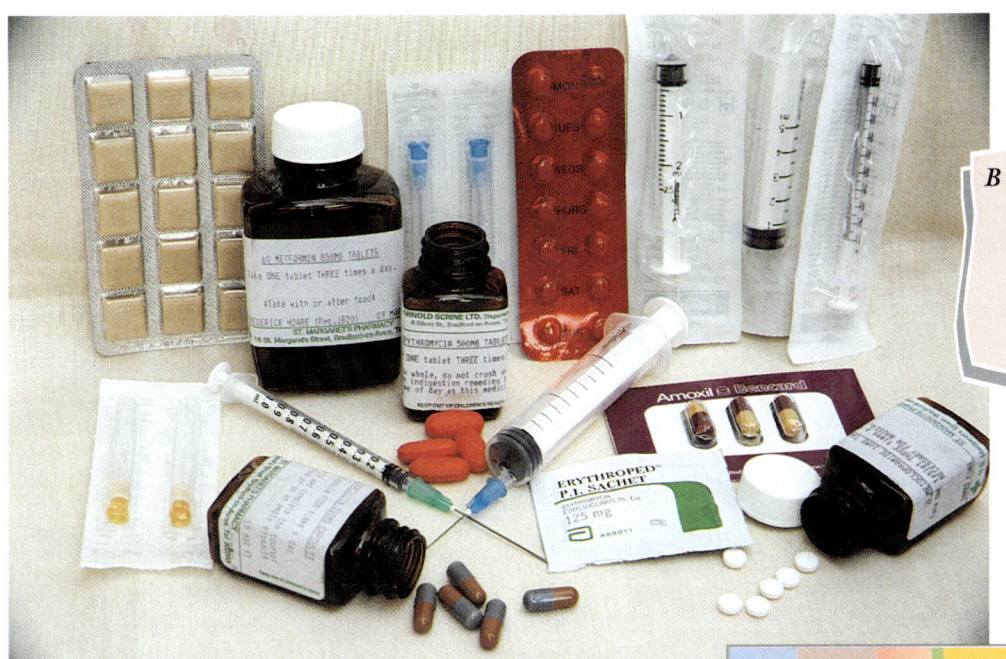

B *In this photograph you can see many legal drugs. Do you think that society as a whole has become too casual in its attitude to drug taking – even those prescribed by a doctor?*

ANSWER IN YOUR BOOK ...

1. Can you think of any other reasons, apart from those given in the text, for young people being drawn towards drug-taking?
2. Do you think that young people know enough about the dangers of drug abuse? If not, how would you set out to get the message across?
3. What do you think the difference is between a physical and a psychological dependency on drugs?

READ AND DECIDE ...

Here are two opinions for you to consider:

a) 1. Corinthians 3.16-17.
   'Surely you know that you are God's temple, where the spirit of God dwells. Anyone who destroys God's temple will himself be destroyed by God, because the temple of God is holy; and you are that temple.'
   ❖ Paraphrase Paul's words here and explain how these words could apply to the illegal taking of drugs.

b) Gregory (19) in a B.M.A. leaflet:
   'We used to take heroin together. When we decided to come off we had to support and encourage one another. We knew that if one of us continued, it wouldn't take long for the rest of us to start using again. We even started a self-help group near our estate with some of the other kids who wanted to come off. You've got to find things to do when you come off, something to keep you busy so you don't want that buzz again. I started thinking about what I really wanted to do...'
   ❖ What do you think are the key-points in Gregory's campaign to give up drugs?

9.10 WORK

For the 25,000,000 adults in England and Wales who are in paid employment, work is a natural part of their lives as well as the means by which they and their families can survive. It is tempting, therefore, to simply define 'work' as:

'...any activity for which we are paid...'

Tempting, but inaccurate. Many leisure activities, such as working out in a gym or running a marathon, are extremely hard word but unpaid. So, too, are the arduous hours put in by millions of housewives and carers of dependent relatives. Work, in fact, is any 'meaningful or purposeful activity', whether there is a financial rumuneration attached to it or not.

Why work?

There are several reasons why people go out to work:

1. *To survive* – as the Bible says:

    'The Lord God took the man and put him in the Garden of Eden to till it and look after it.' (Genesis 2.15)

    To survive human beings need food, shelter and clothing – and that is where the need to work comes in.
2. *For self-respect and satisfaction* – a person's own identity is closely bound up with their work. Such work requires effort and discipline. Loss of work, through unemployment, often brings depression, a loss of status and a lack of enthusiasm for life.
3. *To enjoy a sense of achievement, fulfilment and self-worth* – many Christians believe that all work is a 'vocation' – a gift from God – although that word is more often applied to the 'caring' professions such as teaching and nursing.
4. *For social contact with others* – many people enjoy the 'social' aspect of work with its daily contact with colleagues in a busy working environment.

Unemployment

Nearly all Western countries have an unemployment problem and there are several reasons for this:

a) There was a marked decline in manufacturing industries in the 1970s and the 1980s.

A What do you think this woman hopes to gain from her work? Is she simply seeking financial rewards or is it more complicated than that?

b) There has been a considerable increase in mechanisation and automation within manufacturing and service industries (banking and insurance).

c) There has been a growth in the number of people seeking work – more and more people chasing fewer and fewer jobs.

Working in the local community as they do, the Christian Churches are only too aware of the personal and social consequences of unemployment. Many of them are located in the inner city areas where the problems caused by unemployment are greatest. Among such problems are the following.

- Low morale, depression, poor self-esteem and even suicide.
- Tension within families leading to marital breakdown.
- An increase in alcohol abuse and drug-taking.
- An increase in petty crime.
- An increase in vandalism and violence.
- An increase in racial attacks and abuse.

9 · CHRISTIANITY IN TODAY'S WORLD

B Do we make a distinction between the value of some jobs in our society and others? If so, where would you place road-sweeping on your list of priority occupations? Could it be a 'vocation'?

ANSWER IN YOUR BOOK …

1. What would your own definition of 'work' be?
2. What is a 'vocation'? Discuss the question with members of your class, come up with a definition, and then draw up a list of ten jobs which most feel are vocations. Can you explain what makes the jobs on the list special?
3. Take three of the suggested results of unemployment and try to explain the link between people being out of work and the social problems that you are looking at.

WHAT DO YOU THINK?

The 'United Nations Declaration on Human Rights' says the following about work:

> 'Everyone has the right to work and to just and favourable conditions of employment. Everyone has the right to equal pay for equal work. Everyone has the right to form and join a trades union…'

This declaration raises all kinds of important questions about work:

a) Do you think that everyone has the 'right' to work?
b) Do you think that everyone, male or female, should be paid the same wage for the same work? If so, how does this fit in with the parable that Jesus told in Matthew 20.1-6?
c) Do you think that everyone should have the right to belong to a Trades Union? What is the membership of such a union intended to safeguard?

READ AND DECIDE …

The Bible has a great deal to say about work. Here are just three examples:

a) Ecclesiastes 5.19.
   'This is what I have seen: that it is good and proper for a man to eat and drink and enjoy himself in return for his labours under the sun, throughout the brief span of life which God has allotted to him. Moreover it is a gift of God that everyone to whom he has granted wealth and riches and the power to enjoy them should accept his lot and rejoice in his labour.'
   ❖ What do you think it takes to make a man or a woman happy in their work?

b) 2.Thessalonians 3.10.
   '…anyone who will not work shall not eat…'
   ❖ Do you think that this principle could/should be put into operation in today's world?

c) 1.Corinthians 4.11-12.
   'To this day we go hungry and thirsty and in rags; we are beaten up; we wander from place to place; we wear ourselves out earning a living with our own hands.'
   ❖ Do hard work and wealth necessarily go hand in hand?

IN THE GLOSSARY …

Vocation.

9.11 LEISURE

Most people in Britain today have far more leisure time than their ancestors did a century ago. The average working week is now less than 40 hours compared to 80 – 90 hours during the 19th century. Such statistics, however, can be misleading. Some people, including mothers with young children and those caring for elderly or disabled relatives, have little or no leisure time.

The 'Ages of Leisure'

Leisure can be defined as:

> 'The time that one has at one's disposal.'

In other words, leisure is the time that each one of us has to do exactly what we want with. What people actually choose to do in their leisure time depends not only on their background and interests but also on their age. Sociologists tell us that we all pass through five distinct 'Ages of Leisure':

Age One *The childhood and teenage phase* – we play with friends, watch television and videos, go to the cinema, play electronic games, read etc.

Age Two *Early married life* – spare time is largely spent on setting up a new home, cooking and entertaining, DIY, playing with children etc.

Age Three *Early middle age (35-45)* – as the children are growing up so people are free to spend more time outside the home with friends, eating out, becoming involved in church and other group activities, going on foreign holidays etc.

Age Four *Later middle age (45-65)* – once the children have left home people are free to pursue such interests as golf or bridge, take longer holidays etc.

Age Five *Old Age* – leisure activities are likely to be less physical with knitting, gardening, walking and playing with the grandchildren among the most popular ways of spending time.

The dangers of leisure

For many overworked people the idea of having unlimited leisure time might seem like a dream come true, but for others it comes close to being a nightmare. For the unemployed, those unable to work and many retired people, too much leisure time can lead to boredom, frustration and depression. In many communities boredom and 'enforced leisure' are blamed for a wide variety of social problems including vandalism, car theft and increasing crime rates.

The Bible and leisure

The idea of one day a week being set aside for leisure purposes is a biblical one. The Jews were told by God that the Sabbath Day, the seventh day of the week, was to be a day of rest (Exodus 20.8). There was considerable debate among the Jewish leaders at the time of Jesus as to what exactly constituted 'work' and leisure. The biblical idea of a day of rest underlines two things:

a) That it was God's idea for men and women to have a day of rest each week (Genesis 2.2-4). In the Bible, this principle is built into the very fabric of creation. It makes it clear that humanity suffers considerably if it ignores it.

A What do you think 'leisure' is?

b) That it is in the interests of the human race for a sharp distinction to be drawn between what is work and what is leisure. It is a distinction which humanity often overlooks to its great cost.

> **ANSWER IN YOUR BOOK ...**
>
> 1. How do leisure activities change according to age?
> 2. List five activities which are, without question, leisure activities and five which belong to the work category. Can you think of any activities which you would find very difficult to place in either category?
> 3. What do you think might be some of the personal long-term consequences if you fail to guarantee adequate time for relaxation?

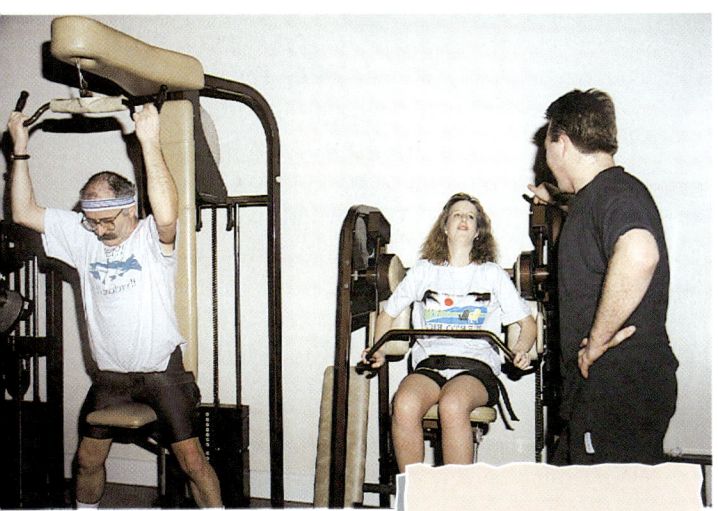

B There is a great deal of emphasis these days on using leisure time to keep fit. Do you think we might have 'gone over the top' a little?

> **WHAT DO YOU THINK?**
>
> **a)** The United Nations Declaration of Human Rights states:
> > 'Everyone has the right to rest and leisure, including reasonable working hours and holidays with pay.'
>
> Do you think that everyone has the 'right' to enjoy reasonable leisure time? Bearing in mind the pressures of modern life, how would you define '...reasonable working hours and holidays with pay'?
>
> **b)** Why do you think that leisure time is considered to be so important in the modern world? What would you say is a 'good' use of leisure? What, in your opinion, would be a 'bad' use of leisure?

> **READ AND DECIDE ...**
>
> Here are two quotations from the Jewish Scriptures on which the tradition of the Sabbath Day was based.
>
> ❖ '...on the seventh day, having finished all his work, God blessed the day and made it holy, because it was the day he finished all his work of creation.' (Genesis 2.2,3.)
>
> ❖ 'Remember to keep the Sabbath Day holy. You have six days of labour to do all your work; but the seventh day is a Sabbath of the Lord God...for in six days the Lord made the heavens and earth, the sea and all that is in them, and on the seventh day he rested.' (Exodus 20.8-11)
>
> **a)** What is the Sabbath Day?
> **b)** Why did God bless the Sabbath day and make it holy?
> **c)** Do you think that it is realistic, or desirable, to set aside one day out of seven for rest and relaxation?

> **IN THE GLOSSARY ...**
>
> Sabbath Day.

9.12 THE ELDERLY

In our society more people than ever are surviving into old age. This is due to great improvements in our standard of living and health care, combined with the wider availability of facilities for the elderly. What are the facts about old age?

A *Can you put into words your own hopes and fears about growing old?*

The facts

The basic facts about old age are these:

a) The life expectancy (the age to which a person can reasonably expect to live) in the UK is now 70 for men and 75 for women.

b) About 17% of the total population in the UK is now past retirement age – more than 10,000,000 people. During this century, the number of people over the age of 65 in the UK has increased by more than 400%.

c) The State pension in the UK has always encouraged men to retire at 65 and women at 60. By the year 2020 the retirement age will be equalised at 65. The State pension is only 30% of the average working wage and, as a consequence, thousands of elderly people live in poverty.

d) Some 2,000,000 households in the UK are made up of old people living alone. Almost 500,000 elderly people have no living relative. One of the major problems, therefore, faced by the elderly is that of loneliness and depression.

e) Obviously, failing health features large in the lives of old people. Those over the age of 65 are seven times more likely to visit a doctor than someone in their thirties. More than 1000 elderly people die from hypothermia (low body temperature) each year in the UK.

Ageism

Just as we have sexism and racial discrimination, we also have ageism. This is active discrimination against people simply because they have reached a certain age. Compulsory retirement at the age of 65 for men and 60 for women is a form of ageism in itself since it is based on the premise that once a person reaches a certain age they must be compelled to retire. Many old people look forward to retirement, but others would like to have the choice.

Another form of ageism in society is when sweeping generalisations are made about the elderly:

'Old people are always living in the past...'
'Young and old can never get along together...'
'When you reach retirement age it is a steady decline down towards death...'

Ageism is also seen in the way in which old people are often treated in our society. Within the old Jewish extended family system, reflected in the Bible, the patriarchal (grandfather/father) and matriarchal (grandmother/mother) figures stood at the head of their clan or family. Younger family members were taught to respect them and see them as the possessors of great wisdom, derived from the experience of many years. This is still the case in cultures and societies which are based on the extended family system. Paul emphasised the responsibility which children have towards their parents when he wrote to Timothy:

'If a widow has children or grandchildren, they should learn as their first duty to show loyalty to their family and so repay what they owe their parents and grandparents...' (1.Timothy 5.4)

Sadly, this is not always the case in our society today. Yet growing old is not as depressing as you might think. Most people can expect several years of retirement with reasonably good health. Free of other responsibilities, they are able to devote their time to hobbies and interests. The majority have the birth of grandchildren to look forward to and this often gives them a new lease of life. Clubs and leisure centres give the elderly the opportunity to remain active – if they wish to do so. That should be the key to growing old. The elderly should retain their independence for as long as possible.

B *Many people dread the idea of growing old. Do you? Can you explain your answer?*

READ AND DECIDE ...

Here are three comments about growing old and being elderly. Read them carefully:

a) Ronald Blythe. A View in Winter.
 'Old age is ... a lot of crossed-off names in an address book.'

b) Jenny Joseph. Warning.
 *'When I am an old woman I shall wear purple
 With a red hat that doesn't go, and doesn't suit me.
 And I shall spend my pension on brandy and summer gloves
 And stain sandals and say we've no money for the butter.'*

c) Dylan Thomas. 'Do not go gently into that good night'.
 *'Old age should burn and rage at close of day
 Rage, rage against the dying of the night.'*

Take each of these extracts in turn. They are each making an important, sometimes morbid, point about growing old. What do you think the point is in each case? Do you agree with it? How does each of the extracts make you feel about old age? Try to sum up in a short poem or paragraph how you feel about old age.

ANSWER IN YOUR BOOK ...

1 What do you understand by 'ageism'? Why do you think that it is very unfair to the elderly?
2 What do you think is the best way of looking after elderly people?
3 Write an essay with the title 'The Elderly in Britain today'.

WHAT DO YOU THINK?

Most of you will have had close contact with some elderly people – grandparents, next-door neighbours etc. Write down and explain five positive aspects of growing old as you observe them in the lives of others.

9.13 RACIAL DISCRIMINATION

For a long time geographical barriers (oceans, deserts, mountains etc) kept the different races apart. Each race developed its own characteristics – physical features and colour among them. This was significant. During this time, human beings, like other animals, developed the strong feeling that they were safest when surrounded 'by their own kind'.

Ever since the races began to intermingle the 'outsider' has been seen as a threat. It is this fear, fuelled by an ignorance of the unknown, which lies at the heart of racism, prejudice and discrimination.

So, what are we talking about?

- *Racism* – this is the belief that one race is superior to another and this leads to antagonism between the races.
- *Prejudice (pre-judging)* – this exists in many areas of life, but colour prejudice is the negative judgment of someone purely on the basis of their skin-colour.
- *Discrimination* – this is active prejudice when people are treated unfairly because of their skin-colour and nationality.

Immigration

Britain is a multi-racial society and has always been so. From the time that the Romans conquered Britain and mingled with the native population, waves of immigrants have come to the UK. There have been two main factors which have driven people to Britain – the need to find work or to escape persecution at home. As long as the immigrants were white the influx was barely noticed. It only became an issue when coloured immigrants from the old British Empire began to come in the 1920s and, particularly, when the UK looked to the Carribbean and Africa for labour in the 1950s and 1960s. Then, in the late 1970s, many Asians came to Britain to escape persecution in Uganda.

Race and the Law

There are now about 2,500,000 black people in Britain of whom about 40% were born here. They represent just over 4% of the total population – 50% of them being African and 25% Caribbean in origin. When the immigrants first arrived they went to areas where work and housing were available, mainly in the inner-city. Most of them have stayed there.

From the beginning these immigrants found themselves faced with prejudice, abuse and

A Growing up together in a multi-racial society. Do you think that this is the way forward?

discrimination. The Race Relations Act of 1976 gave them full legal rights in the areas of education, housing and employment. Despite this, a survey, conducted in 1985, found that:

- 35% of white people in this country saw themselves as colour prejudiced;
- 66% of black people thought that they had lost a job because of their colour.

Racial prejudice, it seems, is still very much in existence in Britain today.

Christianity and race

Christians believe that everyone is equal in God's family. No person or race can be spiritually, morally or intellectually superior to another. This is made clear in Leviticus 19.33-34 and Galatians 3.28 as well as in the parable of the Good Samaritan. Belief, though, is one thing and practice another. Christians have often failed to live up to these ideals. Here are two examples:

a) In South Africa, from the late 1940s when the racist policy of apartheid was set up, through to 1994 when it was finally abolished, the Dutch Reformed Church was a strong supporter of the South African Government.

b) Many of the West Indians who came to Britain in the 1950s were Christians but they received a lukewarm reception from many British churches. As a result, they set up their own churches which have thrived while the established churches have declined in the same period.

B What problems do you think that this mixed-race family, parents and children, might face in modern Britain?

READ AND DECIDE ...

a) How do you think that Jesus, as a coloured man, would be welcomed by people in Great Britain today and by the Christian Church?

b) A Nigerian student wrote that:
   'God is black, a beautiful shining black. It is a wicked white man's lie to say that he is white. The Devil is white.'

- What was your first reaction when you read these words?
- What do you think the student is really trying to say?
- Why do you think he said that 'The Devil is white'?
- Do you agree with him?

ANSWER IN YOUR BOOK ...

1 How did Britain become a multi-racial society from the 1920s onwards? What did the Race Relations Act set out to achieve?

2 How would you explain the meaning of racism, discrimination and prejudice?

3 What do you think lies at the heart of racism, prejudice and discrimination? Why is it 'colour' that arouses such strong feelings?

WHAT DO YOU THINK?

World Council of Churches, 1980:
   'Every human being created in the image of God is a person for whom Christ died. Racism, which is the use of a person's racial origin to determine a person's value, is an assault on Christ's values and a rejection of his sacrifice.'

What do you think?

9.14 WORLD POPULATION

There is one major world problem today that outweighs all others, and that is over-population. The other major world problems such as poverty, homelessness, pollution, illiteracy and hunger cannot be solved unless something is done to reduce the number of babies being born. Otherwise, the pressure on the planet will be simply too great!

Population – the facts

In 1800 there were less than a billion (1,000,000,000) people on earth and it had taken millions of years to reach that figure! By the year 2000 there will be 6,000,000,000 people and by the year 2030 that number will have doubled. This increase, known as the 'population explosion', is set to continue into the foreseeable future.

In simple terms, the population of the world increases by:
- 5 people every second;
- 150 people every minute;
- 200,000 people every day;
- 80,000,000 every year.

This growth is not taking place equally across the world. 90% of these babies are being born in Developing Countries. By the year 2000, for instance, one in every four people on earth will be living in China. In Kenya, the population is increasing by 8% each year compared with 2% in the world generally.

In her book 'How the Other Half Dies', Susan George explains why, in poorer countries, people have more children although it only makes their plight worse. In countries where "...every day is a long grind of many hard jobs just to survive..." there is a less than 50% chance of a baby reaching its fifth birthday. In that situation "...you have got to plan to have many children...". She ends:

> "The poor of the world will start using contraceptive devices very quickly indeed, just as soon as real development and a fairer deal in life lets them do so."

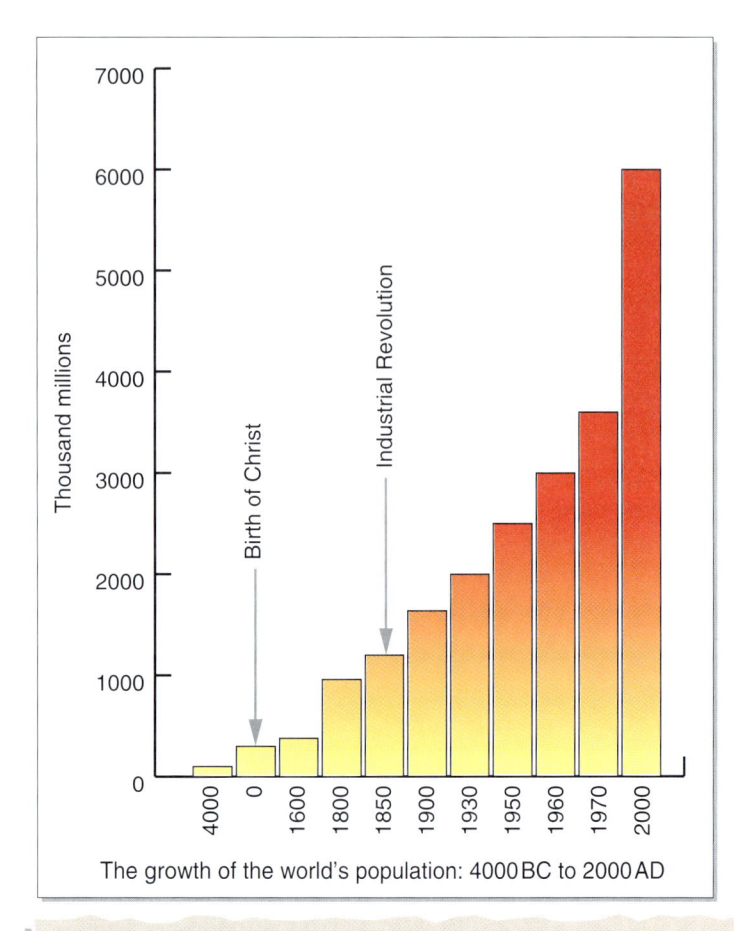

The growth of the world's population: 4000 BC to 2000 AD

A Can you come up with any reasons to explain why the population of the world has exploded in the last two centuries?

Problems

This population explosion is causing many long-term problems which put the future of the human race in jeopardy. In particular:

1. *Overcrowding* – about 50% of the world's population now live in cities with all their pollution, overcrowding and appalling social problems. Mexico City is currently the world's largest city with a population of 15,000,000.
2. *Malnutrition* – each year 20,000,000 people die as a direct result of malnutrition.
3. *Pollution* – pollution of the earth, air and water, together with the problems of disposing of human waste, are directly related to the pressure of an ever-increasing population.

Yet, any attempt to deal with the problems of over population faces many moral and religious issues. Here are a few for you to consider:

a) Should the governments of countries like China (1300 million) and India (625 million) exercise compulsory sterilisation and family limitation programmes?
b) If compulsory sterilisation is rejected, should a much greater effort be made to encourage people to voluntarily limit the size of their families?
c) Should the Roman Catholic Church be put under pressure to end its opposition to all artificial means of birth-control?

B What do you think might happen if the population of the world is allowed to continue growing at its present rate?

ANSWER IN YOUR BOOK ...

1 How would you explain what is meant by the 'population explosion'?
2 What is the link between the 'population explosion' and such major problems as pollution, homelessness and poverty?
3 Why do you think that some countries have greater over-population problems than others?

WHAT DO YOU THINK?

Peter Adamson, United Nation's Childrens Fund, has said:

'It is not that people suddenly started breeding like rabbits, it is just that they stopped dying like flies.'

❖ What point do you think is being made here?

READ AND DECIDE ...

Here are three comments about population. Read them carefully and record your comments:

a) 'Be fruitful and increase...' (Genesis 1.28)
   ❖ Why does this advice sound very hollow today?
b) 'No wonder people in the developing world have their problems – they have far too many children. If they will not limit their family size voluntarily then compulsory sterilisation is the answer.'
   ❖ Is it?
c) 'The Western countries hold the key. If they ate less and consumed less of the world's resources then there would be much more to share with the poorer countries. As their standard of living went up they would see that it was not in their interests to have more children'.
   ❖ Can you see the time coming when Western countries, like our own, will be prepared to see a drop in their own standards of living so that the living standards of developing countries can be raised?

IN THE GLOSSARY ...

Developed country; Developing country.

9.15 WORLD HUNGER

The simple statistics of world hunger are staggering. Each year about 20 million people die from malnutrition, and 50% of these have not reached their 5th birthday. Malnutrition kills approximately:

- one person every 1½ seconds.
- 38 people every minute.
- 55,000 people every day.

Yet there is a frightening contradiction here – there is more than enough food in the world to go around!

What has gone wrong?

Most of the food is in the wrong place. The rich northern hemisphere has enormous grain surpluses while the needy southern part goes hungry. Look at this chart:

THE INDUSTRIALISED WORLD	THE DEVELOPING WORLD
Has 20% of the world's population	Has 80% of the world's population
Uses 80% of the world's resources	Uses 20% of the world's resources
Eats, on average, 3300 calories per person per day	Eats, on average, less than 1000 calories per person per day

Here are three other interesting statistics:

1. The US has just 6% of the world's population (210,000,000 people) and yet consumes 35% of the world's resources.
2. The developed world spends £20 billion each year on helping the poor and £450 billion on military arms.
3. Even when a developing country produces food, its own population cannot afford to buy it. India, for example, with 50% of the world's poorest people, still has a regular grain surplus of 24 metric tons. When their own people cannot buy the food, large landowners turn to growing 'cash crops' – tobacco, tea, coffee, cotton etc. – to sell on the world's markets.

The Brandt Report

In 1980 an important Report, 'North-South, A Programme for Survival' (the Brandt Report), pointed out that the birth-rate is high and the life expectancy low in developing countries – where 75% of the world's population live. Poor people continue to have many children because they need help on the land and security when they grow old. The Report concluded that the only long-term answer is for the rich countries to share their wealth with the poorer ones – a process which has hardly begun.

A *CAFOD is the Catholic Fund for Overseas Development. Can you explain why this text is particularly appropriate?*

Give us ALL this day our daily bread

CAFOD
ON THE SIDE OF PEOPLE IN NEED

9 · CHRISTIANITY IN TODAY'S WORLD

> **B** Why do you think that rich countries are so reluctant to share their wealth with others? Can you ever see things changing? If so, what do you think might bring the change about?

What is being done?

Many international agencies exist to help developing countries. Among the most well-known are Oxfam, Save the Children Fund, Tear Fund and Christian Aid. These relief organisations seek to provide the following:

a) *Short-term or emergency aid* – after natural disasters such as floods and earthquakes supplies of food, shelter and medicine are always needed quickly.
b) *Small-scale aid* – such as farming equipment and water purification units to help people set up their own improvement schemes.
c) *Long-term aid* – such as health projects and education schemes to secure a better long-term future for people.
d) *Trade reform and political pressure* – many agencies recognise that the poorer countries are treated very badly in the world's markets which are controlled by the West. If Western countries have a surplus of a particular commodity, such as sugar-cane, this will depress the world price – to the great disadvantage of the poorer countries.

ANSWER IN YOUR BOOK ...

1. Can you explain why 20 million people die each year from malnutrition when there is a world surplus of food?
2. What was the main recommendation of the Brandt Report?
3. What kind of aid do relief organisations try to provide?

READ AND DECIDE ...

How would you reply to people who made each of the following comments:

a) 'We must grow more food, there is simply not enough to go around.'
b) 'World over-population lies at the heart of the hunger problem. If people from the poorer countries had fewer children there would be enough food to go around.'
c) 'Hungry people need better contraceptive advice – then there would be fewer mouths to feed and we would end world hunger.'
d) 'People living in rich countries would never to prepared to eat less. Besides which, many of us would then end up dying from malnutrition.'

WHAT DO YOU THINK?

Susan George. Quoted on 'The Politics of Food'. Channel 4 T.V:

a) There are 3500 calories per kilo of grain so a ton of grain supplies an average of 3,500,000 calories.
b) About 2300 calories a day is adequate for proper nutrition.
c) At 2300 calories a day for 365 days a person needs 839,500 calories a year. This means that a ton of grain could feed four people for a year.
d) A million tons would feed more than 4,000,000 people. Five million tons would feed 20,000,000 people – the number who die from malnutrition each year.

If the governments in the developed world decided to cut down on the consumption of their people and send the surplus to developing nations, what problems do you think they would face? Can you suggest any way that these might be overcome?

IN THE GLOSSARY ...

Developing country.

9.16 WAR AND PEACE

During the 20th century more than 100,000,000 people have died as a result of war and organised violence. During the First World War (1914-18), 95% of the casualties were soldiers, but in recent conflicts over 90% of those killed have been civilians. The balance and nature of armed conflict has changed out of all recognition.

Wars of different kinds

Since the end of the Second World War in 1945 there have been more than 250 wars throughout the world. A 'war' is any armed conflict which lasts longer than 60 minutes and in which regular forces from at least one side are involved. There are two broad categories for such conflicts:

a) *Civil wars and wars of liberation* – in 1994 alone civil wars were raging in Bosnia, Rwanda, Somalia and the Yemen. A civil war is an internal conflict within a country although outside forces might also find themselves drawn in. It is thought that as many as 500,000 civilians were killed in the conflict in Rwanda alone.

b) *Wars between nations* – since 1945 there have been wars in the Middle East and South East Asia – including the Korean War (1950-53); the Vietnam War (1965-73); the Iran/Iraq conflict (1980-88) and the Gulf War (1991).

The cost of these wars is immense. It can be measured in the following terms:

1. *Destruction*. The number of people killed and injured, the destruction of towns and countryside and the number of families shattered all have to be taken into account.
2. *Refugees*. There are now some 15 million refugees (people without a home or a country) throughout the world and almost all of them were forced to leave their homes through war.
3. *Economic cost*. War inevitably destroys homes, crops, water and power supplies, industry, hospitals and schools. All of them have to be replaced once the war is over. It also uses up vast amounts of money. Developed countries spend 20 times more on their military weapons than they do on alleviating world poverty and hunger. In a civilised world that cannot be right.

A Just part of the cost of war? Who do you think pays the highest price in an armed conflict?

In 1945 two atomic bombs were dropped on the Japanese cities of Hiroshima and Nagasaki – killing over 140,000 people. Thousands more suffered the appalling after-effects for the rest of their lives. Before long the so-called 'Nuclear Club' included the USA, Great Britain, the USSR, France and China. Now at least 20 other countries either have nuclear weapons or the capability to build them. Even though the USA and Russia have destroyed thousands of nuclear warheads in recent years, they still have the capacity to destroy each other twenty times over.

Just and Holy Wars

While most people feel that war should be avoided if at all possible, few are genuine 'pacifists'. Jesus told his disciples that they should not use violence in any circumstances – Matthew 5.39. In 1250 St Thomas Aquinas laid down four conditions which would enable a Christian to fight with a clear conscience – in a 'Just War'. They still form part of the teaching of the Catholic Church. The conditions are:

a) There must be a 'just' cause for going to war. (Refer to READ AND DECIDE...)
b) Every other alternative must have been tried.
c) The war must have a 'just' aim and be halted when that aim has been achieved.
d) Only as much violence may be used as is strictly necessary, and it must never be directed against civilians.

When one side in a war believes that it has God on its side then it might claim to be fighting a 'Holy War'. The claim was made, for instance, in the 11th and 12th centuries during the Crusades, when Christians were fighting against the 'pagan' Muslims.

ANSWER IN YOUR BOOK ...

1. Why do you think that a modern war is much more likely to cause a high level of civilian casualties?
2. What is the difference between a 'just' war and a 'holy' war?
3. Collect as much information as you can about a war that is going on at the present time. In the course of writing up your information, try to explain the reasons behind the conflict and the objectives of both sides in fighting the war.

DISCUSS AMONG YOURSELVES ...

These four quotations are from the Bible:

a) 'Declare a holy war, call your troops to arms.' (Joel 3.9)
b) 'I pursue and overtake my enemies; until I have made an end of them I do not turn back. I strike them down and they can rise no more... I wipe out those that hate me.' (Psalm 18.37-39)
c) 'You have heard that they were told, "An eye for an eye, a tooth for a tooth." But what I tell you is this: Do not resist those that wrong you. If anyone slaps you on the right cheek, turn and offer him the left also.' (Matthew. 5.38-39)
d) 'But Jesus said to him: Put up your sword. All who take the sword die by the sword.' (Matthew 26.52)

Do you detect a clear change of emphasis between the Old and New Testaments? Do the two sayings of Jesus here suggest that a pacifist approach to violence is also the Christian one?

READ AND DECIDE ...

Read the following quotation carefully:
'War or violent struggle can never be just except in the very special circumstances that it is the only way of restraining a very great injustice; that it will not itself bring about greater injustice than the evil it opposes; that it has a reasonable chance of success; that it does not involve acts of injustice such as the deliberate killing of non-combatants and that those who wage it are authorised to do so by a large degree of popular support.'
(Hebert. The Teaching of the Catholic Church.)

a) What, according to this quotation, needs to be present before a conflict can be declared a 'just' war?
b) Is there any difference between these conditions and those laid down by St Thomas Aquinas in the 13th century?
c) Can you think of any war in modern times which would seem to meet all of the conditions laid down in the quotation?
d) Write an essay of some 500 words on 'The Just War'.

IN THE GLOSSARY ...

Developed country.

9.17 HUMAN RIGHTS

On December 10th 1948 the United Nations drew up the 'Universal Declaration of Human Rights'; one of the most important documents of the 20th century. Among the many articles in the document are:

Article 1	All human beings are born free and equal in dignity and rights.
Article 2	Everyone is entitled to these rights without any distinction of race, colour, sex or religion.
Article 3	Everyone has the right to life, liberty and security of person.
Article 4	No one shall be held in slavery.
Article 5	No one shall be subjected to torture.
Article 7	All are equal before the law.
Article 11	Everyone charged with a criminal offence is presumed innocent until proved guilty.
Article 13	Everyone has the right to freedom of movement.
Article 16	Men and women of a full age have the right to marry and to have a family.
Article 18	Everyone has the right to freedom of thought, conscience and religion.
Article 19	Everyone has the right to freedom of opinion and expression.
Article 20	Everyone has the right to peaceful assembly.
Article 23	Everyone has the right to work.
Article 24	Everyone has the right to rest and leisure.
Article 26	Everyone has the right to an education.

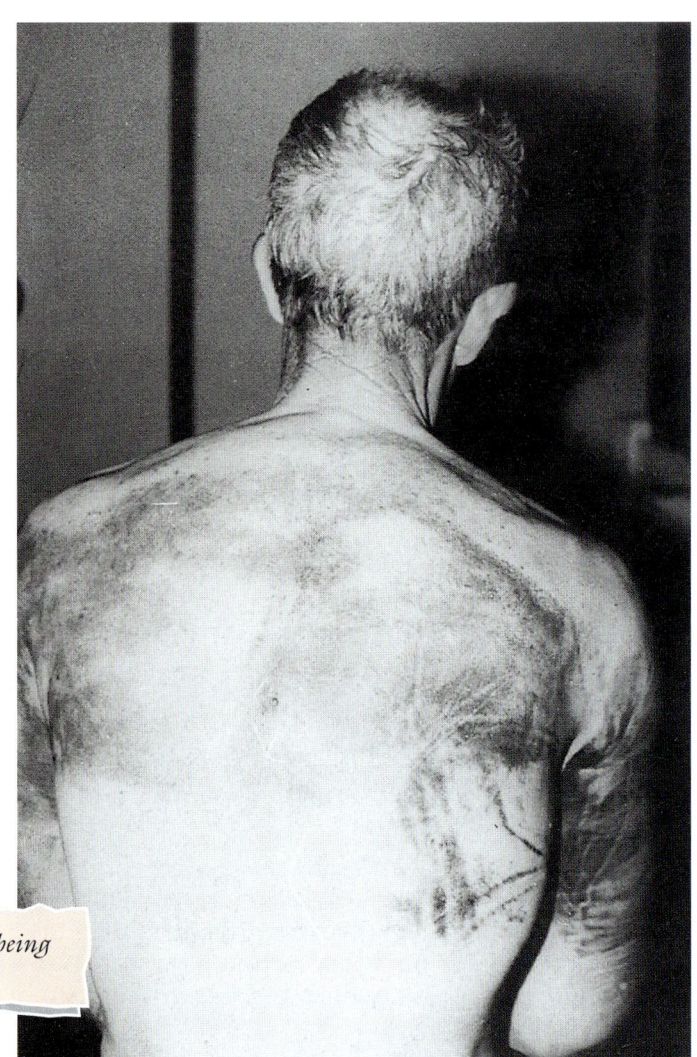

A What do you think makes one human being do this to another?

Fighting for human rights

Many of those countries which voted for the Declaration in 1948 have since denied basic human rights to their citizens. There are many countries in today's world which do not allow freedom of expression, oppress minorities, use torture against their own people, suppress religion and restrict the movements of their citizens.

Amnesty International, an organisation which is active in over 150 countries, is the most well-known body working for human rights.
Founded in 1961, Amnesty does not specifically support any government, ideology or creed.

It supports any government which upholds basic human rights and opposes any which does not. It works independently across all national and international boundaries and this is where most of its strength comes from. In recent years it has severely criticised Albania, Bulgaria, the Ivory Coast, Iraq, Iran, Indonesia and Turkey, among many other countries, for their human rights record. Surprisingly, it has also criticised countries where, you might think, human rights were safe. This includes Britain which has, over the years, been criticised for denying human rights to prisoners in Northern Ireland, its treatment of remand prisoners, and for introducing laws to prevent wives and children joining immigrant husbands and fathers in this country.

The widespread use of torture is an alarming fact of life in the 20th century. ACT (Action by Christians against Torture) was set up in Great Britain to mount a concerted attack on this barbaric practice – wherever it is still used. Such torture, ACT maintains, is an affront to decent human values and an attack on everything that a Christian believes.

B Find out all that you can about the work of Amnesty International.

ANSWER IN YOUR BOOK ...

1. Read through the 'Rights' again and copy them into your book. Do any of them surprise you? What do you think are the three most important 'rights' that human beings have?
2. What do you think ACT has in mind when it calls torture an attack on everything that a Christian believes to be true?
3. Although nothing has been said in this chapter about the rights of children and animals, can you draw up five basic 'rights' for each of them?

FIND OUT AND NOTE ...

Here is a statement by Prince Sadruddin Aga Khan, former U.N. High Commissioner for Refugees:

'The Universal Declaration of Human Rights adopted on 10th December 1948 promised a better world. The aspirations set out in the thirty articles, however, remain largely unfulfilled. The right to life, to an adequate standard of living, to freedom of expression, to protection from torture, inhuman treatment, or arbitrary arrest, and many of the 'common standards of achievement for all peoples and nations' are as far from realisation as ever.'

Six clear infringements of human rights are mentioned here. During the next two weeks gather examples from the mass media of ways in which these rights are being infringed across the world.

WHAT DO YOU THINK?

This is how Amnesty International describes its aims: 'Amnesty International is engaged in what is very often a life and death struggle to defend human rights in many countries of the world...only by becoming a mass movement for human rights can we hope to play our full part in ending this international hypocrisy which surrounds the plight of so many – many who suffer alone or collectively amidst a deafening silence from some of the very people who pay lip service to the International Declaration of Human Rights...Amnesty's reason for existence is to campaign against torture and execution and for the release of men and women imprisoned for their beliefs, colour, ethnic origins, language or religion...'

a) Why do you think that many governments who signed up to the Declaration on Human Rights allow people in their own countries to suffer? What does this statement mean when it calls such countries hypocrites?

b) Someone has described execution as 'the ultimate infringement of human rights'. What do you think they meant? Are you surprised that some countries which trumpet their support of human rights loudest, such as the USA, still carry out executions?

9.18 THE WORLD IN DANGER

We know the damage that we have already done to the world in the name of progress. We have polluted its atmosphere, poisoned its rivers, destroyed its forests and brought about the extinction of species that we have never even managed to name! We are aware that we must change our attitudes and way of life. We also know that it is becoming harder and harder to feed the world's ever-expanding population. Yet, all the indicators show that we are still determined to rush headlong down the slope towards destruction.

Indicators of decline

Everywhere that we turn in today's world there are clear indicators that the world as we know it is in sharp decline.

Here are just five examples:

1. Indigenous tribes around the world are facing the imminent prospect of extinction. Those that remain face the loss of their land and culture.
2. Each day humankind destroys between 50 and 100 species of plant, insect and animal life. Many of these are found in the world's rainforests which are being bull-dozed so quickly that 50% of those remaining may disappear by 2035. This will have a potentially disastrous effect on the world's oxygen supply.
3. Pollution (car exhaust fumes, aerosol sprays etc.) is destroying the ozone layer in the upper atmosphere which protects the earth from lethal ultra-violet radiation.
4. Motor-cars, one of the greatest pollutants, are set to increase in number by some 15 million a year between now and 2015. The corresponding rise in CO_2 emissions can only increase what scientists call 'The Greenhouse Effect'. Already there is a marked increase in the number of cases of skin-cancer as a result of people being exposed directly to the sun's rays. In many parts of the world sun-bathing is now a very great risk.
5. Uncontrolled fishing has brought about such a depletion of fish stocks that many of the species are only 10% of what they were 20 years ago.

The future?

The planet on which we live is in a state of real crisis. The human race finds itself at a cross-roads. Decisions that it makes now will determine whether it has any kind of future or not. Christians, like everyone else, are involved in deciding which way humankind will go.

Here are some points to consider:

a) In its opening chapters the Bible suggests that God made the world – and then appointed 'man' to be his steward or representative on earth. This has not prevented the human race from exploiting the earth and its resources for its own greedy gain.
b) Some of the emphases in the Bible have been deliberately exploited in the past – to the detriment of the planet's health. In particular, the idea, supported by one of the two creation stories in Genesis, that humanity stands at the centre of all life – and that everything is there for humanity's benefit. It is very difficult to avoid this impression from a reading of Genesis 2.15-25.
c) Over the centuries the Church has done little to build up a positive attitude to the earth among believers. Instead of encouraging a simple lifestyle among its members, it has often been a bastion of wealth and privilege. Even today it does little to

A A simple act of vandalism or a real threat to the future well-being of our planet?

challenge the waste and over-consumption which are such strong features of our society. This should be one of the roles which the Church undertakes in the future.

ANSWER IN YOUR BOOK ...

1. Write an essay of some 500 words on the topic 'The world in great danger'.
2. Which of the dangers facing the planet in the future concerns you most? Can you explain why? Do you think that the planet will survive the many attacks being made on it?
3. Draw up what you would consider to be a 'Christian plan' for the survival of the planet beyond the 21st century.

FIND OUT AND NOTE ...

Two technical terms are mentioned in this unit which are very important in trying to understand what is happening to our planet. Can you find out the meaning and importance of the following:

a) The Ozone Layer
b) The Greenhouse Effect

B Find out as much as you can about recycling. Write your notes up and include references to the recycling facilities available in your area.

READ AND DECIDE ...

Read this poem carefully:

If the Earth were only a few feet in diameter
floating a few feet above a field somewhere
people would come from everywhere to marvel at it.
People would walk around it marvelling at its big pools of water, its little pools
and the water flowing in between.
People would marvel at the bumps on it and the holes in it.
They would marvel at the very thin layer of gas surrounding it
and the water suspended in the gas.
The people would marvel at all the creatures walking around
the surface of the ball and at the creatures in the water.
The people would declare it as sacred because it was the only one,
and they would protect it so that it would not be hurt.
The ball would be the greatest wonder known,
and people would come to pray to it,
to be healed,
and to gain knowledge.

(**Joe Miller.** *Quoted in Save the Planet.* J.Porritt. Dorling Kindersley. 1991)

The writer suggests that if the earth was just a few feet in diameter, floating above a field, people would come to marvel at it. Would they? What point is he making? Do you think he is right?

WHAT DO YOU THINK?

Read this carefully:

'It is easy to say that it is up to Governments and industry to put things right but, in practice, it is what we do and what we buy or reject that dictates what industry and Governments do. We are all, in some small way, responsible for what happens to the world as a whole. We can no longer ignore the fact that if each of us in our everyday life does not do something about it, we may not have a world fit to live in.'
('Doing our bit – a practical guide to the environment and what we can do about it.' **Hugh and Margaret Brown**)

Do you agree with this? Are we all responsible for what happens to the world? If so, what should everyone be doing about it?

THE GLOSSARY

A

Abortion – an operation carried out to remove a baby (foetus) from the womb of the mother before 24 weeks of pregnancy.

Adult Baptism – the Baptist Church chooses to baptise adults rather than infants because it believes that a person must profess their own faith before the ceremony.

Advent – (the coming) the time of contemplation of the mystery of Christ's incarnation.

Altar – the raised table in an Anglican, Catholic or Orthodox church from which Holy Communion is conducted.

Alternative Service Book – introduced in 1980 to replace the Book of Common Prayer in the Church of England.

Anglican Church – the Church of England and other Episcopal Churches, such as the Church of Australia, which accepts the Archbishop of Canterbury as their leader.

Anglo-Catholics – members of the Church of England who are closest to the Roman Catholic Church in their worship and beliefs.

Apocrypha – derived from the Greek word for 'hidden', this refers to a collection of books written between the two Testaments.

Apostles – derived from the Greek word 'to send', the twelve disciples of Jesus were later called this.

Apostles Creed – the oldest statement of Christian belief going back to the 2nd or 3rd century.

Archbishop – the senior bishop in the Church of England and the Roman Catholic Churches.

Ascension Day – forty days after Easter, this is the time when Christians celebrate the ascension of Jesus into heaven.

Ash Wednesday – the first day of Lent.

Authorised Version – Bible published in the reign of King James I in 1612.

B

Baptise – the word means 'to dip', referring originally to the practice of dipping sheep to kill the insects on them.

Baptists – a worldwide Protestant denomination which practises adult baptism.

Benedictines – members of a monastic order founded by St Benedict around 530.

Bible – Old and New Testaments: it is the sacred Scriptures for all Christians.

Bishop – the highest of the three major orders in the Church, the others being deacon and priest.

Bodily Assumption of Mary – the belief of Roman Catholic and Orthodox believers that at the end of her life the Virgin Mary was taken bodily up into heaven.

Book of Common Prayer – after three revisions in the 16th century this was published in 1662.

Breaking of Bread – Nonconformists often call their service of Holy Communion this.

C

Cardinals – the senior bishops in the Roman Catholic Church. Together they form the College of Cardinals.

Celibacy – refers to the practice of priests, and others, who remain unmarried as part of their vocation or calling.

Charismatic Movement – includes those churches which emphasise the gifts and baptism by the Holy Spirit.

Chrismation – the service in the Orthodox Church at which infant baptism and confirmation are combined.

Christmas – the festival at which Christians celebrate the birth of Jesus.

Church of England – the Established Church in this country, first formed by Henry VIII.

Citadel – a Salvation Army place of worship.

Confirmation – the service which admits a person into full membership of the Church of England, the Roman Catholic Church and the Orthodox Church.

Creed – an official statement of Christian belief.

Crucifix – a cross which contains the body of Jesus, this is displayed in church and worn around the neck.

D

Deacon – in the Church of England and Roman Catholic Church a person must be this before they can be ordained as a priest.

Developed World – in the northern hemisphere, this contains the richest countries in the world.

Developing World – in the southern hemisphere, this is that part of the globe where the standard of living is far lower than that in the Developed World.

Diocese – an area within the Christian Church which is governed by a bishop.

Divine Liturgy – the Orthodox equivalent of Holy Communion. A 'liturgy' is any Divine service which follows a prescribed ritual.

Dominicans – a Roman Catholic monastic order started by St Dominic at Toulouse in 1212.

E

Easter – the time of the year when Christians celebrate the death and resurrection of Jesus.

Eastern Orthodox Church – the branch of the Christian Church which is dominant in Eastern Europe.

Ecumenical Movement – the movement, supported by many Churches, towards closer co-operation and even unity.

Epiphany – (manifestation) – a festival held on January 6th to commemorate the manifestation of Christ to the Gentiles.

Epistle – a letter that refers to those books in the New Testament written by Peter, James, John and others.

Established Church – the Church of England in this country. This means it enjoys many privileges which the other Churches do not have.

Eucharist – (thanksgiving) – one of several terms used for the central liturgical act of worship in the Church.

Evangelical – a Christian who believes that the Bible is inspired and that each person must respond individually to Christ as their Saviour.

Evangelism – the activity which involves Christians sharing the Gospel of Christ with others.

Excommunication – a penalty imposed by the Catholic Church which prevents a person taking the sacraments.

Exodus – of the Jews from slavery in Egypt: it is the most important event in Jewish history.

Exorcism – the casting out of demons from those people believed to be demon-possessed.

Extra-marital Sex – this takes place when one, or both, of those involved are married to someone else.

F

Fasting – the discipline of the body's natural appetite for food as a form of worship.

Font – a stone receptacle in a Roman Catholic or Anglican church which holds the water used in infant baptism.

Fornication – refers to any sexual activities outside marriage, particularly between two people who are unmarried.

Franciscans – a Christian order of friars founded by St Francis of Assisi early in the 13th century.

Free Churches – Nonconformists who are not bound by any outside authority.

G

Gay – the modern term used for a male homosexual.

Gentile – in the Bible this refers to a 'non-Israelite' but the word has now come to mean 'non-Jew'.

Good Friday – the day, two days before Easter Sunday, when Christians remember the death of Jesus on the cross.

Gospel – a Greek word which means 'Good News'. The four Gospels in the New Testament are our primary record of that Good News.

Great Schism – took place in the 13th century when the Orthodox Church and the Roman Catholic Church split.

H

Hail Mary – an important Catholic prayer directed to the Virgin Mary.

Heretic – a person who believes and teaches doctrines which are contrary to the beliefs of the Church to which they belong.

High Altar – the holiest part of an Orthodox Church where the preparations for the Divine Liturgy are carried out.

High Church – see Anglo-Catholics.

High Priest – at the time of Jesus, Caiaphas was the High Priest, the leader of the Jewish community.

Holy Communion – the title usually given to the central act of worship in the Church of England.

Holy Spirit – the third person of the Christian Trinity.

Holy Unction – the service in the Roman Catholic Church in which a priest anoints a sick or dying person with holy oil.

Holy Week – the central festival of the Christian Church beginning with Palm Sunday and ending on Easter Sunday.

House Church Movement – began when people started to meet for worship in each other's homes rather than in church.

I

Icon – a holy picture widely used in Orthodox churches as a devotional aid.

Iconostasis – the screen in an Orthodox church, covered with icons, which separates the people from the High Altar.

Immaculate Conception – the Catholic belief that Mary was conceived without original sin.

Incarnation – the Christian belief that Jesus Christ, the second member of the Trinity, became a human being in Bethlehem.

Indulgence – an act of merit performed by someone to shorten the time that someone else spends in purgatory.

Infant Baptism – the service performed in many Churches which brings a baby into the family of God – the Church.

J

Jerusalem – sacred to three religions – Christianity, Judaism and Islam. It is the city in which Jesus was crucified.

Jesuit – a member of the Society of Jesus which was formed by St Ignatius of Loyola in 1540.

L

Laity – those members of the Christian community who are not ordained as priests.

Last Supper – the last meal that Jesus shared with his disciples before he was arrested.

Laying on of Hands – a traditional act used in Confirmation and Ordination to signify the passing on of the Holy Spirit.

Lent – the time of fasting and spiritual preparation which leads up to Easter. This lasts for a period of 40 days or 6½ weeks (Sundays not counted).

Liturgy – see Divine Liturgy.

Lord's Prayer – the prayer which Jesus taught his disciples as a model prayer for all believers.

Lord's Supper – the term used by Paul (1.Corinthians 11.20) to refer to Holy Communion and the term adopted for this service by the Free Churches.

Low Church – refers to Evangelicals whose style of worship is very different from the Anglo-Catholics.

M

Mass – the central act of worship in the Roman Catholic Church.

Maundy Thursday – the day set aside to commemorate the institution of the Eucharist by Jesus Christ.

Meditation – a form of prayer used by many Christians.

Meeting-House – the place in which Quakers gather for worship.

Mercy-Seat – the place where penitents kneel to seek God's forgiveness in a Salvation Army citadel.

Messiah – ('anointed one') – the leader expected by Jews to deliver them from their enemies. This is a Hebrew word as opposed to Christ (Greek).

Methodist Church – formed after the death of John Wesley and based on his teachings.

Missionary – someone who is sent to take with them the 'Good News' of Jesus.

Monastery – the traditional home of monks.

Monk – a member of a male religious order who lives under the vows of poverty, chastity and obedience.

N

Nave – area of the church where the congregation sit, running from the western wall to the chancel.

New Testament – that part of the Bible which tells the story of Jesus and contains letters written about him.

Nicene Creed – resulted from a meeting of 318 bishops at Nicea in 325.

Nonconformist – a Christian who does not 'conform' to the teachings of the Church of England.

Nun – a woman living in a convent under the disciplines of poverty, chastity and obedience.

O

Old Testament – books in the Christian Bible – the same as those found in the Jewish Scriptures but in a different order.

Ordination – the ceremony by which a lay-person becomes a priest.

Original Sin – the traditional belief that there is a link between the sin of the first man and woman in the Garden of Eden and people's sinful disposition today.

Orthodox Church – originally the Church of the eastern region of the Roman Empire – separated from the Roman Catholic Church in 1054.

P

Palm Sunday – when Christians celebrate the entry of Jesus into Jerusalem riding a donkey.

Parable – a human story which has a moral or a spiritual message.

Paschal Candle – lit in Catholic and Orthodox churches on Holy Saturday to symbolise the resurrection.

Passover – the most important Jewish festival celebrating the release of the Israelites from Egyptian slavery.
Penance – (penalty) that the priest decides on in the Roman Catholic Church after a person has confessed their sins.
Pentecost – the Jewish festival celebrating the giving of the Ten Commandments by God to Moses on Mt Sinai.
Pentecostal Movement – formed in 1901 this emphasises the work and gifts of the Holy Spirit.
Pontius Pilate – the Roman Governor of Judea (26-36 CE) who condemned Jesus to death.
Pope – the Bishop of Rome and the chief bishop of the Roman Catholic Church.
Priest – someone ordained in the Anglican and Catholic Churches and authorised to administer the sacraments.
Prophet – a person called by God to deliver a message to the people.
Protestants – those Christians who do not owe any allegiance to the Catholic or Orthodox Churches.
Pulpit – the raised platform in a church from which the sermon is delivered.
Purgatory – according to Roman Catholic belief, this is a state after death for those not yet ready for heaven.

R

Relic – the remains of saints or holy people which have become venerated.
Reserved Sacrament – in the Catholic Church, this is the keeping of bread which has already been blessed in the Mass to take to people who are sick.
Roman Catholic Church – the community of believers throughout the world who owe their allegiance to the Pope, Peter's successor.
Rosary – a string of 165 beads which encourages Roman Catholics to meditate on the 15 mysteries of Christ.

S

Sabbath Day – the Jewish day of rest at the end of a week.
Sacrament – an outward and visible sign of an inward and spiritual blessing.
Salvation Army – a Protestant organisation founded by William and Catherine Booth in 1880.

Satan – Hebrew word meaning the 'accuser', this is the fallen angel who became the leader of the evil spirits opposed to God.
Shrine – originally a place containing the bones of a saint – now refers to any holy place with religious associations.
Sign of the Cross – the tracing of the shape of a cross by a priest or a bishop as a sign of God's blessing.
Stations of the Cross – the fourteen places at which, according to the scriptures and tradition, Jesus stopped on his way to be crucified.
Sunday – the Christian Sabbath – a day set aside for rest and worship.
Synagogue – the Jewish meeting-place for prayer and instruction in the Scriptures.
Synoptic Gospels – ('seeing together') – Gospels written by Matthew, Mark and Luke, since they present a similar picture of Jesus.

T

Thirty-Nine Articles – a statement of doctrine first accepted by the Church of England in 1574.
Torah – ('teaching') – refers to the first five books of the Bible and is the most sacred part of the Jewish Scriptures.
Transubstantiation – the Roman Catholic belief that during the Mass the bread and wine change into the actual body and blood of Jesus.
Trinity – the Christian belief that there is one God in three persons – Father, Son and Holy Spirit.

V

Virgin – a man or a woman who has never had sexual intercourse.
Virgin Birth – the Christian belief that Jesus was miraculously conceived in the womb of Mary by the Holy Spirit.
Virgin Mary – the mother of Jesus Christ.
Vocation – a 'calling' which a person believes to have received from God.

W

Whitsun – the festival commemorating the coming of the Holy Spirit on the first disciples.

INDEX

A
Abbot: *82, 84*
Abortion: *21, 126, 128, 130*
Adultery: *123, 124, 126*
Advent: *100, 102, 123*
Ageism: *142*
Aids: *123, 126, 128, 134, 137*
Altar: *58, 62, 78*
Alternative Service Book: *24, 66, 74, 96*
Anglican Church: *30, 32, 34, 62, 63, 66, 67, 68, 72, 74, 78, 84, 90, 91, 92, 96, 100, 106, 122, 123*
Anglo-Catholics: *62, 74*
Anti-Semitism: *10*
Apocrypha: *50*
Apostles: *22, 23*
Apostles Creed: *34, 48, 116*
Archbishop of Canterbury: *24, 68, 88*
Ascension Day: *74, 112, 114*
Ash Wednesday: *100, 106, 108*
Assumption of the Blessed Virgin Mary: *19, 48*
Authorised Version: *55*

B
Baptism: *25, 62, 64, 90, 91, 92, 94, 114*
Baptist Church: *16, 64, 94*
Bible: *24, 28, 50, 56, 57, 62, 64, 70, 80*
Bishop: *16, 18, 20, 25, 68, 92, 108, 125, 130*
Bishop of Rome: *18, 22*
Book of Common Prayer: *24, 66, 74, 96*
Breaking of Bread: *72, 80*

C
Cardinal: *18, 20*
Celibacy: *68, 126*
Chapel: *64*
Charismatic Movement: *30, 40, 67*
Chastity: *82*
Christmas: *100, 102, 104*
Church of England: *16, 24, 25, 26, 68, 74, 125*
Citadel: *64*
Confirmation: *42, 92, 93*
Constantine: *15, 86, 104*
Contemplation: *70*
Contraception: *126, 128*
Creed: *16, 25, 34, 38, 104*
Crucifix: *58, 59, 62*
Crucifixion: *38, 110, 111*

D
Day of Pentecost: *13, 30, 36, 40, 94, 114*
Devil: *30, 44, 106*
Divine Liturgy: *23, 61, 72, 73, 78, 79*
Divorce: *124, 125*
Dominicans: *83*
Drugs: *134, 136*

E
Easter: *59, 100, 108, 110, 112, 114*
Ecumenical Movement: *32*
Epiphany: *100, 105, 106*
Epistles: *50, 52, 57, 62, 76*
Eucharist: *68, 72, 74, 106, 112*
Euthanasia: *21*
Evangelicals: *28, 56, 62*
Evangelism: *29*
Exodus: *50*
Extended family: *120, 142*

F
Font: *58, 62, 90*
Free Churches: *42, 72, 112, 125*

G
Gentiles: *15, 100, 105*
Good Friday: *89, 101, 106, 108, 110, 111, 112*
Gospel: *29*
Gospels: *5, 6, 8, 12, 38, 51, 52, 53, 60, 72, 76, 78, 102, 110, 112, 114, 121*
Great Schism: *16, 22*

H
Harvest: *101, 116, 117*
Holocaust: *10*
Holy Communion: *25, 38, 42, 64, 72, 73, 74, 78, 80, 93, 108*
Holy Land: *86, 87, 88, 89*
Holy Scriptures: *22, 25, 57*
Holy Spirit: *26, 28, 30, 34, 36, 40, 48, 68, 70, 76, 79, 90, 92, 102, 112, 114*
Holy Week: *106, 108*
Homosexuality: *130, 134*

I
Icon: *23, 49, 60, 105, 110*
Iconostasis: *60, 61, 78*
Immaculate Conception: *19, 48*
Incarnation: *36, 104*
Iona: *84, 85*

J
Jerusalem Bible: *50, 55*
Jesuits: *83*
Jesus: *4, 23, 38, 87, 99, 121, 130*
John the Baptist: *8, 90, 94, 99, 102, 106*
Just War: *151*

K
Kingdom of God: *4, 6, 8, 40, 105*

L
Laying on of hands: *18, 42, 92*
Lent: *57, 100, 106*
Lord's Prayer: *70, 76*
Lord's Supper: *42, 64, 72, 80, 118*
Lourdes: *86, 88*
Love: *46*
Luther, Martin: *16, 24, 28, 57*

M
Marriage: *122, 126*
Mass: *19, 38, 59, 72, 73, 74, 76, 78, 96, 99, 108, 118*
Meditation: *70, 110*
Messiah: *4, 7, 8, 10, 13, 14, 15, 48, 52, 102, 108, 110, 118*
Methodist Church: *16, 26, 32, 64, 80, 93, 130*
Miracles: *8*
Missal: *66*
Monastery: *82, 84*
Monk: *82, 126*

N
Natural disasters: *44*
New Testament: *38, 40, 50, 51, 54, 57, 62, 72, 90, 92, 94, 114*
Nicene Creed: *34, 76*
Nonconformist Churches: *16, 26, 34, 62, 64, 66, 80, 96, 100, 125*
Nun: *82, 83, 126*

O
Old Testament: *38, 50, 51, 52, 54, 56, 57, 62, 76, 102*
Oral Tradition: *6, 53*
Ordination: *42*
Original Sin: *28*
Orthodox Church: *16, 22, 32, 42, 48, 57, 60, 66, 67, 72, 78, 84, 92, 104, 106, 110, 112, 122*

P
Palm Sunday: *106, 108*
Parables: *6, 10*
Paschal Candle: *112*
Passover: *10, 14, 108, 114*
Paul: *14, 28, 30, 31, 40, 46, 52, 72, 87, 94, 96, 123, 130, 142*
Pentecostal Movement: *30, 40, 67*
Peter: *10, 14, 18, 94*
Pope: *16, 18, 21, 24, 57, 128*
Prayer: *70, 83*
Priest: *26, 42, 58, 62, 68, 73, 74, 76, 78, 90, 96, 98*
Protestant: *16, 18, 21, 24, 26, 30, 32, 38, 42, 54, 72, 74, 80, 81, 86, 105, 119, 122*
Purgatory: *19, 99*

Q
Quakers: *16, 26, 42, 64, 67, 68*

R
Racism: *21, 32, 144*
Reformation: *16, 18, 54, 57, 62, 81*
Refugees: *32*
Roman Catholic Church: *16, 18, 20, 21, 24, 30, 32, 34, 42, 48, 53, 57, 58, 62, 63, 66, 67, 68, 76, 78, 84, 86, 88, 89, 90, 91, 96, 97, 98, 100, 101, 105, 106, 108, 110, 112, 118, 122, 123, 125, 128, 130, 132*
Rosary: *19*

S
Sabbath Day: *112, 113, 118*
Sacraments: *23, 25, 42, 65, 68, 96*
Salvation Army: *16, 26, 42, 64, 65*
Satan: *30, 44*
Second Coming of Christ: *28, 36, 80, 102*
Second Vatican Council: *18, 20, 68*
Sex: *126, 128*
Sign of the Cross: *58*
Stations of the Cross: *59, 89, 110*
Suffering: *44*
Sunday: *23, 62, 118, 119*

T
Taize: *84*
Thirty-Nine Articles: *25*
Torah: *6, 50*
Transubstantiation: *73, 81*
Trinity: *22, 36, 40*

U
Unemployment: *138, 140*
United Reformed Church: *32*

V
Virgin Birth: *48*
Virginity: *124, 126*
Virgin Mary: *19, 21, 48, 59, 87, 88, 99, 101, 105*
Votive Candles: *59*

W
Wesley, John: *64*
Whitsun: *101, 114*
Women Priests: *68*